THE MIDDLE EAST BEDSIDE BOOK

THE MIDDLE EAST
BEDSIDE BOOK

edited by

Tahir Shah

THE OCTAGON PRESS
LONDON

ISBN 0 863040 60 8

Published 1991
First published in this edition 1992

Photoset, printed and bound in Great Britain by
Redwood Press Limited, Melksham, Wiltshire

Contents

TRAVELLERS' TALES

Baksheesh for the Englishman

People are constantly asking what things and situations really mean. There has to be a single meaning for everything, one often feels, otherwise people cannot endure thinking about it.

But what a situation, a thing or even a person 'means' can hardly be divorced from its context, which includes what people desire to think about it.

Now suppose this anecdote, published in a newspaper, is important – that is, it is valuable to know what it means:

> An Arab in London, seeing an Englishman wearing a dinner-jacket, thought he was a servant at the establishment he was visiting, and handed him a twenty-pound note. The Englishman, who was a fellow-guest waiting for his wife, put the money in his pocket.

I have been asking people what they think of the story, and in two days I have received these replies:

1. It is not true. Everyone makes up jokes about rich Arabs.
2. It is a disgrace that Englishmen have become beggars.
3. It shows the height of politeness: the Englishman did not want to embarrass the Arab by refusing the money.

Each interpretation gives you an insight into the mind of the interpreter: each one has a bias, each bias is employed to explain and to analyse the 'meaning' of the story.

The Pasha Speaks

Pasha: The Englishman is welcome; most blessed among hours is this, the hour of his coming.

Dragoman (to the Traveller): The Pasha pays you his compliments.

Traveller: Give him my best compliments in return, and say I'm delighted to have the honour of seeing him.

Dragoman (to the Pasha): His Lordship, this Englishman, Lord of London, Scorner of Ireland, Suppressor of France, has quitted his governments, and left his enemies to breathe for a moment, and has crossed the broad waters in strict disguise, with a small but eternally faithful retinue of followers, in order that he might look upon the bright countenance of the Pasha among Pashas – the Pasha of the everlasting Pashalik of Karagholookoldour.

Traveller (to his Dragoman): What on earth have you been saying about London? The Pasha will be taking me for a mere Cockney. Have I not told you *always* to say, that I am from a branch of the family of Mudcombe Park, and that I am to be a magistrate for the county of Bedfordshire, only I've not qualified; and that I should have been a deputy-lieutenant, if it had not been for the extraordinary conduct of Lord Mountpromise; and that I was a candidate for Boughton-Soldborough at the last election, and that I should have won easily if my committee had not been bribed. I wish to heaven that if you *do* say anything about me, you'd tell the simple truth!

The Dragoman is silent.

Pasha: What says the friendly Lord of London? Is there aught that I can grant him within the Pashalik of Karagholookoldour?

Dragoman (growing sulky and literal): This friendly Englishman – this branch of Mudcombe – this head purveyor of Boughton-Soldborough – this possible policeman of Bedfordshire – is recounting his achievements and the number of his titles.

Pasha: The end of his honours is more distant than the ends of the earth, and the catalogue of his glorious deeds is brighter than the firmament of heaven!

Dragoman (to the Traveller): The Pasha congratulates your Excellency.

Traveller: About Boughton-Soldborough? The deuce he does! But I want to get his views in relation to the present state of the Ottoman Empire. Tell him the Houses of Parliament have met, and that there has been a speech from the Throne pledging England to maintain the integrity of the Sultan's dominions.

Dragoman (to the Pasha): This branch of Mudcombe, this possible policeman of Bedfordshire, informs your Highness that in England the talking houses have met, and that the integrity of the Sultan's dominions has been assured forever and ever by a speech from the velvet chair.

Pasha: Wonderful chair! Wonderful houses! – whirr! whirr! all by wheels – whiz! whiz! all by steam! – wonderful chair! wonderful houses! wonderful people! – whirr! whirr! all by wheels – whiz! whiz! all by steam!

Traveller (to the Dragoman): What does the Pasha mean by all that whizzing? He does not mean to say, does he, that our Government will ever abandon their pledges to the Sultan?

Dragoman: No, your Excellency, but he says the English talk by wheels and by steam.

Traveller: That's an exaggeration; but say that the English really have carried machinery to great perfection. Tell the Pasha (he'll be struck with that) that whenever we have any disturbances to put down, even at two or three hundred miles from London, we can send troops by the thousand to the scene of action in a few hours.

Dragoman (recovering his temper and freedom of speech): His Excellency, this Lord of Mudcombe, observes to your Highness, that whenever the Irish, or the French or the Indians rebel against the English, whole armies of soldiers and brigades of artillery are dropped into a mighty chasm called Euston Square, and, in the biting of a cartridge, they rise up again in Manchester, or Dublin, or Paris, or Delhi, and utterly exterminate the enemies of England from the face of the earth.

Pasha: I know it – I know all; the particulars have been faithfully related to me, and my mind comprehends locomotives. The armies of the English ride upon the vapours of boiling cauldrons, and their horses are flaming coals! – whirr! whirr! all by wheels! – whiz! whiz! all by steam!

Traveller (to his Dragoman): I wish to have the opinion of an unprejudiced Ottoman gentleman as to the prospects of our English commerce and manufactures: just ask the Pasha to give me his views on the subject.

Pasha (after having received the communication of the Dragoman): The ships of the English swarm like flies; their printed calicoes cover the whole earth, and by the side of their swords the blades of Damascus are blades of grass. All India is but an item in the ledger-books of the merchants whose lumber-rooms are filled with ancient thrones! – whirr! whirr! all by wheels! – whiz! whiz! all by steam!

Dragoman: The Pasha compliments the cutlery of England, and also the East India Company.

Traveller (to the Dragoman): Tell the Pasha I am exceedingly gratified to find that he entertains such a high opinion of our manufacturing energy, but I should like him to know, though, that we have got something in England besides that. These foreigners are always fancying that we have nothing but ships and railways, and East India Companies; do just tell the Pasha that our rural districts deserve his attention, and that even within the last two hundred years there has been an evident improvement in the culture of the turnip; and if he does not take any interest in that, at all events you can explain that we have our virtues in the country – that we are a truth-telling people, and, like the Osmanlees, are faithful in the performance of our promises. Oh, and by-the-by, whilst you are about it, you may as well just say, at the end, that the British yeoman is still, thank God! the British yeoman.

Pasha (after hearing the Dragoman): It is true, it is true: through all Feringhistan the English are foremost and best; for the Russians are drilled swine, and the Germans are sleeping babes, and the Italians are the servants of songs, and the French are the sons of newspapers, and the Greeks are the weavers of lies, but the English and the Osmanlees are brothers together in righteousness: for the Osmanlees believe only in one God, and cleave to the Koran, and destroy idols; so do the English worship one God, and abominate graven images, and tell the truth, and believe in a book; and though they drink the juice of the grape, yet to say that they worship their prophet as God, or to say that they are eaters of pork, these are lies – lies born of Greeks, and nursed by Jews.

Dragoman: The Pasha compliments the English.

Traveller (rising): Well, I've had enough of this. Tell the Pasha I am greatly obliged to him for his hospitality, and still more for his kindness in furnishing me with horses, and say that now I must be off.

Pasha (after hearing the Dragoman, and standing up on his divan): Proud are the sires, and blessed are the dams of the horses, that shall carry his Excellency to the end of his prosperous journey. May the saddle beneath him glide down to the gates of the happy city like a boat swimming on the third river of Paradise! May he sleep the sleep of a child when his friends are around him; and the while that his enemies are abroad may his eyes flame red through the darkness – more red than the eyes of ten tigers! – Farewell.

Dragoman: The Pasha wishes your Excellency a pleasant journey.

From *Eothen*, by Alexander Kingslake (died in 1891).

Travel Notes
by *Idries Shah*

_____

Darkest London

It is not necessary to be a foreigner before one can appreciate England, but it probably helps. While one may not get the range nor richness of experiences which are to be had in more colourful places, darkest London has given me encounters which match many that I have had in the mysterious East.

Once, for instance, when I was standing in the street near Trafalgar Square, dressed in a manner appropriate to the very humble work in which I was engaged, I saw a well-dressed Englishman, with bowler hat and furled umbrella, walking purposefully towards me.

When he was still about twenty yards away I recognised him as one of my father's most distinguished and oldest friends: someone who had seen me in very different circumstances in the past. What would he do when we came face to face? I now hardly looked like anyone whom he would feel inclined to talk to. But could he ignore me?

I just stood there, keeping my eyes on his face.

His expression never changed. When he was a few feet away he paused, stopped, brandished his umbrella, and said to me, as if to a complete stranger with whom he had decided to share a sudden thought:

'Do you know, it has struck me that nothing ever goes on forever. You may be up, you may be down. But *change* comes, do you see? Yes ... Change.'

Twirling his umbrella he went on his way.

Could anyone have thought of a more civilised way to communicate sympathy, support, recognition, without any of the awkwardness which one would have thought inseparable from such an encounter?

If I wanted to regard his comments as an accident, I was free to do so. If I cared to take the thing a stage further, ask for help, borrow money, I might try, since the ice had been broken. If I wanted to carry on, taking some encouragement from his words, I could do so.

I still have no actual proof that he recognised me at all.

That experience and its consequences for me match almost anything seen or accomplished which I can report from journeys to unusual and inaccessible fastnesses in Central Asia...

Travel notes can be generated by all kinds of events, in England or elsewhere. I was at an English country house for a weekend when one of the guests whom I did not yet know came up to me and said: 'I say, are you from Trinidad?'

Thinking that he might have some interest in the place, I said: 'No, are you?'

He looked at me, shocked:

'No!' he said huffily, 'I most certainly am *not*!'

About-turns provide some of the best travel notes I have. When I had a flat in London, I threw a rather noisy party. At the height of it a squad of police forced their way in, led by a white-haired and red-faced sergeant. He shouted: 'Who's in charge here?'

I told him that I was. As soon as he saw my face he started to give me the treatment:

'We let you fellows into this country and this is how you behave! You may have to leave the country for this ... Let me see your Alien's Book.'

When he saw my British passport his attitude changed completely, he was even apologetic...

Once I was plodding down the road near my house in London, notebook and pen in hand, when I saw a knot of people on the pavement, overflowing into the road. I did not notice at first that this was happening in front of a studio, where prominent musical performers frequently went to make records.

I ploughed through the crowd. In the middle of it were three or four youngish men with long hair. One of them said to me: 'Autograph?' and gestured towards my notepad.

I said: 'Sorry, I'm in too much of a hurry.'

It was only after I had passed through the crowd that I realised that a current pop-idol had offered *me* his autograph – and certainly didn't want mine...

Television has added another dimension to the possibilities of travel-note encounters in England. When I was put into a television programme I learned how well-known one can become even after one exposure on the screen. Taxi-drivers started to ask me for my photograph, for their teenage children. The only unflattering thing about this was that, upon enquiry, I discovered that though they had indeed seen me on television, they were generally under the impression that I was a bandleader or singer – 'or something'...

The almost fantastic interchanges in the West are equally matched in the East. In Central Asia a man asked me: 'What are they saying in the Great Bazaars of London about our new Five Year Plan?' But a club hall porter in London, in his turn, said once: 'You're a college man aren't you, Sir? Then tell me how football-pool permutations work.'

And, again in England, people are always saying: 'You are from out foreign, like. What's it like in the Philippines (or Burma, or Patagonia ...)?' More readily understood was the policeman in Piccadilly Circus giving me directions. He was convinced, because of my foreign appearance and since I asked him the way, that I only understood pidgin-English: 'You very good savvy right-left, quick-quick, on foot, foot, get there in no time, straight like I make with hand now...'

Two or three attempts at explaining that I understood were impatiently brushed aside. *He* knew, obviously what foreigners were like...

Cairo

Misunderstanding seems to be one of the best sources of Travel Notes. Dressed in Arab robes one day in Cairo, I once could not resist telling some serious Scandinavian folklorists an 'ancient Arabian tale' which they insisted upon identifying as a typical Eastern story of a kind which had been typed and numbered by some eminent professor ages ago. They were most excited and wanted to write a monograph on it: so I had to reveal that I had just read it, in the form of a science-fiction story, in the current issue of the *Saturday Evening Post*.

Jerusalem

In Jerusalem I heard this amazing exchange between a stallkeeper and a Western woman tourist:

10

'This is genuine representation, in beaten silver, of the Last Supper of our Lord.'

'What about it?'

'You buy, relic of Holy Land.'

'Certainly not! Now, if you could get me a picture of the *first supper*, that would be something to show the folks back home.'

Silence.

Then, again from the traveller: 'When is the *next* supper, anyhow ... ?'

Fez

Another woman in a shop, this time in Morocco, provided such a powerful Travel Note that I feel the original experience all over again every time I think of it.

I was looking at fabrics and pottery in a merchant's shop in Fez. A woman came in, well-dressed and carrying a basket full of excellent fresh fruit and vegetables.

The shopkeeper gave her a coin and she went out.

I asked: 'Is she selling vegetables?'

'No,' he said, 'she is a beggar.'

'But where does she get those clothes and that marvellous produce?'

'People give them to her.'

'To a *beggar* – things of that quality?'

He looked me straight in the eyes:

'Do you then think that just because a person is a beggar she should be given things of low quality? We aren't like that here.'

Tangier

On one trip to Morocco, my wife took a fancy to a princess's robe, beautiful and ancient which was for sale in one shop. The price asked was enormous, and we used to go every day to look at it, explaining that we had too little money and try to see whether the shopkeeper would reduce the price.

He did come down a little, but it was still tremendously costly, although it was worth it, being perhaps unique.

The day before we were leaving the town we went to say good-bye, and I did not mention the robe. The shopman asked me whether I wanted it. I said that I did, and that my wife wanted it more. Then I showed him what I had in my pocket: about twenty percent of the lowest price that he had asked. He shrugged, and we said goodbye.

As we walked away down the hill, my wife was not too pleased, but I thought that something would soon happen. Within a couple of minutes we heard someone running after us. It was the brother of the shopkeeper. He asked us to come back.

The man accepted our offer. Then he said to me:

'It is bad luck for me if a woman in a certain state covets something I have and does not get it. Why don't you keep your women in the house when expecting a child?'

'I don't believe in that kind of bad luck,' I told him.

'Yes, I *know* you don't, but I do, and *I* can't shake off the belief!'

So superstition can be a great leveller. Many of those shopkeepers buy such heirlooms as we had secured from impoverished noble families for shockingly small sums...

Beirut

Shopkeepers have their ways, all over the world.

I could not make out the basis on which a certain seller of foreign newspapers ordered his papers, and asked him how he predicted his sales.

He said that he just thought of a number, and people came and ordered them all.

But did he not get left with surplus stocks?

No, he did not. People came first and bought the ones they wanted most. Then they came, later, and bought 'the ones they did not want'.

How could he get them to do that?

'Because they know that I will not get in a fresh batch until all the old ones are sold. So it is in their interest to clear my stock.'

'But,' I asked, 'supposing someone set up in opposition to you and actually took orders and even delivered them?'

'I'll think about that problem if and when it happens. I have been here for eleven years and nobody has yet done what you suggest. Besides, it would not be moral.'

Mykonos

I spent only a few days in Mykonos; and if I went there because it was reputed to be a paradise for superior internationalistic intellectuals, I deserved all I got.

The moment I stepped ashore from the ship from Piraeus and was looking around at the cafés and streets full of foreigners, the scene closely resembling a film-set in which the extras had been told to talk endlessly and aimlessly on the cry of 'action!' until someone said: 'Cut, now first positions!' – I was buttonholed by a Greek.

'You speak English?'

'Yes.'

'Why are you wearing Dimitri's shoes?'

'I am not wearing Dimitri's shoes.'

I was, in fact, wearing a pair of Afghan sandals which had already got me into an argument with a Spaniard in Deya, Majorca, a year before. That exchange had run:

'I see you have a pair of Mexican sandals on.'

'They are not Mexican sandals, they have been worn by Afghans for thousands of years.'

'Then how did I manage to buy a pair just like them in Mexico City?'

A man of culture and intelligence, too, and quite sober at the time.

But to return to Mykonos.

I was taken to a Tourist policeman, where my new Greek friend and various local well-wishers and general advisors who had collected started to tell him their version of what had happened, at the top of their voices. I could only understand 'Dimitri'.

The policeman heard them out. It seemed to take hours. Then he turned to me and said:

'They say that you are wearing Dimitri's shoes.'

'I know they do,' I said, 'but I am not.'

I had to go to his office to see his superior. The witnesses and several more well-wishers came too. Acting as their spokesman, and not neglecting to give volume, subtlety and quantity to his words, the policeman explained, in Greek, the situation.

The chief policeman turned to me from his desk. He said, slowly and ponderously, in good enough English:

'They say that you are wearing Dimitri's shoes.'

It took half an hour, cigarettes, back-slapping and shouting – and certain other customary things – to arrive at what had at first seemed intensely illogical to the citizenry and officials of Mykonos alike: that there might be another pair of shoes like the sainted Dimitri's on the island.

Anyone with a taste for that kind of social encounter, I reflected, would have enjoyed the incident immensely. Everyone except me certainly seemed greatly restored after it.

When I was about to leave Mykonos I heard someone call out 'Hi, Dimitri!' and nearly jumped out of my skin. But it was only a porter pushing a cart loaded with baggage. He was wearing Afghan-type sandals ...

Khartoum

But if people can't always learn from a traveller, he can often pick up useful information. How to replace a lost library book, for instance.

One day I was talking to an aged librarian in the Sudanese capital, about borrowing books.

'You can never tell what will happen to your books,' he said, 'and that is why I do not want to lend them. A lot of people pass through here from various parts of Africa, on the way to Mecca. Once a man borrowed a manuscript of which I had only one copy. I heard later that he had died on the Pilgrimage, and – as often happens in such cases – the book had been buried with him.'

'Whatever did you do? Nothing, I suppose.'

'No, it was all right, I happened to know it by heart, so I wrote out a fresh copy ...'

Khyber Pass

But travellers, it seems, do not always get away with whatever tales they have collected. There is a village in the Khyber area whose people greatly envied their neighbours, because buried there they had nothing less than a genuine Sayed, a descendant of the Prophet.

One day, as luck would have it, a Sayed on a pilgrimage called at their village.

'Stay and spend the rest of your days here,' said the people, 'and we will build you a magnificent tomb when you die.'

'No, thank you,' said the holy man, 'I have to travel north, and must waste no time.'

So they killed him. Now they have their very own Sayed, and they can justifiably feel that they also are especially blessed...

Granada

I got away with one piece of information which has not yet reached the encyclopaedias: this time in Granada. I was sitting in the grounds of the Alhambra watching a gardener spraying some flowers and chattering to a labourer in that Andalusian dialect of Spanish which – five hundred years after the Moors left – still has the sound of Arabic.

As soon as I could, I got into conversation with him, remembering that a British professor had noted Arabic as still used in parts of Spain.

Did he know any Arabic words? Yes, indeed. 'Usted', for instance, now, people said that it was a contraction for 'Vuestra Merced' – something like 'Your Worship'. It means 'You'. But if it was not Spanish, which Arabic word was it from?

'You may not know any Arabic, caballero, but it is the same, my grandfather told me, as the Arabian word for "Master".'

I had been racking my brains for all the possible Arabic words standing for 'You'. But 'Master' – sure enough, through five hundred years of oral tradition, unknown to and unrecognised by even the most erudite contemporary lexicologists of Spanish, there it was – *Ustad* in Arabic means *Master*.

Emboldened by this discovery, I started to talk to a magnificent-looking old fellow, a typical ancient and wise peasant, whom I saw sitting by a water-channel. What wisdom was his? I spoke Spanish, and so was able to put into action that tourist dream: 'If only I could speak his language, I would be able to share his wonderful thoughts...'

So I asked him:

'Caballero, what are you thinking about?'

He raised his head from contemplation of the sunset, and delivered himself of timeless wisdom:

'What I really want in life is a veritable plastic dustbin.'

15

Afghanistan

Afghanistan is a comparatively small country, certainly small for Asia, about the size of France or Texas; and since it has only sixteen million people, quite a lot of them know each other.

One day, however, I found myself in a corner where nobody knew me.

In a certain teahouse near Jalalabad, an ancient was talking about people of the past as if they were still alive. He was especially communicative about the almost-legendary Jan-Fishan Khan, a mystic, prince and mighty warrior about whom he spoke as if he had known him well.

'One of his favourite practices,' he said, 'was to go into a shop and ask how much something was. Supposing the shopkeeper said: "One silver piece," he would answer: "Well, I'll give you ten golden *ashrafis* for it, you rascal, for that is what it is worth to *me*. I see no reason why I should pay a price equal to *your* insensitive under-valuation of this magnificent object!" But,' continued the old man, 'that was generations ago. You youngsters have never even heard of men like that ...'

I took the force out of his argument and did not really mend matters by hastening to assure him that indeed I had heard of the Great Khan, and even his shopping habits. He was my great-great grandfather.

The Philosopher

I went to a party. A man I had never seen before came up to me and, as is usual under such circumstances, started to talk. We talked about all kinds of things; about shooting, about clothes, about world affairs, and so on. Then he said: 'I'm glad I came tonight; let's meet again and have a talk at my Club. I nearly didn't come: in fact I am only here because of curiosity.'

I asked him what kind of curiosity.

He said: 'Well, you see, there's some extraordinary kind of oriental philosopher coming tonight. They say he's clever enough, and I dare say he is. After all, they've got nothing else to do, have they? His name is Idries Shah ...'

A moment later, when the conversation had drifted to legal anomalies, our hostess came up and introduced us. My new friend started to stutter — and I never did get to his Club ...

Letters from Morocco

An Invitation to Dinner

'To my gracious master, my respected lord...

'This evening, please God, when the king of the army of stars, the sun of the worlds, will turn towards the realm of shades and place his foot in the stirrup of speed, thou art besought to lighten us with the dazzling rays of thy face, rivalled only by the sun.

'Thy arrival, like a spring breeze, will dissipate the dark night of solitude and isolation.'

An Invitation to a Carousal

'To my noble and venerated friend...

'Please God, this evening, when the silver circle of the moon fourteen days old will present itself on the surface of the blue sky, spreading all around it rays of love and tenderness, we will hold a gathering in the village of Sidi Kasem, that place so full of delight, and all night, until the rising of the day we will indulge in inexpressible pleasures. We do not admit of the delay of the thickness of a hair. Let the force of sails and oars hasten thine arrival, which will be a source of delight for all your friends.'

From *The Moors*, by Budgett Meakin, London 1902.

The English Through Eastern Eyes
by *The Sirdar Ikbal Ali Shah*

An Eastern Visitor's Impressions in the 1930s

Many foreigners, some with greater names than mine, have attempted to describe the mind and character of the English and their country. Some have been so lyrical as to express more love for England than for their own homelands; others, blinded by prejudices, have found comfort in destructive criticism, and portrayed an ugly image of all that they saw after landing at Dover. And there are yet those in a third group, who, over-awed by the mightiness of London were simply struck dumb. Consequently, in a vast volume of literature presented by these foreigners, we find a picture of England more false than true.

The above reminds me of an Eastern legend, in which three blind men were taken to an elephant and asked to describe it. The first, feeling the legs of the animal, said that the elephant was made of thick soft columns; the second, touching only its belly, thought that it was like a large water tank; while the third, stroking the trunk, likened the elephant to a giant tapering water hose. The analogy is pertinent because each of them conjectured according to his own imagination, and true definition of the object was lost in a haze of unreality.

This lack of positive analysis regarding the English people and the country in which they live is due to the fact that many foreigners, who write or speak on England and the English, do so only after casual acquaintance with those whom they endeavour to delineate. But to know a people one must enter into their life-fibre, feeling as they feel, acting as they act, and at least appearing to love and hate what they love and hate.

It is of the essence of the high philosophy of Oriental Sufism to be in the world, and not be of it; thus, if all that I have said demands integration, then integration let it be before you can see into the soul of an Englishman; for without that insight, it is at best a superficial portrait that will be presented of the English.

Staying at a first-class London hotel, or motoring round the Lake District, and then writing about the English is so much waste of time. You can never penetrate into the depths through such surface roaming; and therefore, to believe that watching the Derby or the Lord Mayor's Show, or being invited to lunch at a London club, or shopping in Bond Street, or having a suit made in Savile Row constitutes knowing the English – all this is mere illusion.

I do not suggest, of course, that you do not meet at such gatherings or locations the English men and women of quality who represent their race and traditions; but the real son of England 'does not lie on the surface of things', so to speak. He requires a thorough search; and, the search is long and discriminating, because one of the fundamentals of an Englishman's make-up is his shyness. He speaks of himself least of all. You have to look him up in *Who's Who*, or ask about him from his friends. The more eminent he is the more painfully silent he will be about his qualifications.

I believe that this trait is due to his country's insularity; being of an island race, he has through centuries of self-sufficiency developed an acute sense of nationhood. Yet, strangely enough, the national character was never aggressive even in the hey-day of greatness, despite the Palmerstons, Beaconsfields, Curzons and others known as Empire Builders. The reason, perhaps, is that an Englishman is essentially an individualist. He will act within a group, but that group acts in the interests of the individual, and not as a despotic clique against all others. Parliament is a mirror of English society where the human rights of man are voiced and protected. This forum of debate and discussion, evolved through centuries of struggle, is the best fruit of human endeavour that the English have given to the world; and although copied by other countries, it is true to say that its system is not fully applied yet by others who adopted it. The House of Commons is a Mother of Parliaments, and the mother still remains the best of her family.

The parliamentary institution has grown out of another deep-rooted English conception, that of toleration, meaning that you permit the right of free speech and would like to hear another man's point of view. But we must note a delicate difference here. There is toleration only so long as one does not interfere with the legitimate rights of another man; for instance, one is completely free to listen to one's radio, but one may not open the windows and let it blare full blast, if one's neighbour in the adjoining garden is resting upon his lawn. Again, on a train journey, one has no right to pester a fellow-traveller with conversation, if the latter has no inclination to talk. I have heard it said that the English are cold and reserved. They are not really, and, in fact, I have greatly benefited by emulating their mode of living. That silence in the train is so soothing to the nerves – as those who travel on the continental trains will readily agree.

One sometimes hears of intolerance shown towards the foreigner among a certain class of the English people; but few have gone to the root cause of the matter. The fact is that the English strive to make their homes as comfortable as possible. There is the bedroom, the little garden patch, the sitting-room and a well-managed kitchen, where the mother works while the father toils in an office or a factory; and at night they want undisturbed rest. For the English are a home-loving people; father's slippers repose beside his big chair, the cat sits before the fire; mother is knitting, the children have been put to bed, and peace descends upon the castle of the Englishman. If anybody then disturbs the even tenor of his placid life, he is vexed. It is for this reason that average Englishmen never feel at home outside England.

Despite occasional instances of snobbery, a curious fellow-feeling exists among the English; whatever others say, 'Don't hit a man when he's down'. I have done some research in the field of social service, and I find that since 1910 no fewer than eight hundred foreign delegations have visited England in order to enlighten public opinion so that this or that 'wrong' might be removed. Not all have succeeded, but none has failed to get a hearing somewhere, from the Odd Fellows Hall in Edinburgh to the Albert Hall in London. Were these delegations of any value, and was the public opinion which they awakened effective? I know of several which made a stir; and with one in particular I was actively associated, when a mission of Indian Muslims headed by the late Aga Khan, by addressing meetings in Britain created a mass of highly pro-Turkish sentiments after the first World War, whereby the harshness of the peace terms offered to the Turks was greatly mitigated.

Then, too, a noble feature characterises the English; they are very human. There are 1,400 Cats' and Dogs' Homes, supported by either a group of like-minded people, or by some recognised organisation, where stray and homeless animals are cared for; and I know of many of the older generation who have left legacies for such animal welfare. In the like manner, I was once amazed that a lady had telephoned to the fire-brigade to come and rescue a cat which, frightened by a dog, had climbed a tree, and would not come down. In the case of a wayside accident, no one will hesitate to help an injured person. Charity also is one of the virtues of English society. There is a large number of charitable institutions – both public and private – whose activities and disbursements have grown so vast as to require the creation of a Charity Commission in London.

So many foreign elements have come, one way or another, as settlers in England – Saxons, Normans, Danes, Dutch, French and others – that it is hard to say as to what is true stock. But the soil of England, in some mysterious way, has converted them all into Englishmen. I believe that in this process of 'digesting' the foreign elements, the uncanny trait of compromise that they have has helped them. In most of their dealings, governmental or personal, there is always a feeling of give-and-take, which accounts for their being the best diplomats in Europe.

I remember an incident germane to this skill in compromise; when I attended a conference after the last Anglo-Afghan war. The discussion was leading nowhere between the Afghan and the English delegate, when the Afghan Sirdar, rather exasperated by the stalemate, asked me to tell his English opposite number that the discussion was at an end. Placing his revolver on the table, he said: 'This weapon will decide the issue, and the conference should be considered over.' This forthright statement, however, did not ruffle the Englishman. He merely smiled; and said quietly, 'No, Sirdar Sahib, the conference is not ended. No diplomatic conference is ever finished. We shall meet again tomorrow.' The whole matter was amicably settled between Kabul and London. No fireworks were needed; it was all ironed out at further diplomatic conferences in London.

Another remarkable instance of compromise is the granting of independence to India. There might have been discussions between India and England for quite twenty-five years during which heat would have developed – heat, if not open war, as in the case of some other European colonial powers – but ultimately the good sense of the English secured a friendly and co-operating India instead of a mass of over 400 millions of hostile subjects. The grace with which the English stepped out of Hindustan affords a singular example of high political morality.

The result, of course, is that there are now more English in India than before as honoured and respected guests of the Indian Republic and her people.

Tourists and Missionaries

The Mummy's Hand

A tourist guide once told me that he offered to take a party, as a side-trip, to one of the places in Egypt with the most extraordinary atmosphere and authentic sights: but it would mean a long and uncomfortable climb. All 35 of the people on his tour accepted with alacrity, and they discussed the treat excitedly for the three days of routine sightseeing which were left before the 'free day', for which the excursion was planned.

They started out at dawn and the tourists' enthusiasm drained as they climbed towards the caves where my friend was taking them: a very ancient hide-out of anchorites. After an hour and a half, during which they had demanded two halts and various arguments had broken out, they decided to return to their motor-coach without visiting the caves. By popular decision the whole group spent that afternoon watching a British horror movie, *The Mummy's Hand*, which was showing locally. They expressed themselves delighted with it.

I said: 'So much for their interest in the real thing, eh?'

The guide said: 'I am an Egyptian Copt, and I am sure that the spiritual influence of those ancient Christian anchorites intervened, to deny their holy place to those who were unworthy.'

The Missionary's Death Curse

After spending many years in Egypt as a missionary, Canon Temple Gairdner suddenly realised that the Egyptians were opposing his community, converting his flock to their own beliefs. This enterprise, he found, was 'organised, deliberate, resourceful, supported by the highest in the land, heavily financed'. He decided that there was only one course to take: he would pray that the devil should take the soul of his main adversary, by means of a death curse attributed to St. Paul.

Dr. Harpur, his associate, describes how, on the prompting of the reverend Canon, a number of members of the mission went into the desert, near the Pyramids. They went to a deserted place where there was a cave used by dervishes for their exercises, and a portion of the Christian scriptures was read out by one of the party.

Gairdner's biographer, apparently approving the cursing service, alludes to the severity of his words, by quoting it as 'only the right of those who have gone all lengths in love and prayer'. He continues, 'And this right was surely his, for his wife remembers that he felt so deeply the attack on the Church and the losses it sustained that he said to her (devoted father as he was), "I believe I should have felt it less even if one of our own little ones had been taken!"'

The admiring biography* continues:

'In the right of this love he proposed to his comrades that, for the saving of the Church, all calls to repentance having been rejected by the seducer, they should make the terrible act described by Saint Paul:

> 'In the name of the Lord Jesus Christ, when ye are gathered together, and my spirit, with the power of our Lord Jesus Christ, to deliver such an one unto Satan for the destruction of the flesh, that the spirit may be saved in the day of Jesus Christ.'

The terrible curse, invoking the Devil, was agreed, and 'the man was laid under a power he could not resist'.

It must be recorded that not everyone present agreed unreservedly to this curious rite: though 'only one or two fell away'. These are the words of Gairdner, who continued to hope that his curse would work. If it did, we are not told so. All that Gairdner says after that is, 'We breathed again and are now praying for and believing for a manifestation of divine power...'

---

* Constance E. Padwick: *Temple Gairdner of Cairo*, London (Society for Promoting Christian Knowledge), second, revised, Edition, 1930, pp. 221-2.

THROUGH OTHER EYES

Through Eastern Eyes

The English Ambassador is received at Court

The English *elchi* (ambassador) had reached Tehran a few days before we arrived there, and his reception was as brilliant as it was possible for a dog of an unbeliever to expect from our blessed Prophet's lieutenant. Indeed, the city was almost shocked at the honours paid him, and some of our most violent mollahs declared that, in treating a *Giaour* so well, we were ourselves in some measure guilty of his infidelity, and preparing our own damnation. At different stations on the road, the throats of oxen had been cut before his horses' feet; in many places his path was strewn with sugar-candy, and on the day of his entry he was permitted to have his trumpets sounded in the procession, all of which were honours that could be exacted by none save our own princes.

Then all the proper attentions of hospitality were shown. The house of a khan was taken from him and given to the ambassador, and whatever furniture was wanting was demanded from the neighbours and placed therein. A handsome garden was levied upon another, and added to the house. The Lord High Treasurer was commanded to feed the strangers at his own expense as long as they chose, and clothes and shawls were collected from the courtiers and servants of the court, for the dresses of honour which it is the custom to make on such occasions. The princes and noblemen were enjoined to send the ambassador presents, and a general command issued that he and his suite were the Shah's guests, and that, on pain of royal anger, nothing but what was agreeable should be said to them.

All these attentions, one might suppose, would be more than sufficient to make infidels contented with their lot; but, on the contrary, when the subject of etiquette came to be discussed, interminable difficulties seemed to arise. The *elchi* was the most

27

intractable of mortals. First, on the subject of sitting. On the day of his audience with the Shah, he would not sit on the ground but insisted upon having a chair; then the chair was to be placed so far, and no farther, from the throne. In the second place, of shoes, he insisted upon keeping on his shoes, and not walking barefooted upon the pavement; and he would not even put on our red cloth stockings. Thirdly, with respect to hats: he announced his intention of pulling his off to make his bow to the King, although we assured him that it was an act of great indecorum to uncover the head. And then, on the article of dress, a most violent dispute arose: at first, it was intimated that proper dresses should be sent to him and his suite, which would cover their persons (now too indecently exposed) effectually, that they might be fit to be seen by the King; but this proposal he rejected with derision. He said that he would appear before the Shah of Persia in the very same dress he wore when before his own sovereign. Now, as there was not a Persian who had ever been at the court of a Frank king, nobody could say what that proper dress was; and, for aught we knew, the *elchi* might put on his bed-gown and night-cap on the occasion.

This was a difficulty apparently not to be overcome, when, turning the subject over in my own mind, I recollected that among the paintings in the palace of Forty Pillars at Ispahan, there were portraits of Europeans who, in the days of the great Shah Abbas, flocked to his court, and even established themselves in the city. In particular, I well recollected one in the very same painting in which Shah Abbas himself is represented, whose dress is doubtless the only proper costume to wear before a crowned head. I immediately suggested this to my master, who mentioned it to the Grand Vizier, who ordered that a copy of it should, without loss of time, be made by the best artist of Ispahan, and sent to Tehran.

So soon as it arrived it was officially presented to the English *elchi*, with a notification that the Shah was satisfied to receive him in the same dress as he wore before his own sovereign, a model of which was now offered to him, and to which it was expected that he and his suite would strictly conform.

The shouts of laughter which the infidels set up upon seeing the picture and hearing the message are not to be described. They asked if we thought them monkeys, that they should dress themselves as such at our bidding, and were so disagreeably obstinate in their resolution of keeping to their own mode of attire, that at length they were permitted to do as they chose.

The audience of the Shah passed off much better than could have been expected from such rude and uncivilized people, and we were all astonished that men, so unaccustomed to the manners and forms of the world, should have conducted themselves on this difficult occasion without committing some act that was flagrant and improper. The King was seated on his throne of gold, dressed with a magnificence that dazzled the eyes of the strangers, and made even his subjects exclaim, 'Jemshid! who was he? or Darab? or Nûshirvan? that they should be mentioned in the same breath?'

On the right and left of the throne stood the princes, more beautiful than the gems which blazed upon their father's person. At a distance were placed the three Viziers of the state, those depositaries of wisdom and good counsel; and, with their backs to the wall, each bearing a part of the paraphernalia of the crown, were marshalled in a row the black-eyed pages of royalty, who, with their unhidden legs, their coats cut to the quick, their unbearded chins, and unwhiskered lips, looked like birds moulting, or deceased apes, or anything but human creatures, when contrasted with the ample and splendidly dressed persons by whom they were surrounded. And they stood their ground, not in the least abashed by the refulgent presence of the great King; but their attitude, manner, and expression of countenance would have made us suppose they were quite as good and as undefiled as ourselves.

The speech made on the occasion by the *elchi* was characteristic of the people he represented; that is, unadorned, unpolished, neither more nor less than the truth, such as a camel-driver might use to a muleteer: and, had it not been for the ingenuity of the interpreter, our Shah would never have been addressed by his title of 'King of Kings', or of 'the Kebleh of the Universe'.

It would be taking up the pen of eternity were I to attempt to describe the boundless difference that we discovered between the manners and sentiments of these people and ourselves. Some of our sages endeavoured to account for it upon philosophical principles, and attributed much to the climate of those dark, watery, and sunless regions in which they were bred and born: 'For,' said they, 'how can men living surrounded by water, and who never feel the warmth of the sun, be like those who are never a day without enjoying the full effulgence of its rays, and do not even know what the sea means?'

But the men of the law settled the question in a much more satisfactory manner, by saying that 'It was owing to their infidelity that they were doomed to be cursed even in this life; and that if the ambassador, his suite, and even his whole nation, would submit to become Mussulmans, and embrace the only true faith, they would immediately be like ourselves, their defilements would be washed clean, and they might even stand a chance of walking in the same storey of the heavens as the genuine children of Islam would in the world to come.'

From *The Adventures of Hajji Baba of Ispahan*, by James Morier.

Arabia in Europe

Arabs and the English

Those who treat the traditional affinity between the Arabs of Arabia and the British as a myth, are unaware of its well-established historical origin. In the sixth century A.D., before Islam, the tribes of Arabia passed their lives fighting one another. These interminable battles might have ended in their mutual extermination had they not developed a code of honour governing their wars. According to the rules which they developed, the object of war was not to win battles or destroy the enemy, but to provide a field for the performance of deeds of valour, which were subsequently immortalised in poetry. To fight honourably was more important than to win the battle.

In the eighth century, the Arabs conquered Spain, invaded France and brought to Western Europe their idea of chivalry, which was enthusiastically imitated in France and England. They remained seven hundred years in Spain, after which contact was severed in Europe, though it was prolonged by the Crusades. Thereafter in England the spirit of 'chivalry' was continued in sport, in which to play the game was more honourable than to win the match, so when the nineteenth century British explorers discovered the Arabian tribes, they immediately recognised about them something akin to their own moral codes – to fight honourably was better than to win. These feelings were no myth but were based on a genuine historical cultural inheritance.

Studying for Pleasure

We often refer to our European culture as 'the legacy of Greece and Rome', ourselves as heirs to 'the glory that was...' and I can remember no other suggestion from the days of my education to modify this belief. That may have been because I was not listening,

31

but if that was the reason then neither were a lot of my contemporaries; it still seems to be the tradition that the main line of the Occident Express runs from Athens via Rome, passing on the way through one or two junctions of only moderate importance, serving interesting but much less significant branch lines.

What emerges from *The Arab Heritage* – it probably emerges from a dozen textbooks as well, but that isn't quite the same – is that at the period when we were still Saxons, there existed in the Arab world, monarchies of a splendour which might possibly have been equalled if six of the wealthier medieval kings in Europe had decided to pool their resources. The interesting thing is that we are inclined to deprecate this unbelievable magnificence: your Saracen in his riches is cruel and luxurious, a stereotype which must surely have gone into circulation no later than the Crusades and which that complex of pleasures and envies adding up to Puritanism has doubtless done much to preserve.

Yet this picture conflicts with what we learn from the more influential European courts: their rulers were a mixed lot, the worst of them touching levels of cruelty and excess which your Arab might equal but certainly not surpass; their wealth and conditions attracted regiments of the most brilliant men of the day. It would be curious if the same sort of pattern were not to be observed in Arab lands and very strange indeed if these concentrations of prosperity and excellence had not exported to the relatively dark areas around them a good deal of fuel.

To the civilized Arab, his European counterparts must often have seemed only slightly preferable to the Mongols. An illustration of this is the report of a physician witnessing the treatment meted out by a Frankish colleague: having encompassed the death of a knight through a butchered amputation, the learned Frank turned his attention to a madwoman. First he had her head shaved; when that failed, he diagnosed demonic penetration of her head, made a cruciform incision in the scalp, peeled it back like the skin of an orange and rubbed the exposed skull with salt. 'The woman,' writes the Arab laconically, 'also expired instantly … I returned home, having learnt of their medicine what I knew not before.' The Frank, it seems, learnt nothing at all and his descendants are with us even to this day.

Tales: Eastern or Western?

Legal and Illegal

Both the East and the West have much in common in their traditional tales, sometimes humorous, sometimes instructional, about justice: or, at any rate, about the law.

A Persian tale, published also in Don Quixote, in the medieval Latin of the monks, and in the Italian tales of Malespini, shows that one and the same story has been shared for centuries by peoples of Europe and the East:

A woman went to a judge and complained that she had been annoyed by the attentions of a young man in a public place; though he denied the charge. There were no witnesses.

The verdict was that the youth should compensate the woman by giving her ten silver pieces.

When the woman had gone, the young man started to complain bitterly to the judge, who said:

'Obey my instructions! Follow her and take the money away.'

When the man tried to take the money back she fought him bitterly, raising such a commotion as she held on to the money, that both of them were seized and brought before the court again.

'Why,' enquired the judge, 'did you make such a hue and cry?'

'He was trying to take the money away,' said the woman.

'Now we have seen how you can fight,' the judge told her, 'it is proof enough that you could have defended your virtue as strenuously if you had been attacked in the first incident. Return the money.'

Dogs and Stones

The drift of Middle Eastern literature into the traditions of the West has often been noted by folklorists and literary researchers, but in general the ordinary reader knows little about this. He may know

Middle East Bedside Book

that, for example, 'Aladdin' is from *The Arabian Nights*, but he will not realise that many tales — and extensive ranges of ideas — have been so naturalised into the culture of the West that people in Europe and America think that these things are rooted in their own local lore.

Sometimes, however, the borrowing is so clear that examples can be extracted. One such is the story of the dogs and the stones.

In the thirteenth century the great poet, Saadi, wrote his tale of a poet who presented himself to a robber band and declaimed some verses which he had composed in honour of its chief. Instead of rewarding him, as was the custom, the bandit chief gave orders that the poor poet was to be stripped of his clothes and driven out of the village.

As he was fleeing pursued by dogs, this unhappy man of letters bent down to take up a pebble from the ground: but found that all the stones were frozen to the soil. 'What foul people these are,' he exclaimed, 'when they fasten down the stones and let loose the dogs!'

The seventeenth-century English poet, John Taylor, in his book of *Wit and Mirth*, includes just this tale, as one which he had collected in London, from the oral tradition . . .

Abou Ben Adhem and the Angel

Ibrahim, son of Adhem was born in Balkh, present-day Afghanistan, of Arab stock. A Sufi mystic — one of the most illustrious, in fact — he, like Buddha, was a prince who renounced his throne to follow the path of higher wisdom. He died in 782.

Leigh Hunt (died 1859) has immortalised in English literature one of the outstanding teaching-tales, presented as personal experiences, recited by Ben Adhem, in the poem which countless schoolchildren remember for the lines:

'Abou Ben Adhem (may his tribe increase!)
Awoke one night from a deep dream of peace . . .
The angel . . . showed the names whom love of God had
    bless'd,
And lo! Ben Adhem's name led all the rest.'

The original story recounts how Ibrahim, son of Adhem, saw Gabriel, who had descended from heaven with a book containing

34

the names of the friends of God. Gabriel refused to include Ben Adhem's name as one, so he asked to be included as a 'friend of the friends of God'.

After a pause, Gabriel said: 'The order has come. I am to write Ibrahim's name at the very beginning, since on the Path, hope comes from hopelessness.'

In Leigh Hunt's version, taken from Fariduddin Attar, the Sufi author:

'Abou Ben Adhem (may his tribe increase!)
Awoke one night from a deep dream of peace,
And saw within the moonlight in his room,
Making it rich, and like a lily in bloom,
An Angel writing in a book of gold:-
Exceeding peace had made Ben Adhem bold,
And to the Presence in the room he said,
'What writest thou?'. The vision raised its head,
And with a look made of all sweet accord,
Answered 'The names of those who love the Lord'.
'And is mine one?' said Abou. 'Nay, not so',
Replied the Angel. Abou spoke more low,
But cheerily still; and said, 'I pray thee, then,
Write me as one who loves his fellow men.'
The Angel wrote and vanished. The next night
It came again with a great wakening light,
And showed the names whom love of God had bless'd,
And lo! Ben Adhem's name led all the rest.'

From *Abou Ben Adhem and the Angel* by James Henry Leigh Hunt.

The Girl who had Seven Divs for Brothers

Now, *Divs* are very interesting creatures and they are found in many countries of the East. They are enchanted beings, not in any one size or shape, but come in all sorts of disguises. They can look like men or women, or be huge and monstrous, as big as giants, with long pointed teeth and large wild eyes, and claws instead of hands and feet.

Once upon a time, high up on a mountainside in old Iran, there lived a girl, who was adopted by seven Divs who found her one day in the woods when they were out hunting. They took her home to their castle, and she was brought up by their old nurse until she reached the age of seventeen. On her seventeenth birthday she was as beautiful as the loveliest princess in all the land, and she looked out of the window to see someone coming up the path to the castle.

'Nurse, nurse,' she cried to the old woman. 'What sort of thing is this walking up the hill towards our castle? I have never seen anything like it before.'

'Lady Fatima,' cried the nurse, who was a large and ugly female Div with a wart on her chin, 'come away from that window, for it is a human being that you can see, and you must not speak to him or your seven brothers will be angry.'

'Nonsense, nurse,' said Fatima, for she was rather wilful and liked getting her own way, 'I will open the window and call to him, for he looks so tired and hot. I am sure he is lost and hungry.'

The nurse began to hiss and snarl in anger, but Fatima took no notice of her, and opening the window, she called out in a melodious voice:

'Come into the castle, Man, so that you may have something to eat and drink, for I am all alone here, with my brothers away hunting all day long.'

It so happened that the stranger was a prince, whose name was Nureddin, and he had lost his horse while riding nearby. So he was delighted when he looked up and saw the girl staring down at him from above. The nurse opened the gate, and within half an hour Nureddin was sitting with Fatima, eating grapes and cheese and delicious sweet hulwa.

Fatima was delighted with him, and asked him a hundred questions, and he told her about the outside world.

'I must see all those wonders,' she said, 'if only my brothers would let me go . . .'

'Nay, Lady Fatima,' reproved the nurse, who was waiting upon them. 'You know that my seven masters would never let you leave the castle, for they are very jealous and would kill this human if they saw him here.'

'Then I will escape and run away myself,' Fatima vowed, 'and I shall see all the wonders of the world as this young man has described.'

The prince was overjoyed, and promised Fatima that he would take her with him to his father's kingdom as soon as he had rested from the journey. But at that moment, before Fatima could reply, there were loud shouts from the road outside, and the barking of dogs mingled with the neighing of horses.

'O Human Being!' cried the nurse, 'conceal yourself in this chest, for my masters have returned and they will tear you to pieces the minute they set eyes on you.'

For though she was a Div, and usually hated humans, she knew that her mistress liked the young man, and she wanted to help her.

Quickly, the prince got into the chest, and Fatima closed the lid down upon him with trembling hands.

No sooner had the prince been concealed than the door flew open and the seven Divs came into the room.

'Sister Fatima, Sister Fatima, what have we to eat tonight?' cried the first Div, and the others all began to shout and laugh as they pulled off their big boots, and the nurse and Fatima began to help them to take off their fur coats.

'Nurse, bring us wine to drink, we are parched with thirst!' they ordered, and the aged female Div hurried away.

The servants were putting the horses away in the yard, and the dogs were growling over their bones in the kitchen.

Suddenly, one after the other, the Divs began to sniff with their large noses, and one shouted angrily: 'A man! A man! I can smell a man.'

Fatima went pale, and her heart began to beat wildly. Inside the chest the prince was huddled in the clothes which hid him from sight.

'Someone has been here! Sister Fatima, where is he?' All the Divs were on their feet now, their voices loud and angry. They began to rush from one room to the other, throwing open one door after another, sniffing and snorting like wild beasts. Somehow, they had grown so excited that they never thought of looking in the chest in which Prince Nureddin lay, so as soon as they were all out of the room, Fatima opened the chest and pulled him out.

'Quick, quick, I will show you a secret way out of the castle, or my brothers will tear you to pieces!' As night was falling, and the Divs were still searching everywhere, Fatima was getting frightened.

Together they ran, hand in hand, towards the fireplace, and Fatima helped the prince into the chimney. He found his feet on small, dark steps.

'Come with me, Fatima, I will save you from this terrible place,' he whispered, and she silently nodded. Down the slippery stone steps they went, emerging at last into the starry night air.

'Where are the horses?' said the prince urgently, and Fatima took him to the stables. As silently as two shadows, they crept behind the castle. The grooms were preparing their part of the day's spoils, and so they did not know that two of the finest stallions were being saddled by Nureddin for Fatima and himself.

When they were both mounted, the noise from the castle grew louder, and the seven Divs saw them in the moonlight riding out of the huge gates.

'After them!' roared the eldest Div. 'Bring them back alive, and we will roast them like chickens upon the spit!'

The horses galloped like the wind and flew down the hillside like enchanted animals, as indeed they were. Soon in full pursuit came the seven Divs, riding horses just as swift and strong.

'Fatima! Come back! We will forgive you, but let us have the human!'

The frightened girl could hear them shouting behind her, and knew it would be only a matter of minutes before the galloping Divs would be upon them. So she reached into her pocket and found a magic grass seed there, which she threw over her left shoulder. In a trice, a great grassy plain sprang up between the Divs and the runaways, and the Divs' horses could not run as fast as before until they were through the thick, high grasses, which caught at their legs and slowed them down. But within half an hour they were catching up again, and Nureddin called out:

'Fatima, what shall we do? We must try and stop them, for we are just halfway towards my father's kingdom, and we should reach it by dawn if the Divs could be stopped somehow.'

'Never fear,' said Fatima bravely, reaching into her pocket again, 'I think I can do it,' and she threw over her shoulder a pine cone. In a trice a fine thick pine forest had sprung up, and the runaways were able to gallop on without seeing the Divs behind them.

The gallant stallions were bearing them nearer and nearer to the prince's country, and Fatima, with her hair streaming in the wind, was just beginning to feel safe at last, when the prince, who had glanced behind, cried:

'Alas, they have made up on us once more. They will catch us in a matter of minutes unless something stops them . . .'

Fatima searched her pockets, and nearly lost her hold upon the reins of her horse. She was almost in despair, when her fingers closed upon a grain of salt in the corner of her pocket. She threw it behind her, and immediately a huge foaming sea sprang up behind her horse's hooves, plunging the seven Divs and their mounts into the mountainous waves. And so they were drowned, for Divs cannot safely swim in salt water.

Then Fatima and Nureddin rode on a little while longer, until as day was breaking they came to the beautiful city of Nishapur, where the royal palace was all shining in gold and turquoise splendour and peacocks strutted upon the garden paths, their splendid tails outspread. Then the soldiers on the battlements, seeing their prince approaching, sounded their silver trumpets, all set with rare and precious gems.

And so Fatima was treated as a princess, which indeed she soon became in reality, when she married Prince Nureddin at a magnificent feast lasting seven days and seven nights.

As for the enchanted horses which had brought them there, they disappeared a month later, when the moon was full. They knew that their young mistress was after all a human being and they preferred to live in the service of Divs rather than humans, for such is the law of magic, laid down when the world began by Suliman, King of Magicians and Enchanted Beasts, (Upon whom be Peace!).

From *Folk Tales of Central Asia* by Amina Shah.

Treaty Between France and Turkey

Headed with a star, this document of 1740 is regarded as 'a thoroughly typical example of the official phraseology of the East.'

'The Emperor Sultan Mahmoud, son of the Sultan Moustapha, always victorious.

'This is what is ordered by this glorious and imperial sign, conqueror of the world, this noble and sublime mark, the efficacity of which proceeds from the divine assistance.

'I, who by the excellence of the infinite favours of the Most High, and by the eminence of the miracles filled with benediction of the chief of the prophets (to whom be the most ample salutations, as well as to his family and his companions), am the Sultan of the glorious Sultans; the Emperor of the powerful Emperors; the distributor of crowns to the Chosroes who are seated upon thrones; the shade of God upon earth; the servitor of the two illustrious and noble towns of Mecca and Medina, august and sacred places, where all Mussulmans offer up their prayers; the protector and master of holy Jerusalem; the sovereign of the three great towns of Constantinople, Adrianople, and Brusa, as also of Damascus, the odour of Paradise; of Tripoli in Syria; of Egypt, the rarity of the century, renowned for its delights; of all Arabia; of Africa; of Barca,' ... and eight other cities; 'particularly of Baghdad, capital of the Caliphs; of Erzeroum the delicious,' ... and eleven other places; 'of the isles of Morea, Candia, Cyprus, Chio, and Rhodes; of Barbary and Ethiopia; of the war fortresses of Algiers, Tripoli, and Tunis; of the isles and shores of the White and the Black Sea; of the country of Natolia and the Kingdom of Roumelia; of all Kurdistan and Greece; of Turcomania, Tartary, Circassia, Cabarta, and Georgia; of the noble tribes of Tartars, and of all the hordes which depend thereon; of Caffa and other surrounding districts; of all Bosnia and its dependencies; of the fortress of Belgrade, place of war; of Servia, and also of the fortresses or castles which are there; of the countries of Albania; of all Walachia and Moldavia, and of the forts and battlements which are in those provinces; possessor, finally, of a vast number of towns and fortresses, the names of which it is unnecessary to enumerate and boast of here; I, who am the Emperor, the asylum of justice, and the king of kings, the centre of victory, the Sultan son of Sultans, the Emperor Mahmoud, son of Sultan Moustapha, son of Sultan Muhammed; I, who, by my power, origin of felicity, am ornamented with the title of Emperor of the two Earths, and, to fill up the glory of my Caliphat, am made illustrious by the title of Emperor of the two Seas.'

There ends the description of the Turkish monarch: the document then turns westward, and begins to designate the King of France, who is catalogued as follows: 'The glory of the great princes of the faith of Jesus; the highest of the great and the magnificent of the religion of the Messiah; the arbitrator and the mediator of the affairs of Christian nations; clothed with the true marks of honour and of dignity; full of grandeur, of glory, and of majesty; the Emperor of France and of the other vast kingdoms which belong thereto; our most magnificent, most honoured, sincere, and ancient friend, Louis XV, to whom may God accord all success and happiness, having sent to our august Court, which is the seat of the Caliphat,' – (here we revert to Turkey) – 'a letter containing evidences of the most perfect sincerity, and of the most particular affection, candour, and straightforwardness; and the said letter being destined to our Sublime Porte of felicity, which, by the infinite goodness of the incontestably majestic Supreme Being, is the asylum of the most magnificent Sultans, and of the most respectable Emperors; the model of Christian Seigneurs, able, prudent, esteemed, and honoured minister, Louis, Marquis de Villeneuve, his Councillor of State and his Ambassador to our Porte of felicity (may the end thereof be filled up with joy), has demanded the permission to present and hand in the aforesaid letter, which has been granted to him by our imperial consent, confirmably to the ancient usage of our Court; and consequently, the said ambassador having been admitted before our imperial throne, surrounded with light and glory, he has given in the aforesaid letter, and has been witness of our Majesty in participating in our power and imperial grace; and then the translation of its loving meaning has been presented, according to the ancient custom of the Ottomans, at the foot of our sublime throne, by the channel of the most honourable El Hadji Mehemmed Pacha, our first Minister; the absolute interpreter of our ordinances; the ornament of the world; the preserver of good order amongst peoples; the ordainer of the grades of our empire; the instrument of the glory of our crown; the road of the grace of royal majesty; the very virtuous Grand Vizier; very venerable and fortunate minister, lieutenant-general, whose power and prosperity may God cause to triumph and to endure.'

Then begins the treaty, which goes on through eighty-five articles, and finishes with these words: 'On the part of our imperial Majesty I engage myself, under our most sacred and most inviolable august oath, both for our sacred imperial person and for our august successors, as well as for our imperial viziers, our honoured pachas, and, generally, all our illustrious servitors who have the honour and the felicity to be in our slavery, that nothing shall ever be permitted contrary to the present articles.'

From *Curiosities of Ceremonials ... or International Vanities* by Frederick Marshall, London (J.C. Nimmo & Bain) 1880. pp.82ff.

Moslem Art in Europe

by *Bibi Amina*

A time comes in the lives of all interested in the whys and wherefores of life as we know it today, to ponder upon origins and inspirations. To study thus long enough and to some purpose, the quest must take us into the past. We seek to ask ourselves: 'Just what is beautiful, and how can we know it for what it is? Is there any law by which we may reach a decision?'

A scholar and student of art and architecture can scarcely define the true difference between ugliness and beauty; and it is truly said that beauty can be in the eye of the beholder. In the words of a contemporary philosopher: 'Significant form is the one quality common to all works of art'. Perhaps it could be more adequately expressed thus: art is craftsmanship plus inspiration. Without inspiration, there is only craftsmanship. More usually, of course, the artist starts with inspiration, and only rarely with any capability in the field of craftsmanship. *It* is the urge and the drive, given to him by the desire adequately to express his inspiration, that forces him to become a master of his medium; an inspired craftsman.

One can agree: with the vision before the eye of glorious columns; carved and inlaid, inlaid with colours never before or since surpassed, in the Hall of the Ambassadors in the Moorish paradise of Spain.

One fact emerges, and plainly so, from a study – however cursory – of the fundamental differences between architecture before and after the Moslem era in Spain. And this is that a great deal of artistic expression owes its birth to efforts at honest realism, efforts sincerely dedicated to the reproduction of natural lines. One finds in the columns and cloisters and the pure spreading arches of the time of the Moors, that inner perception of the artist and master-builder which grasped the significance of the power of the tree and the forest glade over civilised man. Is not a softly rounded pillar like the

43

trunk of a sheltering tree, and the finely spread archway above and on either side of it, the symbolic branches?

To primitive man, within the forest there was safety. Is it not quite conceivable that inside the heart, too, lies the dormant feeling of the need for sanctuary of a similar sort granted by the tree to mankind? Harun al-Rashid is said to have had a room painted with trees and bushes and flowers of fabulously strange design, in order to have a favourite daughter cured of what we would today call claustrophobia. The ceiling was dark blue, and golden stars were affixed at artistic intervals in the corners, to give the effect of a starlit sky.

The influence of oriental art on the formation of what is known to the present-day West as *Gothic*, has long been perceived; Wren, in his writings on architecture, calls it the *Saracen* style. In the Gothic architecture native to France, there appears a highly conspicuous orientalising strain. Centuries before the time of the Crusaders the art, literature and philosophy of the Moslem schools had been deeply affecting the West. This knowledge made an impression because it was energetic, refined, civilised. At the time, life in the North was rough in most forms of native culture.

Saracenic art expanded further and further west, via Spain to other parts of Europe; on contact with it, most of the stagnant pools of artistic complacency disintegrated. With aspiring heights, with branching forms, with every conceivable trick of building on a grand scale, the Arab and his other Moslem workers made new conquests in the field of Northern and Western aesthetics. By the end of the sixteenth century, there flashed the blinding light of beauty and reason: with previous generations of philosophical thought to press home the truth. Here was fineness of line and unlimited expression; yet, if lines were to be shown, so far as they indicated anything, they gained the power of expression rather than opposing the general direction of the character of the object, be it wall, doorway or enormous lofty-ceilinged hall. There was no economy in the long, sweeping line, the rounded curve, rather more pinched at the corners than the Roman arch. There is a grand feeling of generosity in the Moorish halls, and in halls which were their offshoots, their European descendants; but a controlled generosity, a generosity bounded by reason.

It was as if the presiding genius, like the donor of the legend, gave freely in the right direction, where food was needed, not merely wanted: as if an insistence on detail took place, providing beneath a subdued grandeur, a mere suggestion of studied unconsciousness without overfilling the space provided.

Let us now turn to another branch of aesthetic culture; the influence of the art of the Moslems upon the art of the West. Here we have in many cases, especially in Fra Lippo Lippi's glorious masterpiece, the *Coronation of the Virgin*, an unmistakable Moslem influence in the decorative motifs of the veiling; where the eye of the artist has been faithful in reproducing the beautiful Kufic Arabic script as a decoration upon the scarfs held by the angels. In the work of Rembrandt, we have many examples of the fact that he was fascinated by oriental splendour, and surrounded himself with objects of Moslem life. He painted himself in interestingly colourful garments and turbans, such as might have come from *The Thousand and One Nights*. In a masterpiece of his art, called *David before Saul*, in which the boy David plays his harp to the great king in one of his hours of mad reflective introspection, it is interesting to note how the artist has been at pains to give that sombre theme the close attention to detail consistent with the depth of paint used to suggest shadows; and to throw his light upon the royal apparel, especially the gorgeous headdress. And in the fold of curtaining drawn behind the lavishly turbaned head of the majestic melancholic, there lies the corresponding depth of the shaded tone.

The depth and perception of the East may be seen in several other Rembrandt groups; for instance the detailed descriptive power of the *Descent from the Cross*, in which the eye finds, on the right foreground, relief from the central tragedy in the splendid and majestic strength of a strangely pasha-like figure, bearing a resemblance to Rembrandt himself; again attired in Eastern robes, with a staff and the curling beard of an oriental sage. In many another painting, full use has been made of the powerful strength of carpets from the East.

In the field of pure design, there stands out that design known since Elizabethan times as *arabesque*; this, consisting as it does of interlacing and symmetrical motifs of geometrical and other shapes, is seemingly perfect except for one link which appears irregular. It became popular after the decline of panelling as house decoration, and during the era of plaster, it took the shape of tapestry which rich families had on the walls. Flowers and fruits, such as roses and grapes, may be regularly introduced within the lattice, and when finished it makes a most pleasing and harmonious whole.

These are but a few instances of the everlasting debt which the art of the West owes to the influence of Islam.

Middle East Facts and Fallacies : I

- The most often used name in the world is Mohammad, which means 'The Praised One'.
- The only wild camels in the world are in Australia. They were originally taken there by Afghans, who provided early transport.
- In the Middle Ages, the Latin Christians used to study the works of a sage whom they called Doctor Maximus. Many of them did not know that this was a translation of the Sufi teacher Ibn al-Arabi's title: 'Al-Sheikh al-Akbar'.
- The word *coffee* is derived from the Turkish *Kahve*, from the Arabic *Qahwa*, meaning both 'beverage' and 'wine'.
- Alcohol was first distilled by the tenth-century alchemist Jabir ibn Hayyan, el-Sufi. The first translation of his work was by an Englishman, Robert of Chester, in 1144.
- The first critical historical study was made by Ibn Khaldun, born in Tunis in the fourteenth century. His *Muqaddima* is still a classic.
- Mint sauce was a delicacy imported to England from Arab Spain, and is believed to be the only relic of a once comprehensive Eastern cuisine prepared here.
- Paper was brought to Europe by the Arabs from China.
- Printing apparatus used in Afghanistan 1,000 years ago is still extant.
- *Traffic, cheque, tariff, magazine* are all Arabic words.
- Shakespeare uses stories found in Arabic; and Chaucer's 'Pear-Tree' tale is found in the Persian of the mystic Rumi.
- The earliest form of the Dick Whittington tale is attributed to Persia.
- *Tabby* (cat) is an Arabic word. So are *filly, algebra, troubadour* and *admiral*.
- Frederick II of Sicily was so Arabised that he was called 'The Baptised Sultan'.
- Much of Dante's work is found in earlier Arabian legends.

• The British King Offa of Mercia (757-96) struck a dinar in gold with his name on it and 'There is no God but Allah' as a part of the inscription. One of these coins is now in the British Museum.

• On Fra Lippo Lippi's *Coronation of the Virgin* (Uffizi Palace, Florence), the angels are shown holding a scarf covered with Arabic lettering.

• The first book printed in England (*The Dictes and Sayings of the Philosophers*) is a translation from an Arabic work.

• Arabic figures are the figures used in arithmetic (1, 2, 3, etc.,) and transmitted to the West by Arab mathematicians, to replace the clumsy Roman Numerals, I II III, etc. Scholars have argued whether the Arabian name for the figures is *Hindi* (from India) or *Hindasdi* (engineering figures). The former explanation is the most favoured.

• Many Western reference books, including some of the most famous, teem with errors about the Middle East. One standard work has 19 errors, at least, in the first 25 pages: and this is a general reference work, not even one about the Middle East!

• King John of England offered to become a Moslem and to hand over fealty of his kingdom to the Moors, if they would help him. The Moorish King refused the offer.

• The British Prime Minister, Harold Macmillan's, phrase about 'A Wind of Change' occurs in the poems of Hariri.

• Sir Winston Churchill's statement (in Tehran, November 1953) about truth needing a 'bodyguard of lies' may have come from the Arabic proverb: 'Truth needs no bodyguard; lies are a bodyguard, but a weak one.' Churchill's sayings are often found in earlier books of collected sayings.

• The Italian dictator Mussolini's claim to be 'Protector of Islam' worried statesmen in the democracies. They need not have been concerned: since only Allah is the Protector of Islam, this boast made *Il Duce* hated throughout the Moslem world.

• During the Second World War, the British Ministry of Information (sometimes also called 'The Mystery of Misinformation') made an almost fatal blunder. They sent, to the Middle East, thousands of posters intended to show British-Islamic friendship. The picture showed a British Tommy sitting at a café table with an Arab. The soldier's beer-mug was resting on the Koran. The ship carrying this cargo was torpedoed in the Mediterranean.

• The percentage of Arabs who believe that *Idris* cannot be a

Welsh name is said to be equalled only by the proportion of Welshmen who deny that it is Arabic.

• Al-Razi (c. 865–925) of Rayy, northern Iran, first introduced the classification 'animal, vegetable, mineral'.

• The first history of religions was written by Ibn Hazm of Cordoba (died 1064). He is honoured in the West as the founder of the discipline of comparative religion.

• The British Royal Family is of Arabian extraction, through the line of Pedro the Cruel.

THE PROPHET

The Prophet Mohammed
by *Carlyle*

Out of all that rubbish of Arab idolatries, argumentative theologies, traditions, subtleties, rumours and hypotheses of Greeks and Jews, with their idle wire-drawings, this wild man of the desert, with his wild sincere heart, earnest as death and life, with his great flashing natural eyesight, had seen into the kernel of the matter. Idolatry is nothing:

> These wooden idols of yours, ye rub them with oil and wax, and the flies stick on them – these are wood, I tell you! They can do nothing for you; they are an impotent blasphemous pretence: a horror and abomination, if ye knew them. God alone is; God alone has power; He made us, He can kill us and keep us alive; '*Allah akbar*', God is great. Understand that His will is the best for you; that howsoever sore to flesh and blood, you will find it the wisest, best; you are bound to take it so; in this world and in the next, you have no other thing that you can do!

And now, if the wild idolatrous men did believe this, and with their fiery hearts laid hold of it to do it, in what form soever it came to them, I say it is well worthy of being believed.

Sayings of the Prophet Mohammed: I

From the collection of three thousand Authoritative Traditions called the *Sahih of Imam Muslim* (826–883 of the Christian Era).

Prayer and Fasting

The Prophet said:

'How many fast who know nothing of fasting except its thirst, and how many pray who know nothing of prayer but sleeplessness!'

Abu Huraira, in *Darmini's Collection*.

Weakness and Strength

The Prophet said:

'The son of man becomes feeble in his old age: but within him two things grow strong – greed for wealth and eagerness for life.'

Anas, in the *Collections of Bukhari and Muslim*.

In the World

The Prophet said:

'Be in this world as one who is a stranger, or who is a traveller on the way.'

Abdullah ibn Umar, in *Bukhari's Collection*.

Holy Struggle

The Prophet said:

'The best of holy wars is his, who speaks a just word in the presence of tyranny.'

Abu Sa'd, in the *Collections of Tirmidhi, Ibn Maja*.

God and Man

The Prophet said:

> 'God will say, on the Day of Requital:
> "Son of Man! I was sick, and you did not visit me."
> The man will say: "My Lord! How could I visit you, Lord of the World?"
> God will say: "Did you not know that such and such a one of my servants was ill, and you did not visit him? Did you not know that if you had visited him you would have assuredly found me with him?"
> God will say: "Son of Man! I asked food of you, and you did not feed me."
> The man will say: "My Lord! How could I feed you, Lord of all the world?"
> God will say: "Did you not know that such a one of my servants asked food of you, and you did not feed him? Did you not know that if you had fed him, you would have found me with him?"
> God will say: "Son of man! I asked drink of you, and you did not give me to drink."
> The man will say: "O Lord! How could I give you to drink, when you are Lord of all the world?"
> God will say: "Such and such a one of my servants asked drink of you, and you did not give him to drink. Assuredly, if you had given him to drink, you would have found me with him."'

Abu Huraira, in *Muslim's Collection.*

Charity, Knowledge, Children

The Prophet said:

> 'When a man dies, his works also cease, except for three:
>   Acts of charity which continue;
>   Knowledge from which others benefit;
>   Righteous children who pray for him.'

Abu Huraira, in the *Collections of Muslim, Tirmidhi, Sajistani and Nasai.*

Mercy

An Arab came from the desert, and saw the Prophet kissing some children. The bedouin said: 'What – do you kiss children, which we do not do?'
The Prophet said:

'Have I the capacity to give you that mercy which God has taken from your heart?'

Aisha, in the *Collections of Bukhari and Muslim.*

The Best of Islam:

A man asked: 'O Prophet of God! What is the best part of Islam?'
The Prophet said:

'That you should give food to the hungry, and give greetings to all, whether you know them or not.'

Ibn Amru ibn al As, in the *Collections of Bukhari and Muslim.*

The Day of Reckoning

The Prophet said:

'A man shall be asked about five things on the Day of Reckoning:
How he passed his life;
About his youth and how he grew old;
About where he obtained his wealth and how he spent it;
What he did with the knowledge that he had.'

Ibn Mas'us, in *Tirmidhi's Collection.*

A Donation

Abu Lubaba said that he intended to give away, in charity, everything he had.
The Prophet said:

'One-third of that will be sufficient from you.'

Malik, in *Malik's Collection.*

Creation

The Prophet said:

> 'All of creation is the family of God, and the most beloved to God is whoever does good to his family.'

> Anas and Abdullah, in *Baihaqi's Collection*.

Heedlessness

The Prophet said:

> 'Why should one of you laugh at someone for what he himself does?'

> Abdullah ibn Zam'ah, in the *Collections of Bukhari and Tirmidhi*.

Paradise

An Arab came out of the desert and asked the Prophet:
'Teach me works which will enable me to enter paradise.'
The Prophet said:

> 'Even though you have been brief, you have asked a large question.
> Set free all beings which breathe; set free men from servitude; love your kinsmen who do you wrong.
> And, if you are unable to do that, then feed the hungry and give drink to the thirsty, and enjoin what is good and forbid wrongs.
> And, if you are unable to do that, then do not speak unless you say what is good.'

> Bara'ibn Azib, in *Baihaqi's Collection*.

The Disciple

A man went to the Prophet and said: 'Verily, I love you.'
The Prophet said:

> 'Be careful of what you say.'

The man repeated, three times: 'By God, I love you!'
Then the Prophet said:

> 'If you are sincere and speak the truth, prepare yourself for
> poverty; for poverty speeds faster to whoever loves me than the
> river in its extreme spate.'

Abdullah ibn Mughaffal, in Tirmidhi's Collection.

Hospitality

A man said: 'O Prophet of God! There is a man who does not accept
me as a guest when I am travelling. Do I still have a duty towards
him as my guest when he is on a journey?'
The Prophet said:

> 'Yes, receive him with hospitality.'

Auf ibn Malik, in Tirmidhi's Collection.

The Camel

The Prophet was sitting with some of his companions and helpers
when a camel came up and went down on its forelegs before him.
The people exclaimed: 'O Messenger of Allah! Even animals
worship you. Surely it is even more fitting that we should worship
you!'
The Prophet said:

> 'Worship God, your Lord, and honour your brother.'

Aisha, in Ahmad Shaibani's Collection.

Servant

> 'Do not eulogize me,' said the Prophet, 'as the Christians
> eulogize the Son of Mary: for verily, I am a servant of God. So
> call me a servant of Allah, and his messenger.'

Ibn Abbas, in Abdari's Collection.

Preferment

Abu Musa stated:
'I went to the Messenger, taking two of my nephews with me.

'One of them said: 'Messenger of God! Give us [governorships] out of what God has given you to administer'. And the other said the same.'

'By God!' said the Prophet, 'I do not give a position of command to anyone who asks for it, or to anyone who covets it.'

Bukhari, Muslim, Sajistani, Nasai.

The Best

The best among you is he who is the best in treating his wife.

Aisha, in the *Collections of Tirmidhi and Darimi.*

Austerities

The Prophet said:

'Do not be austere with yourselves, for if you are it will go hard with you. There was a people who were severe with themselves, and it went hard for them. Their remnants are the monks in cloisters and in convents.'

Sahl ibn Abu Umama, in *Sajistani's Collection.*

Interference

'It is one of the beauties of Islam,' said the Prophet, 'that a man leaves off what does not concern him.'

Ali ibn al Husain, in *Tirmidhi's Collection.*

The Just Leader

'Verily, on the Day of Requital,' said the Prophet, 'the most beloved of men in the sight of God will be the leader who has been just: and he will be seated nearest to God. Verily, on that day, the most hated, the most severely punished, and the farthest from God will be the leader who was a tyrant.'

Abu Sa'id, in *Tirmidhi's Collection.*

A Prayer of Mohammed

'O God! By Thy knowledge of the secret, and by Thy power

59

over creation, let me live for so long as Thou knowest life to be best for me; and let me die when Thou knowest death to be better for me.

'O God! I beg of Thee to be able to heed Thee in private and in public, and to be able to speak the truth both in pleasure and in anger; and I beg of Thee an excellent way both in poverty and in affluence; and I beg of Thee a pleasure which does not fail; and I beg of Thee a joy of the eyes that is everlasting; and I beg of Thee pleasure in (Thy) commands; and I beg of Thee repose in life after death; and I beg of Thee the delight of seeing Thy face, and a passionate love to meet Thee without adversity to afflict me, or a trial that might lead me astray.

'O God! Adorn us with the adornment of faith, and make us guides, as rightly-guided ones.'

Ata ibn al Sa'ib, in *Nasai's Collection.*

The Password and The Builders

At the sound of the hammers striking upon the brazen gongs to call the workmen, Adoniram tore himself away from his thoughts, passed through the host of assembled workers, and, to preside over the payments, went into the temple, whose eastern door he partly opened, taking up his post at the foot of the column *Jakin*.

The lighted torches under the peristyle sent up showers of sparks when some drops of tepid rain touched them, and the panting workmen gaily offered their bosoms to its caresses.

It was a mighty crowd, and Adoniram, in addition to the book-keepers, had other men to help to pay, each according to his proper order. The three degrees were distinguished by a secret word instead of the manual signs which would have taken too long. Each man received his wage when he pronounced the proper password.

The secret word of the apprentices had hitherto been *Jakin*, the name of one of the bronze columns; the secret word of the companions, *Booz*, the name of the other pillar; and the word of the masters, *Jehovah*.

Arranged in categories, and drawn up in lines, the workmen presented themselves at the counters, before the overseers, over whom Adoniram presided. He touched the hand of each, and in his ear they whispered a word. This last day the password had been changed. The apprentices said *Tubal-Cain*; the companions, *Schib-bioleth*; and the masters, *Giblim*.

Little by little, the crowd grew thinner, the place was deserted, and when the last man to be paid had withdrawn, it was realised that everybody had not come forward, for there was still money in the chest.

'Tomorrow,' said Adoniram, 'you will send out and discover whether any of the workers are sick, or if death has come to any of them.'

As soon as all had gone away, Adoniram, vigilant and zealous

61

even on this last day, took a lamp and went his accustomed rounds through the deserted workshops, and into the different parts of the temple, to make sure that his commands had been obeyed, and the fires extinguished. His steps sounded sadly upon the flagstones: once again, he looked upon his work, and stopped for a long time before a group of winged cherubim, young Benoni's last work. 'The dear child!' he murmured with a sigh.

This pilgrimage over, Adoniram found himself in the great hall of the temple. The thick darkness around his lamp rolled away in reddish spirals, marking the ribs high up in the roofs, and the walls of the hall, wherein were three doors, looking to the north, the west and the east.

The first, that of the north, was reserved for the people; the second was the entrance for the King and his warriors; the eastern door was that of the Levites, and outside it stood the bronze columns of Jakin and Booz.

Before going out by the western door, which was nearest to him, Adoniram looked down towards the dark end of the hall, and his imagination, fired by the many statues which he had just been looking at, called forth from the shadows the phantom of Tubal-Cain. Steadily, he tried to pierce the darkness; but the chimera grew larger as it faded away, reached the top of the temple, and disappeared in the depth of the walls, like the shadow of a man lighted by a torch and moving away. A plaintive cry seemed to echo through the beams of the roof.

Then Adoniram turned, and made ready to go. Suddenly a human form stepped from behind a pillar, and, in a furious voice, said:

'If you would leave this place, give me the password of the masters.'

Adoniram had no weapons; the object of everyone's respect, and accustomed to secure obedience by a sign alone, he never even thought of defending his sacred person.

'Wretch,' he answered, recognising the companion Methousael. 'Away with you. Only when reason and crime are honoured shall you be received among the masters. Fly with your accomplices before the justice of Soliman falls upon your heads.'

Methousael heard this, and, raising his hammer with a strong arm, brought it down heavily on Adoniram's skull. The artist faltered; by an instinctive movement, he tried to escape by the second door, that on the north. There stood the Syrian Phanor, who said to him:

'If you would leave this place, give me the password of the masters.'

'You have not served for seven years,' answered Adoniram in a weak voice.

'The password!'

'Never!'

Phanor, the mason, buried his chisel into Adoniram's side, but he could not repeat the blow, for the architect of the temple, aroused by the pain, ran like a flash to the eastern door, to escape his assassins.

But there, Amrou the Phoenician, companion among the carpenters, was waiting for him, and he, in turn, cried:

'If you would leave this place, give me the password of the masters.'

'It was not thus I gained it,' Adoniram answered with difficulty, for he was exhausted. 'Ask it from him who sends you.'

As he tried to force a passage for himself, Amrou plunged the point of his compasses into Adoniram's heart.

At that moment the storm burst, signalled by a tremendous burst of thunder.

Adoniram lay upon the pavement, and his body covered three flag-stones. At his feet, the murderers stood together holding each other by the hand.

'This was a great man,' murmured Phanor.

'In the tomb, he will not need a greater space than you,' said Amrou.

'May his blood fall upon Soliman-Ben-Daoud!'

'Let us rather give thought to ourselves,' replied Methousael; 'the King's secret is our secret. Let us do away with the proof of this murder; the rain is falling, and the night is dark. Eblis protects us. Let us take this body far from the city, and bury it in the earth.'

So they wrapped up the body in a long apron of white skin, and, raising it in their arms, went silently down to the banks of the Medron, making their way to a solitary hillock beyond the road to Bethany. As they reached there, anxious and with fear at their hearts, they suddenly came upon an escort of horsemen. Crime is fearful: they halted; men who are fleeing are always timid . . . and at that moment the Queen of Saba passed in silence before the startled

63

assassins who were carrying the remains of her husband Adoniram. Then they went farther, and hollowed out a hole in the earth in which they put the body of the artist. Methousael, plucking a young branch from an acacia-tree, planted it in the freshly moved soil beneath which their victim rested.

Meanwhile, Balkis was dashing on through the valleys; the lightning split the heavens open, and Soliman slept.

His wound was the more cruel for he had to waken.

The sun had made its journey round the world, before the lethargic effect of the philter he had drunk was dissipated. Tormented by terrible dreams, he fought against visions, and it was with a violent shock that he returned again to the realm of life.

He rose in wild astonishment; his roving eyes seemed to be in search of their master's reason. At last he remembered.

The empty cup was before him; the Queen's last words came back to his mind; he saw her no more and became anxious; a sunbeam that played ironically upon his forehead made him tremble; he realised everything, and uttered a cry of rage.

It was in vain he questioned everyone. Nobody had seen her go, and her people had disappeared in the plain, only the traces of her camp had been found.

'This then,' cried Soliman, casting a look of wrath at Sadoc the high priest, 'this is the help your god sends to his faithful servants! Was it this he promised me? He delivers me as a plaything to the spirits of the abyss, and you, you imbecile, who reign in his name through my lack of power, you have abandoned me, without foreseeing anything, preventing anything. Who will give me winged legions to reach that perfidious Queen. Spirits of the earth and the fire, rebellious powers, spirits of the air, will you obey me?'

'Blaspheme not,' cried Sadoc. 'Jehovah alone is great, and he is a jealous god.'

In the midst of this disorder there appeared the prophet Ahias of Silo, dark, terrible and burning with divine fire – Ahias, poor and feared, whose greatness was only of the spirit. To Soliman he spoke: 'God marked the brow of Cain the murderer with a sign, and he declared: "Whosoever shall seek the life of Cain shall be punished seven times". And Lamech, the son of Cain, having shed blood, it was written: "The death of Lamech shall be avenged seventy times seven". Now hear, O King, what the Lord has bade me say to you:

"He who has shed the blood of Cain and Lamech shall be chastised seven hundred times seven times".'

Soliman bowed his head; he remembered Adoniram, knew that his orders had been carried out, and remorse drew from him the cry: 'Wretches! what have they done? I never said that they should kill him.'

Abandoned by his God, at the mercy of the genii, disdained and betrayed by the Princess of the Sabeans, Soliman in despair looked down upon the disarmed hand, upon which the ring he had received from Balkis still shone. The talisman gave him a gleam of hope. When he was alone, he turned the bezel towards the sun, and towards him came all the birds of the air, save *Hud-Hud*, the magic hoopoe. Three times he called the hoopoe and forced her to obey, then bade her take him to the Queen. At once the bird took flight again, and Soliman, stretching out his arms to her, felt himself lifted from the ground, and carried in the air. Fear took possession of him, he withdrew his hand, and came to earth again. The hoopoe went on across the valley, and, at the top of a hillock perched upon the frail bough of an acacia-tree, and Soliman could not compel her to leave it.

Then, mastered by a wild frenzy, King Soliman dreamed of raising countless armies and putting the kingdom of Saba to fire and sword. Often he shut himself up alone to curse his fate and to conjure spirits. An *afrit*, genius of the abyss, was constrained to serve him and go with him in his solitudes. To forget the Queen, and stamp out his fatal passion, Soliman sent everywhere for strange women whom he married with unholy rites, and they initiated him into the idolatrous worship of images. Soon, to bend the genii to his will, he peopled the high places and, not far from Tabor, built a temple to Moloch.

So was fulfilled the prophecy, which the shade of Enoch had uttered in the realm of fire to his son Adoniram, in these words: 'You are destined to avenge us, and this temple which you are raising to Adonai shall bring about the fall of Soliman'.

But the King of the Hebrews did still more, so the Talmud tells us, for the noise of the murder of Adoniram being spread about, the people in their wrath demanded justice, and the King ordered that nine masters should make sure that the artist was truly dead, by finding his body.

Seventeen days went by. The investigations made in the neighbourhood of the temple produced nothing, and the masters searched in vain through all the countryside. And then, one day, one of them, wearied by the heat, thought to grasp a branch of an acacia-tree from which some strange unknown bird of brilliant plumage had just flown, that so he might climb more easily. He was surprised to find that the whole tree gave way beneath his hand, and was not fully rooted in the ground. The earth had recently been moved, and the astonished master called to his companions.

At once the nine set to digging with their nails, and found the shape of a grave. And one of them said to his brothers:

'Perhaps the murderers were felons who wished to learn the password of the masters from Adoniram. Perhaps they succeeded; would it not be prudent to change the word?'

'What word shall we choose?' said another.

'If we find our master here,' said a third, 'the first word which one of us shall utter shall be the password. It shall immortalise the memory of the crime, and the oath we swear here to avenge it, we and our children after us, upon those murderers and their posterity while the earth shall endure.'

The oath was sworn; their hands were joined above the grave, and they began to dig with eagerness.

When they had recognised the corpse, one of the masters took it by one finger, and the skin stayed in his hand; so too a second; a third seized it by the wrist, in the manner of the masters to the companions, and still the skin came away, whereupon he cried: *MAKBENACH*, which means: *'The flesh leaves the bones'*.

Immediately they agreed that this, henceforth, should be the word of the masters and the rallying cry of the avengers of Adoniram, and God's justice has determined that this word, through many centuries, should rally the peoples against the lineage of kings.

Phanor, Amrou and Methousael had taken to flight; but, recognised as false brothers, they perished at the hands of workmen in the states of Maaca, the King of the country of Geth, where they had hidden themselves under the names of Sterkin, Oterfut, and Hoben.

Nevertheless, the guilds, by a secret inspiration, still continued to seek the vengeance which had been denied them upon *Abiram* or the murderer. And the posterity of Adoniram was sacred in their

66

eyes; long afterwards they swore by *the sons of the widow*, for so they called the descendants of Adoniram and the Queen of Saba.

On the express order of Soliman-Ben-Daoud, the illustrious Adoniram was buried beneath the very altar of the temple he had raised; and it was for this that Adonai left the Ark of the Hebrews and brought to slavery the successors of Daoud.

*   *   *   *

Greedy for honours, might and pleasure, Soliman married five hundred wives, and finally constrained the reconciled genii to serve his designs against the neighbouring nations, by the virtue of the famous ring, once carved by Irad, father of Maviael the Cainite, and owned in turn by Enoch, who used it to command the stones, then by the patriarch Jared, and Nimrod, who bequeathed it to Saba, the father of the Hemiarites.

This ring of Soliman's made the genii, the winds and all the animals obedient to him. Surfeited with power and pleasures, the wise Soliman kept on repeating: 'Eat, drink and love; for all the rest is but vanity'.

Yet, by a strange contradiction, he was not happy. This King, whom material things had brought so low, aspired to become immortal.

By artifice, and with the help of his great knowledge, he hoped to secure this immortality by observing certain conditions: in order to purify his body from mortal elements without encompassing its dissolution, it must sleep the profound sleep of the dead for two hundred and twenty-five years, beyond the reach of attack from any corrupting principle. After that, the exiled soul would return to its envelope, which would be made young again with the splendid virility whose blossoming is marked by the age of thirty-three years.

When he had grown old and feeble, as soon as he saw the signs of an approaching end in the failing of his strength, Soliman ordered the genii whom he had made his slaves to build for him, in the mountain of Kaf, an inaccessible palace, and in the middle of it a massive throne of gold and ivory, raised upon four pillars made from the lusty trunk of an oak.

There, Soliman, the prince of the genii, had determined to pass this time of trial. The last days of his life were spent in charming away, by magic signs, by mystic words, and by the virtue of the ring, all the animals, all the substances, all the elements, all the substances endowed with the power to decompose matter. He laid a spell upon the vapours of the clouds, the dampness of the earth, the rays of the sun, the breath of the winds, the butterflies, the insects and larvae. He laid a spell upon the birds of prey, the bat, the owl, the rat, the noisome fly, the worm, and the family of insects which creep and gnaw. He laid a spell upon metal; upon stones, alkalis and acids, even the emanations that come from plants.

Having done all this, when he was sure that he had withdrawn his body from all the agents of destruction, pitiless ministers of Eblis, he had himself carried for the last time to the heart of the mountains of Kaf, and there, gathering the genii together, he set them tremendous tasks, enjoining upon them, under pain of the most fearful punishments, to respect his slumbers and watch over him.

Then he seated himself upon his throne, and there settled himself comfortably, and his limbs, little by little, grew cold; his eyes grew dim; his breathing stopped, and he went to sleep in death.

And his genii slaves continued to serve him, to carry out his orders and to prostrate themselves before their master, for whose awakening they waited.

The winds respected his face; the larva which engender worms could not draw near him; the birds and quadrupeds of prey were forced to remain away from him: the water turned aside its vapours, and, by the strength of the spells, the body remained intact for more than two centuries.

Soliman's beard grew and rolled down to his feet; his nails pierced the leather of his gloves and the golden material of his shoes.

But how shall human wisdom, in its narrow limits, bring about the *Infinite*? Soliman had forgotten to charm one insect, the most insignificant of all ... he had forgotten the mite.

Mysteriously, invisibly, the mite advanced. It settled itself in one of the pillars that upheld the throne, and gnawed there slowly, slowly, without ever stopping. Not the acutest ears could have heard that atom scratching, as every year it scattered behind it a few grains of tiny dust.

It worked for two hundred and twenty-four years. Then suddenly the pillar that had been gnawed away, broke beneath the weight of the throne, which crashed to the ground with a tremendous noise.*

It was the mite which vanquished Soliman, and the first to know of his death; for the King of Kings, thus cast upon the flag-stones, never woke.

Then the humbled spirits recognised their mistake, and recovered their liberty.

And here endeth the story of the great Soliman-Ben-Daoud, which is to be welcomed with respect by all true believers, for it is shortly told by the sacred hand of the Prophet, in the thirty-fourth *fatihat* of the Koran, the mirror of wisdom and fountain of truth.

---

* According to the Orientals, the powers of nature can only act by virtue of a common agreement. It is this agreement between all creatures that makes the power of Allah himself. It is interesting to observe the similarity between the mite which triumphed over Soliman's ambitious arrangements, and the legend of Edda. Odin and Freya had, in the same way, put a spell upon all creatures so that they should respect the life of Balder, their child. But they forgot the mistletoe, and this humble plant caused the death of the son of the gods. It was for this reason that the mistletoe was sacred in the religion of the Druids, which succeeded that of the Scandinavians.

EASTERN CUSTOMS –
WESTERN TRAVELLERS

Greetings & Salutations
by *Robert Stanford*

One of the commands of the Prophet Mohammed is that Moslems must greet each other with the words *Assalam-alaikum* – Peace upon you. The singular form, used familiarly, is *Assalam-alaik*. In most places it is not regarded as correct for non-Moslems to use this salutation, and it is therefore best avoided by them.

The greetings used by Arab Christians, and by some Moslems as well, can be employed:

Sabahal-khair – Good Morning; to which the answer often is: *Sabah-an-noor* – a shining morning. You can ring the changes with: *Baharkum saeed* – May your day be happy; and answer it with: *Saeed wa mubarak* – Happy and Blessed!

'Good night' is *Lailatkum saeeda* – Happy Night!

Ahlan wa sahlan, heard in every Arab land, is an all-purpose greeting, standing roughly for 'How are you?', 'Welcome' and 'Do come in'. *Tafaddul,* however, means 'Come in' or 'Have a cup of tea or coffee' or 'Sit down'. Literally it means 'Honour me'.

Arab greetings may go on for several minutes, with questions about one's health, business, and so on. It is not considered polite to ask any questions at all about an Arab's womenfolk: remember that the word *Harim,* ('harem' in the West) is a cognate of 'Sacred'.

Useful and continually heard phrases:

Bismillah = In the name of God.

Said when starting anything, going out of the house, beginning a meal, and so on.

Alhamdulillah = Praise God.

Answer to 'how are you?' (*Kaif halkum, kaif al-hal?*) and when good news is heard or the aversion of evil is desired.

Fi aman Allah = With faith in God.

'Goodbye'.

Shukran = Thank you.

Also *ashkurak*, *ashkurkum* (singular and plural).

La illaha illa Allah, Muhammad ar-Rasul-Allah = There is no God except Allah, Mohammed is the Messenger of God.

This is the Islamic Profession of Faith. To repeat it once is to testify to one's conversion to Islam.

La haula wa la quwwatah illa billahi al aali wa'l azeem = There is no power or might except in God, the High, the Great.

This is sometimes said as an expression of great surprise.

Astaghfirullah = I seek refuge in God.

Expression of alarm, disgust, etc.

*   *   *   *

Never learn oaths and experiment with them. In some Western countries, people swear jocularly. This is never safe in the Middle East. The sense of honour is very high. Words like fool, dog, swine, bastard, and so on can be invitations to the most extreme action.

Some Westerners try to talk 'biblical' English to Middle Easterners, under the impression that they understand it better. This is completely untrue. I have heard a European businessman asking a baffled, Western-educated sheikh: 'Art thou of the Faith, Brother?', apparently in an attempt to ingratiate himself.

Finally, perhaps the words you will hear most in the Arab countries are: *Ahlan wa Sahlan*, 'At home and at ease!', the welcoming phrase originally said by bedouins to travellers when inviting them to accept hospitality. *Marhabba* is another one: it means: 'Welcome!'

Middle East Business

- NEVER, on any account, put into a contract something which might look like sharp practice. I have seen many contracts evaporate just because of that. Example: if you are paying exploratory costs and have agreed to do so, do not try to recover them by slipping in a clause which reimburses you, unless this has been agreed verbally or in writing beforehand. The Western habit of putting in all kinds of clauses and letting the other man's lawyer sort out those which he should not accept is regarded as immoral.
- Get quite clear in your head what you mean by commissions and suchlike payments. If an official expects a percentage for signing or negotiating, this is in many countries because he is allowed it in lieu of salary. To call this a bribe, or to bargain about it seldom helps, so you should make as full enquiries as possible beforehand.
- Never ask a top man directly to get you a contract or to negotiate preliminary matters. As in top-level transactions in the West, the top people come in only for signing: underlings do the negotiating. By asking a Middle-Eastern big shot to negotiate or agree something before it has been through the lower levels is to make him think that you are a small man trying to get a favour. This is because direct requests are made to big people in the East only by underlings or beggars and similar.
- If a top man says: 'I am not empowered to decide,' he means that he is too big to do deals. He may authorise them, but he cannot initiate them without losing face.
- You must give something before you get anything. This is not a bribe, but a way of showing respect and the desire to be friends. A gift is never a small token: it must be worthy of the recipient. This means that if you are dealing with someone important who will smooth your way at contract stage, you have to avoid stinting – or don't start at all.

Never mention his womenfolk.

You are entering a region where the social systems and thinking are similar to medieval and Victorian ones in the West. The only relics now in our culture are the courts of monarchs, presidential circumstances and diplomatic usage at ambassadorial level. If you do not know how to operate under these circumstances, it could pay you to hire someone who is familiar with traditional courtesies. Remember: each present-day sovereign is only a relic of the time when every man (or woman) of importance behaved as they do, with dignity and circumspection, esteeming etiquette and honour above profit or any other form of showing.

Skiving in the Sun
by *Idries Shah*

Visiting the expatriate community in Bahrain for the first time is like walking in on the sons and daughters of all those who peopled the *Family Favourites* programmes of the 1950s; discovering how things turned out for all those names that used to come crackling in over the Sunday joint from the other side of the world. The addresses no longer feature British Forces Post Office 41 or the Sergeants' Mess at Muharraq but the names of engineering and construction firms.

The people have different faces and their motivations are different but only in so far as they represent the changes in Britain itself since it gave up its presence east of Suez. In the 1950s they were the representatives of an empire of sorts; now they have the rather superficial self-confidence of the class that has been running the country in the interim and yet, strangely, their criticisms seem more fundamental now. There is a sense that the new 'rulers' have no commitment to the country that sired them. In the old days the servicemen who represented Britain were largely conscripted, doing their 'bit', one way or the other, perhaps grudgingly but with more than a little secret pride.

Today their spiritual heirs are out from Luton or Manchester making money as fast as they can and any benefit to the country they love to hate is purely by the way. One senses that the very wealth that the privilege of being born in Britain provides has made them despise their country.

Listening to a man in his twenties in a Manama hotel bar boasting of the £25,000 flat he has bought in Brighton, one's mind jumps to his service equivalent of 20 years ago who would most probably have been talking about his leave spent tinkering with a Norton motorcycle and one wonders which of the two was really the better off.

In theory, the serviceman of yesterday was the instrument of imperialism come, if not to subdue the natives, at least to use them. Today's flat-owning son of Britain comes, in theory, about equal with most of those to whom he has come to build, purvey technology, instruct or simply to sell. In practice, he treats the country more like his own backyard than his imperialist forebear ever did. True he doesn't actually practise his English accent into the shaving mirror but a Briton with even a handful of words in Arabic is hard to find and many of the educated Bahrainis with whom he comes into contact will most likely have had a better British education than he has. So pro-British are his hosts, in fact, that when the English popular press portrayed a certain Royal visit as a sort of comic opera with strong racial undertones they were taken aback despite the predictions of some of the more worldly members of the British community who saw it all coming. To their credit the resident Britons, to the last, denounced the scribblers of the British yellow press though even that was a little disingenuous of some of them since the journalists, many of them on their first visits to Bahrain, were merely reporting characterisations of the local people that they had picked up from the British community.

Yet the great contradictions in the *persona* of the overseas Briton are nowhere better illustrated than in this sunny but politically, culturally and physically arid land. Because while the *expats*, as they like to call themselves in the irritating shorthand that abounds, will leap to defend the land that now fattens them from the British press, they seem to delight in tearing to shreds their own country and all that it has ever stood for, for the benefit of the local English language journals. They rant and rave about the declining state of the British economy, how no-one wants to work and how the trade unions are running everything into the ground, blithely unaware of the contribution they might make to solving some of those problems by staying at home and ignorant of the fate of those Bahrainis who have expressed similar, spirited criticism about their own country. They spend their days locked up on a scarcely habitable island off the coast because they feel such things as trade unions and a voice for the people in decision-making are not such bad ideas after all. Such freedom to express ideas and criticise the ruler are not enjoyed to the same extent by Bahrainis in their own press despite the undoubtedly benign rule of the Emir.

The sad fact is that most, or all, of this seems to go completely unappreciated by resident Britons who sometimes have a nasty habit of importing some of the practices that they find so abhorrent in the 'old country'.

Witness the day a British-born engineer promised to show me over one of Bahrain's most successful attempts at industrialisation – the Arab Shipbuilding and Repair Yard – which services not only Arab vessels in the fleets of the Gulf states and Saudi Arabia but also locally-based units of the United States Navy. By all accounts the yard is a joy to work at, being among the most modern of its kind in the world, particularly for all those who learned their trade in the antiquated yards of the North-East of England and on the Clyde. The appointment was set for three o'clock when the working day ends. Arriving about twenty minutes early to make sure that my efficiency matched that of all the hard-working Britons that must people the place, a long wait past the appointed hour produced no sign of my acquaintance. A word with some of his colleagues arriving for the next shift quickly revealed why: 'Still tied up, you must be joking. You wouldn't catch him staying till the final whistle. He's long gone by knocking-off time.'

Go Native

The British, justified or not, have had a reputation in the past for the ability to 'go native', to blend in with local habits and customs despite a general lack of talent at learning foreign languages. Yet most of the Britons in Bahrain display what amounts to a fanatical desire to hang on to every vestige of their home environment and cultural background as though to do anything else would result in the disintegration of personality. One would have thought that having the shops packed with British goods, when available, the newspapers full of British news, written and edited by Britons, a local radio station largely staffed by Britons and with television showing many British programmes not to mention taking most of its international news film from Britain and nightly news from a British newsreader would be sufficient cultural comfort for those finding it hard to tear themselves from Britannia's breast. Not so.

There is the British Club, which looks exactly what it is: a left-over from the British military presence with all the character of a tarted-up Nissen hut. At the weekend it is packed with families trying to recapture Sunday at home. It is a sort of cross between a working man's club and a country pub and it does not quite make it as either. The country pub bar was quite attractive until one discovered the monotony of the company – all discussing job prospects 'back home' – and the fact that the carved beams and white-washed walls were not the work of enterprising Britons who had spent months reshaping and decorating driftwood from some ancient ship-wreck, but all made of fibre-glass. The fact is, as any of the club's older hands will tell you over the self-service Sunday lunch in the main dining room (no roast beef and Yorkshire pudding but plenty of curry and rice), that nowadays the newer members are not interested in the club as a community. They just want to come down for a meal and a drink and use it like a pub. They are not interested in putting anything into the club in return for what they get; not like the old days when all the cooking was done by the chairman and his wife, but everybody chipped in with some kind of a contribution; when every dance or function they had was oversubscribed. Like a slice of the population of Leighton Buzzard translated to Arabia and taking their life style with them.

But the old hands should not really be surprised that the force motivating the majority of their members is self-interest. Most of the expatriate workers are there for the money and most of them, to give them credit, are honest enough to say so.

They do not go to Bahrain for the adventure. Employers paying expensive air fares out to the Gulf don't like surprises, and workers wanting to return home early in mid-contract because they don't like the conditions definitely fall into that category. So the worker is protected against risk and, in many of the jobs they go to, there is precious little challenge either. If they were not in Bahrain making a fast buck they would be anywhere else a fast buck was to be made. Fast money and cheap booze are among the attractions for many but there are those who come to escape restrictive practices at home that stop them spreading their wings. Many lose that drive once they get into Bahrain and find that the local people are not that highly motivated anyway. And if there is not a powerful motivation to work in Bahrain there is little else to do that does not require initiative and a lively interest in what is around you. The long lunch and even longer afternoon siesta soon become, like cirrhosis of the liver, part of the life-style.

The difficulty of filling in the hours for those outside the ultra-busy executive class can be considerable as witness some of the diversions offered by the less-than-scintillating night-clubs and hotels, the latter offering a movie-lunch – a bargain price lunch with a full-length film thrown in. If that does not attract then there is always tennis or swimming at the British Club or a trip to Shaikh Isa's beach on a Friday, a gathering reserved for foreigners, mainly Britons, who get an opportunity for a word in the Shaikh's ear, while the ruler gets an opportunity to cast an eye over the expatriate ladies.

These weekly gatherings have always provided the means for the Emir to gauge the temperature of the foreign community but even these may have to go as an outward manifestation of the 'privileges' extended to foreigners in the new egalitarian spirit which is affecting the Gulf in the wake of the Iranian revolution.

Those wives who do not work and do not have a family to look after, and there are a surprising number among the younger couples, usually end up spending as much time out of the country as possible, especially in the summer when the heat becomes too much for the Bahrainis themselves. One young wife, who could expect probably one foreign holiday a year at home, went off to Hong Kong in the spring and was planning to go to Kenya later in the year.

There are exceptions, of course, to the general run of people who see Bahrain as a short-cut to financial security. It has been almost exclusively Britons who have been responsible for the active preservation and restoration of Bahrain's older buildings and the re-evaluation of the country's architectural heritage as something which is as much a part of the future as of the past; going against the tide in the Arab world which seems intent upon destroying anything with any character and replacing it with futuristic developments which look uninspiring even in their more normal European milieu.

Bahrainis have been more aware of their architectural heritage than other Gulf states and the soukh area of Manama bears witness to this, but it has been left to a Briton, Keith Bailey, actually to restore a typical old Arab town house to its former, some might say 'better than new', condition. Foreigners played a part in the excavation of Bahrain's old Portuguese fort which stands on a promontory overlooking Manama bay, but sadly, since that time, matters have gone very little further and the structure is badly in need of even basic pointing work. Artifacts recovered from the site still litter the floors of the excavators' temporary tents. They are deteriorating fast and only a few have found their way into a local museum. The island's oldest mosque was given a face-lift by the Bahrainis but

81

some might wish that foreign expertise had been called in – after an unauthorised trip up its minaret I was mortified to find out that it was unsafe for such exploits.

Cream Teas

As in Saudi Arabia, the latest fad among the foreign community is to buy video tape machines and buy or swap tapes of the latest films. Television games too tend to get a high rating and, as in any community long on time and money but short on imagination and initiative, eating out becomes something of a ritual. There is no shortage of places to choose from, ranging from good Chinese to sophisticated Arabian eating houses to one which offers genuine English cream teas. But for anyone seriously looking on Bahrain as an opportunity to save money to put into a house or business in Britain, restaurants are an expensive diversion and, anyway, it is far more fun to try and feed yourself cheaply using what is available locally.

Wherever one looks in the expatriate community it is hard to escape an underlying feeling of ennui – the sense that however endless the sunshine, however remarkable the salaries – the life-style of most expatriates, remains an unsatisfactory imitation of what life in Britain is, or is imagined to be, because there is no serious attempt to understand or adapt to the local culture or life-style. The expatriates remain in the position of guests, who may be asked to leave at any time, enjoying privileges unearned, in a country for which they have little real respect, at the beck and call of people to whom they feel superior yet with whom they must maintain a semblance of good relations.

Popularity Through Proverbs

Proverb:

> If you wish to find a good man or woman, seek one who is hated by half the people and loved by the other half.

Few things are such an immediate success in the Arab world as proverbs. Innumerable tales are told of people who have saved their lives – or business deals – through producing an appropriate saying.

The following is a useful selection:-

Haml al-jamaa'at reesh = 'A burden carried by many is a feather'.

Al ajala min ash-shaitaan = 'Haste is from the Devil'.

As sabr miftaah al faraj = 'Patience is the key to success'.

Yakhaf min dhilluhu = 'He is afraid of his shadow'.

Awwal taam, wa baaduhu kalam = 'First the food, then the talking'.

Al aqilu takhfi al ishratu = 'A sign is enough to the wise'.

Al kareem idha wa'ada, wafa = 'The generous perform what they promise'.

Al jenaaza kabeer w'al miyat faar = 'The funeral is large but the corpse is a mouse'.

Al qina'atu kanzun la yufna = 'Contentment is a treasure which does not decay'.

An-naasa ala dini mulukihim = 'People follow the religion of their rulers'.

As-safar sakar = 'Travel is tribulation'.

Jawaab al ahmaq sukoot = 'The answer to a fool is silence'.

Kullu shayin yarja'u ila aslihi = 'Everything returns to its origin'.

La tahmil ala yomika hamal sanatika = 'Don't load on your day your year's burden'.

Man talaba, wajada = 'He who seeks, finds'.

Qaddim al khuruj qabl al dukhool = 'Try the exit before you enter'.

Kathrat ar-riyaas taghraq al-markab = 'Too many captains sink the ship'.

Of these sayings, some are classical and others colloquial: both forms of the language are in use in the Middle East.

Abdesalam Tunisi.

Lokman The Wise

The Arabian sage, Lokman, is represented by tradition to have been a black slave, and of hideous appearance, from which, and from the identity of the apologues in the Arabian collection that bears his name as the author with the so-called Esopic fables, some writers have supposed that Esop and Lokman are simply different names of one and the same individual. But the fables ascribed to Lokman have been for the most part (if not indeed entirely) derived from the Greek; and there is no authority whatever that Lokman composed any apologues. Various traditions exist regarding Lokman's origin and history. It is said that he was an Ethiopian, and was sold as a slave to the Israelites during the reign of David. According to one version, he was a carpenter; another describes him as having been originally a tailor; while a third account states that he was a shepherd. If the Arabs may be credited, he was closely related to the patriarch Job. Among the anecdotes which are recounted of his amiable disposition is the following:

> His master once gave him a bitter lemon to eat. Lokman ate it all, upon which his master, greatly astonished, asked him: 'How is it possible for you to eat so unpalatable a fruit?' Lokman replied: 'I have received so many favours from you, that it is no wonder I should once in my life eat a bitter lemon from your hand.' Struck with this generous answer, the master, it is said, immediately gave him his freedom.

A man of eminence among the Jews, observing a great crowd around Lokman, eagerly listening to his discourse, asked him whether he was not the black slave who had lately tended the sheep of such and such a person, to which Lokman replied in the affirmative. 'How was it possible,' continued his questioner, 'for thee to attain so exalted a degree of wisdom and piety?'

Lokman answered: 'By always speaking the truth; keeping

85

my word; and never intermeddling in affairs that did not concern me.'

Being asked from whom he had learned urbanity, he replied: 'From men of rude manners, for whatever I saw in them that was disagreeable I avoided doing myself.' And when asked from whom he had acquired his philosophy, he said: 'From the blind, who never advance a step until they have tried the ground.'

Lokman is also credited with this apothegm: 'Be a learned man, a disciple of the learned, or an auditor of the learned; at least, be a lover of knowledge and desirous of improvement.' In Persian and Turkish tales, Lokman sometimes figures as a highly skilled physician, and 'wise as Lokman' is proverbial throughout the Mohammedan world.

From *Flowers from a Persian Garden*, by W.A. Clouston, London 1890.

Problems of Language

Public Speaking

An important Western dignitary, who had taken a crash-course in Arabic, was scheduled to speak before an assembly of important opinion-leaders in – shall we call it, the Arabian State of Saracenia?

His visit had been announced many months before, and in the country's capital city a stadium had been set aside for the most significant event of his tour: an address which was to be chaired by no less a personage than the Head of State.

There were three central factors which made this an unusual occurrence, apart from the presence of the Ruler. In the first place, hearing people lecture in their own language was something which few Arabs ever experienced from foreigners. The guest had memorised his speech, with tape-recorders, until he was word-perfect. In the second place, millions of dollars' worth of business hung in the balance: the visitor was an eminent man of affairs, but his country also stood to gain immense contracts if all the sheikhs and other notables would allow pipelines across their territory, and ships to unload at the harbours which their fighting-men protected. Third, but equally important, was the fact that it had taken four years of enquiries to find a date when each and every member of the audience would be free and would be prepared to come to such a meeting.

Eventually the date was fixed, when there would be no cases for the sheikhs to try, none of their sons absent on world tours, no political talks to attend, no visits from relatives, no national celebrations to take their minds off the matter in hand.

When our hero arrived at the stadium, it was packed with amirs and fakirs, sheikhs and wazirs, courtiers and officials – and their heavily-veiled ladies. A sea of faces stared back at the Ruler and his guest, floodlit on the dais, and ten thousand rosaries clicked through perfumed fingers as a hush descended, for the visitor to begin his address.

He had the entire speech word-perfect, and, being an experienced speaker, not a syllable had slipped from his mind as he stood up to begin.

Then he realised that there was something missing: the opening salutation. He knew that it was not recommended for unbelievers to start with the words, 'Peace upon you!' But he did not know the phrase for, 'My friends,' or 'Ladies and gentlemen,' – much less for, 'Your Highness, Noble Amirs, Sheiks and Wazirs: may your days be long!'

But he had, after all, taken a crash-course, and he was a man of resolute courage and initiative and had mastered the Arabic alphabet.

So he looked around for the notices which would, inevitably, in such a well-organised place as this, say the magic phrase: 'Ladies' and 'Gentlemen'. Sure enough, as his eyes moved across the scene, there they were, at every corner of the arena, clear and readable signs. He read out the words:

'*Al-Khuruj w'al Mutamma!*'

In less time than it takes to tell, the entire assembly rose as one man and filed out, leaving the speaker and the Ruler alone on their platform.

Agonisedly, he turned to his host. 'What has happened? What have I said? Are they annoyed at something...?'

The Ruler smiled.

'Your opening words, *Al-Khuruj wa'l Mutamma*, mean "Way out and Restaurant", and also colloquially enough, "To the exits and the food".'

'I knew that there was an Arabic proverb "First the food then the talk," said the guest, 'but this is terrible! What will it mean?'

'It is terrible indeed,' said the Ruler. 'It also means that you owe them twenty thousand dinners!'

Middle Eastern Studies in the Universities

There are a number of elements in the situation which illustrate and perhaps also explain the relative failure of Middle Eastern studies in the universities. The first of these is ignorance – or, to put it differently, a low level of professional competence... Professional advancement in Middle Eastern studies can be achieved with knowledge and skills well below what is normally required in the more developed fields or more frequented disciplines... This has led to low standards of entry at the student level that continue to the professorial level, to low standards of performance, and to low standards of promotion in academic institutions. These defects, in turn, are reflected in the secondary literature of the subject and the acceptance as authorities of books which contain ludicrous errors, even of fact.

From *The State of Middle Eastern Studies*, in *The American Scholar*, Summer 1979, pp. 365–381 inc., by Professor Bernard Lewis, Cleveland E. Dodge Professor of Near Eastern Studies at Princeton University.

Meeting and Mingling

Nicknames

The following names were attributed to various Middle Eastern writers and poets by the English:-

Raymond Lully was known as *Doctor Illuminatus* (1234–1315).

Zakarija ibn Muhammed, a native of Kaswin in the 13th century was known as the *Pliny of the East*.

Sheikh Moslehedin Saadi was the *Nightingale of a Thousand Songs* and the *Oriental Homer*.

Captain Richard Burton (1821) was the *Modern Admirable Crichton* while Avicenna (Abdallah ibn Sina) was the *Admirable Crichton of Arabia* to the Christians because of the variety and extent of his precocious attainments.

Abu Nasr Mohammed Al Farabi in 950 became the *Orpheus of Arabia*.

Francis Bacon was the *Great Verulam* (1561–1626).

Mohammad Hafiz, the poet, was known as *Sugar Lip* or the *Persian Anacreon*.

From Sobriquets and Nicknames by Albert R. Fry.

Lady Mary Visits the Sultana

> The following is an account given by Lady Mary Wortley Montague (who first introduced inoculation against smallpox) in her diary of her visit to the Sultana Hafiten, who became the favourite of Sultan Mastapha after the death of Fatima. This highly descriptive passage affords, on personal veracious evidence, a glowing picture of the splendour, magnificence and richness of Eastern dresses.

I was led into a large room, with a sofa extending the whole length of it, covered with pale blue figured velvet, on a silver ground with cushions of the same; where I was desired to repose until the Sultana appeared who had contrived this manner of reception so as to avoid rising at my entrance; though she made me an inclination of the head when I rose up to her. She did not seem to me to have ever been so beautiful as the fair Fatima (whom I saw at Adrianople) though she had the remains of a fine face, more decayed by sorrow than time. Her dress was something so surprisingly rich that I cannot forbear describing it. She wore a vest called *dualma* which differs from a caftan by longer sleeves and folding over at the bottom. It was of purple cloth, straight to her shape and thick set on each side down to feet and round the sleeves, with pearls, of the best water, being of the same size as their buttons usually are, about the bigness of a pea. And to these buttons large loops of diamonds were fastened in the form of those gold loops so common on birthday coats. The habit was tied at the waist with two large tassels of smaller pearls, and round the arms embroidered with large diamonds. Her shift was fastened at the bottom with a large diamond shaped like a lozenge; her girdle as broad as the broadest English ribbon, was entirely covered with diamonds; round her neck she wore three chains which reached to her knees; one, of large pearls, at the bottom of which hung a fine coloured emerald, as big as a turkey egg: another consisting of two hundred emeralds, close joined together of the most lively green, perfectly matched, every one as large as a half crown piece, and as thick as three crown pieces; and another of small emeralds, perfectly round. But her earrings eclipsed all the rest. They were two diamonds shaped exactly like pears; as large as a big hazel nut. Round her talpoche she had four strings of pearls, the whitest and most perfect in the world, fastened with two roses, consisting of a large ruby for the middle stone; and round them twenty drops of clear diamonds to each. Besides this, her head-dress was covered with bodkins of emeralds and diamonds. She wore large diamond bracelets and had five rings on her fingers – except Mr. Pitts, the largest diamonds I ever saw in my life. 'Tis for jewellers to compute the value of all these things. But according to the common estimation of jewels in our part of the world, her whole dress must be worth a hundred thousand pounds sterling.

The magnificence of her table answered very well to that of her dress. The knives were of gold; and the hafts set with diamonds. But the only articles of luxury which grieved my eyes were the tablecloths and napkins which consisted all of tiffany, embroidered with gold, after the finest manner, in natural flowers. It was with the utmost regret that I made use of these costly silken napkins, which were as finely wrought as the finest handkerchiefs that ever came out of the country. You may be sure that they were entirely spoilt before dinner was over. The sherbet (which is the liquor they drink with their meals) was served in china bowls, but the covers and salvers were of massive gold. After dinner, water was brought in gold basins, together with towels, of the same kinds as the napkins, which I very unwillingly wiped my hands upon; and coffee was served in china with gold spoons.

When I took my leave of her I was complimented with perfumes, as at the Grand Vizier's, and was presented with a very fine embroidered hanky. Her slaves were to the number of thirty, besides ten little ones, the eldest not above seven years old. These were the most beautiful girls I ever saw; all richly dressed; and I observed that the Sultana took a great deal of pleasure in these lovely children, which are a vast expense; for there is not a handsome girl of that age to be bought under a hundred pounds sterling. They wore little garlands of flowers; and their own hair braided with all their head-dresses; but their habits were entirely of gold stuff.

From *Precious Stones*, by W.D. Fernie, M.D., (John Wright & Co.) 1907.

Never Without Charm

While taking a parting cup of coffee with the postmaster I unluckily set my foot on a handsome pipe-bowl (pipe-bowls are always snares to near-sighted people moving over Turkish floors, as they are scattered in places quite remote from the smokers, who live at the farther end of the prodigiously long pipe-sticks) – crash; but nobody moved; only on apologising through Giorgio, the polite Mohammedan said: 'The breaking of such a pipe-bowl would indeed, under ordinary circumstances, be disagreeable; but in a friend every action has its charm!'

From *Journals of a Landscape Painter in Greece and Albania*, by Edward Lear, 1851.

The Merchant and The Frankish Wife

In September, 1187, following the Battle of Hattin, a
disaster for the Crusaders, Sultan Saladin stormed and
took Jerusalem. Events in this narrative take place from
just before Hattin up to the point where the Saracens and
Crusaders agreed to release all prisoners. The holy men,
Junaid and Sari Saqati, mentioned are two classical Sufi
masters. The Judge, Ibn Shaddad, is Saladin's biographer,
author of the celebrated *What Befell Sultan Yusuf*. His full
name was Imam Grand Qadi of the Moslems, Bahauddin
Abu El-Mahasan Yusuf, ibn Rafi, Ibn Tamim, called Ibn
Shaddad, Judge of the Fortified City of Aleppo. He studied
under the great scholars of Mosul, now in Iraq, and was a
disciple of Ibn Saadun of Cordova, Spain. He died on
November 8, 1234, at the age of ninety, leaving his house
as a Sufi centre. His *Life of Saladin* is full of fascinating
eye-witness materials on the period.

Emir Shujauddin Shekurzi, Governor of Cairo, was visiting a man
of substance in Upper Egypt, an ancient who made the Emir and his
retinue welcome, with much hospitality. He was very dark of
complexion. The Governor asked him how it was that his grown-up
sons were so very fair.

'I will tell you,' he said, 'of the time and the circumstances of my
marriage, in my youth, in the days of the Battle of Hattin, won by
the Great Saladin the Victorious.'

And this was the remarkable narrative which he unfolded.

'I had grown,' he said, 'a very large crop of flax, which cost me a
great deal after it had been harvested and cleaned: over five hundred
gold dinars. Nobody would buy it, and the best advice I could get
was to sell it myself. The city of Acre, in Palestine, was in the hands

of the Frankish Crusaders although people were not prevented from doing trade in between the opposing armies. A truce was in being at the time. I went there and opened a shop where I traded my flax.

'I had been occupied in this manner for six months when a wonderfully beautiful Frankish woman, wife of one of their knights, came into my shop and bought some of my wares. I immediately fell in love with her; and my attachment grew as she came again, and again, to buy.

'Now she was always attended by an ancient serving-woman; and at last I said to this crone: 'I am deeply in love with your mistress – can I not find some way to gain her?'

'"Such an enterprise would cost us our lives," said the woman, but I said: "To lose my life for such a lady would be to gain her cheaply indeed, for she is worth my life and several more."

'After a great deal of discussion the hag came to my shop one day and said that she had arranged that the Knight's lady would visit me if I gave her fifty golden dinars of the minting of Tyre. I could hardly believe my good fortune, and I gave her the money at once. She told me to expect her, with her mistress, that very same night.

'I had a house which overlooked the cool sea, and I at once prepared everything: food, drinks, sweetmeats and candles, luxurious furnishings and whatever other delicacy and comfort I could think of for this meeting.

'And she came. We ate and drank, and as the evening darkened we lay down on couches under the starry sky, the moon our lamp and the heavens reflected from the surface of the water.

'Suddenly I began to feel a sensation of the deepest shame. I said to myself:

'"Here, in the open air, beside the sea and under the sky, you are preparing to break the divine Law and earn hell-fire. I declare to Allah that I shall not touch this Nazarene, from respect for his commands."

'So I simply went to sleep. When dawn broke the woman left, showing every sign of anger.

'But that same day I saw her again, as she went past my shop, accompanied by her maid. Her beauty smote me as before, and I realised that I could not resist. I said to myself in my agony:

'"Who am I – the saintly Junaid or Sari El-Saqati, that I can restrain myself and kill my own real love?"

'I ran to the old woman and begged her to bring the lady to me once more.

'"By the Holy Christ!" she rasped, "you could not get her now for less than a hundred pieces of gold!"

'I accepted, and made all ready once again. But when the time came I found that I could not show such disrespect, and again I did not touch her.

'That same day she came to my shop again, and said, in the Arabic which she spoke very well:

'"By Christ and the Virgin, you may be dying of love for me, but if you want my company you will have to find no less than five hundred golden dinars!"

'When she had spoken I trembled and my love for her was kindled again. I swore to spend every penny from my flax to achieve her company, for I was sorely afflicted.

'But then the herald suddenly came through the streets, calling:

'"Know, all ye Moslems, the truce between us Franks and you is now at an end. You have until Friday and no longer to complete your transactions; after that you must return to your own lands!"

'I knew then that we were to be parted, never more to meet, and with a sad heart called in the money owed for my flax, and bought various goods with the money and left Acre in deep gloom.

'Travelling to Damascus, I sold my goods at a great profit, and brought and sold servants for three years, trying to forget my longing for the woman of the Franks.

'After that time Sultan Saladin the Victor fought the Battle of Hattin, and he possessed himself of the towns of the coast and took prisoner the Kings of the Crusaders, and their great commanders fell or were captured, together with their families. One day representatives of the King came to me for a beautiful slave-girl for the Court, whose price was a hundred dinars. They had but ninety and owed me ten. The resources of the Crown were small, and they told the King of this. He ordered that I should be presented with one of the captives from the Franks, as prisoners were traded, in those days, by both sides.

'As I went into the tent where the captives were held, I saw, to my amazement, the Frankish woman with whom I was still besotted, and I claimed her in lieu of the ten dinars.

'I asked her if she remembered me, but she said, "No".

'I am,' I said, 'that miserable flax merchant whose golden dinars you took. Now I find your price to be ten dinars, no more! I was told that I would only be able to have you for five hundred, before Hattin!

'She looked at me closely and extended her arms. As she took my hands she said, "I bear witness that there is but One God, and that Mohammed is his Messenger!"

'I went to Ibn Shaddad, Judge of the King, and he married us, and we lived together and she was with child.

'I returned with her to Damascus, but after some months an order came from His Majesty the All-Victorious Sultan:

'"Peace has been signed and sworn. Wherefore it is enacted that all prisoners shall be restored and each and every captive, both male and female, shall be surrendered. This shall be binding upon the oath and upon the honour of Franks and Believers alike!"

'The fact that I was harbouring a Frank was known, and I received direct instructions to give her back to her own people forthwith.

'I returned to my house in fear and trembling, with a heart of doom, and almost staggered into her presence.

'"Have you had bad news?" she asked. "The worst," I said, and told her what had happened.

'"Take me," she answered, "this very day before the King. I know what I have to say."

'I went with my wife into the presence of the All-Conquering Saladin, sitting in his Court, with the Ambassador of the Franks on his right hand.

'I said, "This is the Frankish woman whom I have been ordered to surrender, may it please the Victorious King. She has made the profession of faith in Islam, and she is, moreover, my legal wife."

'The King turned to my wife. He said, "All prisoners have now been freed. They may return to their own people, and it is a great mercy, for which they should be thankful and joyful. Free decision is the right of the free, and we are celebrating peace."

'She answered, "Mighty Sovereign! God has given you victory and he has given you justice to administer, and this is a holy trust. If you send me back you may please your late enemies and seem generous in their eyes. But if I have rights, hear that I am one of the Moslems, I am a lawfully married woman living with my husband, and I am with child. Decide what is the fairest thing to do with me."

'The Crusader Ambassador, with a face as black as thunder,

cried, "Do you then love this Moslem better than your real husband, the Frankish Knight?"

'She only repeated the same words to him as she had said to the King.

'The Ambassador turned to his suite and said, "You have witnessed her words!" To me he said, "Take your wife and leave us!"

'As soon as we had withdrawn from the presence of the Conqueror, the Crusader Ambassador sent one of his men to me to speak these words: "Your wife was the last of the prisoners unaccounted for. Her mother gave me a chest of her belongings. Collect it, for it is hers."

'Inside we found all her clothes and all her possessions. There, too, were the two sums of money – the fifty and the hundred gold dinars, still wrapped as I had given them to the maid.'

The old merchant went on:

'These men whom you see, fair of face and hair, are the children which she has borne me. The meal which you have just eaten was cooked by her, and our happiness continues into our old age.'

The Emir and his suite rejoiced at the man's good fortune, and complimented him upon the blessing which had descended upon his house and the happy outcome of a strange and delightful tale.

From *The Thousand and One Nights*.

Words and Actions

After the battle for Armenia, the defeated Emperor Romanus Diogenes of Constantinople said to the Turkish conqueror:

'If you are a man, free me!'

Sultan Alp Arslan replied:

'Preachers say: "Follow my words, not my actions". I shall act according to your words, for they are admirable; but not your actions, which have ever been noted for barbarity, stupidity and disrepute.'

Romanus was set free.

The Jews and the Turks

Some Jews in Constantinople were contesting with some Turks about Paradise, saying that no-one would be permitted to enter there but themselves. The Turks asked, 'If it be as you assert, where do you mean to place us?'

The Jews were not so daring as to say that they would be entirely excluded; therefore, only replied, 'Oh, you will be outside the walls, and you will look at us.'

This dispute reached the ears of the Grand Vizier, who said, 'Since the Jews leave us outside the walls of Paradise, it is quite right that they should provide us with tents, so that we be not exposed to the sun and the rain.' Consequently, since that time, the Jews at Constantinople had, in addition to their ordinary tribute, to pay a tax to defray the expense of the aforesaid tents.

From *Paroles Remarquables des Orientaux*, p. 523.

The History of The Adventurer

So to the journey's end. The Gulf was there
Steaming and soundless, and the weary feet
were stayed at last from following the Queen.
The great *dhow* nosed the creek; slow water lapped
About her burnished; burnished in her sat
Unmoving bronze, her oarsmen. Then they rose:
'Hail, Bringers of the Queen!' 'Hail, ship! you bear
What cargo hence?' 'We carry on your charge.'
'But leave us nothing – nothing in exchange?'
'Only the ancient story of a slave.
There lies a secret buried none too deep.'
This the chief rower. This the far-off tale.

I dwelled beside the impulsive Rhone, a child that loved
          to be alone.
The forest was my nursery. My happiness was all my
          own.
I knew by name each cloud that lowers the sunshine
          through in liquid showers.
Deep in the tangled undergrowth I caught the singing of
          the flowers.
Our minstrels sang of rape and arson, all the joys of
          private wars.
The forest wall was calm and tall. My tutor laughed,
          and drank to Mars.
Bald, vulture-like upon its perch, our crag-born castle
          seemed to search
The gorge for prey, its shade to still the bells a-twitter in
          the church
Where, cheek by jowl with fearsome fowl and gargoyle,
          ghostly men, in foul

Incense that tried to stifle me, recited magic formulae.
At home clanked metal psalm and spur; but, oh the
        woods ... ! I tried to tame
A wolf-cub that the gardener called Life. He knew. The
        preacher came.

I see him yet, his visage wet with hot emotion, tears and
        sweat.
Contorted in the market-place he shrieked that all must
        pay a debt
To one Jehovah and His Son, by bursting eastward as
        the Hun
Had scourged the West. In unison we all replied 'twere
        nobly done.
For he explained that heaven was gained more featly –
        wrenching Saint Jerome –
From Palestine than Christendom. That night no
        peasant durst go home.

His words were like a wind that fanned a grass-fire:
        God would lend His hand.
To purge away the infidel whose breath profaned the
        Holy Land.
He showered indulgences, and kissed the brows of those
        who would enlist
To take a chance of martyrdom or give the devil's tail a
        twist.
He promised we should see the light, that cursed Arabs
        could not fight,
Counted them dead since we were 'led by General
        Jesus,' said the Pope.
We saw our path made plain, the hills removed by faith,
        whose foaming course
Flooded the continents like flats. We saw the world
        made one – by force.
Those who were frightened not to go, sold all they had
        to make a show,
Land, tool and ware to pay a fare. The panic made sly
        kings its heir.

In such a gust my tender age availed not with the
                    preaching sage,
For I was born of fighting men; and one of them took
                    me for page,
Only my tutor lay abed, calling us savages, and read
His pagan books. The fever would abate, he sneered,
                    when we were bled.
Sling, crossbow, bludgeon, axe and spud, cilice and
                    vials of sacred blood,
On such equipment we relied . . . Our foes were misery
                    and mud.
Each Norman keep, each Frankish hold, each corner of
                    the Christian fold
Sent forth its sheep to sound of bells. Our prophets
                    might have had them tolled.
Prince, abbot, squire, felt the desire of bliss that
Soft damosels ploughed through the mire with babes at
                    breast and men-at-arms;
And, since this journey was the price of entrance into
                    Paradise,
The gaols blenched out their criminals and beggars all
                    alive with lice.

We took no food, for God is good; besides we heard
                    that convents strewed
Converted Hungary for us. We never dared mistrust His
                    mood.
Heading the mass far up the pass, that led us straight to
                    Calvary.
The preaching-man upon an ass recited magic formulae.
Soon we were joined by northern lords; no few among
                    their folk had swords.
(Walter the Pennyless his rout had gone before and died
                    in hordes,
While Gotschalk's dupes, with geese and goats upon
                    their flags, had found the boats
To pass beyond the Bosphorus, where Kilidj Arslan cut
                    their throats).
Our force could not await the Turk, but in its ardour
                    got to work

That was not mentioned in the breves. It murdered all
the Jews in Treves.
We plodded on for many weeks through mazes where
the Austrian ekes
A bare existence on the slopes of alp below the granite
peaks.

Thus through the months of slapping rain we plunged
into the Hungarian plain,
And paid its mounted bowmen dear for wretched stocks
of fruit and grain.

Yea, often now that I am old and hear how zealous
scribes have told
The zeal that made the first crusade, well – history is
eaten cold.
The locust-swarms were better-drilled than we, the owls
were not so blind.
At every stage we left behind poor simpletons that
moaned and shrilled,
Thinking each swamp Gethsemane. It seemed that at
their agony
The doctors scoffed with cross aloft, reciting magic
formulae.
Alone the princes lightly pranced, as if the pilgrimage
enhanced
Their right to weigh upon the world thereafter. So the
doom advanced.

At last we halted where Constantinople's grandeur puts
to scorn
The villaged west, and challenges the Orient on her
Golden Horn.
Ah, brazen, were your heart as strong as looked your
square-chinned ramparts ... Long
We waited at the gates in dust knee-deep. The Emperor
did not trust
The help that he had craved. He swore he had not asked
so many ... more
Would ruin him ... He let the heat suck out our
strength at every pore.

But we were told great noblemen, Godfrey of Bouillon
        in Ardennes,
Robert of Flanders, 'Sword and Lance of Christians', all
        the flower of France
Were on our side, Hugh Vermandois, Stephen of
        Chartres and Troyes and Blois,
Baldwin and Raymond of Toulouse. The preacher said
        we could not lose.
Our mates streamed in from lands beyond the Adriatic,
        Bohemond
With Tancred; strait Dalmatian bays, Epirus, Scodra,
        devious ways
Bore them with boastful tales of sport and plunder, and
        a vague report
That this was nothing to the spoil that beckoned from
        the Moslem court.
Henceforth impatient ups and downs possessed us.
        Asiatic towns
Flamed to the general vision. We heard less perhaps of
        heavenly crowns
Than flowers and peacocks made of gems, the Caliph's
        crusted diadems
That crushed the head like Guthlac's bell, and tress with
        solid emerald stems.

And I confess Christ counted less to us than tales of
        leash and gess,
Or Harun-el-Rashid's largesse that sent the clock to
        Charlemagne.
Even monks planned theft of saintly scalps; stray hairs
        and chips of nail and chine,
Divinely shielded through the Alps, would make the
        fortune of the Rhine.
The Pope that cursed our tastes had laid the hand of
        blessing on this raid.

Blest chance indeed – as though a man should drink his
        fill and then be paid!
Each set to whet his falchion-pet that only friends had
        tasted yet.

We dressed our hopes in purple silk, wallowed in
                   dreamland's wine and milk.
Yet more than any Sultan's spoil, fair women should
                   repay our toil.
Already some were filled with thoughts that our red
                   cross was meant to foil.
The very Greeks, whose prayers had lured us into this
                   adventure, lodged
Their saviours in a baited trap. Lord, how these foxes
                   turned and dodged.
There lay our army like a log; our camp, our tenets,
                   turned to bog.
We sank. Disorder brought disease that stalked us
                   spectral through the fog.

The Greeks we came to bolster up against their
                   weakness filled our cup
With turpitude; the Byzantine put Circe's poison in our
                   wine.
Our aspirations all became mean as our hosts; the inner
                   flame
Went out. From many a starting-point we found a
                   common ground in shame;
Between our fellow-churches rose the hate that heaven
                   had meant for foes ...
The infidel might well have laughed. Perhaps he did. We
                   came to blows.
And I was sad that Christians had nothing in common,
                   saving bad
Blood, that our highest dizziest heads could all divide
                   but none could add.
To obviate a sinful fate the monks laid on us many
                   weeks
Of penance, wasting us the more with these inventions
                   of the Greeks.

Some paid in cash, some chose the lash – their backs
                   were pitiful to see –
While Bishop Adhemar of Puy recited magic formulae
That lurched us forward to our doom. We cleft the
                   sultanate of Roum,

104

Calling for bread. The peasants fled. We swept the
                  country like a broom.
Our armed migration choked the road. It ran ahead, a
                  stream that flowed
Uphill to glory, so it seemed; and so imagination
                  strode —
O Jack o' lantern! — into the unknown. The Virgin on a
                  silver throne,
Our leaders swore, went on before us. I saw nothing but
                  the Rhone,
The impulsive Rhone that tumbles down, and breaks
                  clean through the grey-walled town.
I heard it rustle in its bed where others heard the
                  Virgin's gown.
The preacher said Jehovah's cloud and pillar would go
                  with us. Yea,
The sky was on our heads alway. The sun rose up and
                  cried aloud,
And stood immobilized at noon. We wondered if at
                  Ajalon
The jews thanked Joshua for the boon of this divine
                  phenomenon.
We came to Nice and formed a seige with tortoise,
                  belfry, catapault,
And curse that brought even less result. Each lordling
                  quarrelled with his liege,
Layman with priest, until the place surrendered, and
                  again we lurched
Forward. I heard our name was made. I only saw how it
                  was smirched.
Alternate famine and carouse brought plague; but
                  doubtless God allows
Expensive trials of faith that we might learn the magic
                  formulae.
Throughout our ranks desertion raged by daily sermons
                  unassuaged.
The preaching man was first in this 'rope-dancing'.
                  Disillusion aged
My youth by years. My master stayed ... If he had erred
                  he promptly paid.

The pestilence ran after him. Despite the fervour I
        displayed
He died of sores, this prince of tilt, though guarded by
        ten hallowed charms,
This subject of all *trouvere*-lilt, lord in an hundred
        ladies' arms.

Oh, how I struggled to be brave when the Pope's legate,
        grey and grim,
Said simply this beside the grave: 'Christ died for you.
        You died for Him.'
I was enamoured of dear Christ; His utter beauty struck
        me dumb,
His face alone could compensate for scenes that almost
        made me long
For blindness. Yea, to Him I turned from all this
        heartache, nightly kissed
His hand with passion. I at least would not betray the
        children's Friend.
Haply His strength has always lain in contrast. I found
        strength to press
Towards the mark. Not so the host: we could not kick
        it to its feet.
Then heaven inspired us to devise a pious fraud – The
        Holy Lance.
We hid it in Saint Peter's crypt, and dug it up. The
        people wept
With rapture at this talisman, and sang the Psalm 'Let
        God arise.'
Also our chiefs – they knew my zeal – bade me
        complete the heartening sign.
White-plumed, white-horsed, with golden shield and
        halo, I contrived to appear
On the horizon, waved my sword while Adhemar
        proclaimed Saint George.
Our men responded with a shout. Through the five
        gates they tumbled out,
An headlong torrent. In a trice the infidel was put to
        rout,

And I joined in to hack and prod. Pure Tancred praised
    me with a nod.
Ascetic Godfrey even spoke to me: 'Lad, you belong to
    God.'

I won my spurs. They *made* me proud. Before my sword
    the wizards bowed,
Though me they washed. In vigil and fast I joined the
    perfect order, vowed
To hold my manhood chaste, to gird on might with
    right and courtesy,
To speak the truth, and so to be at variance with the
    common herd.
I wrenched and wrestled to believe that God had sent us
    here to grieve
Our bodies with this fruitlessness, that only fakirs could
    achieve
His purpose. Then in blind revolt my soul like an
    unbroken colt
Ran round and round an empty field. The hedge was
    thick. I could not bolt,
Though one poor knight on stiffened knee revealed
    beneath his breath to me
His thoughts on women while the monks recited magic
    formulae.
I sought for solace in renown. Men watched me
    swagger through the town
The youngest knight in Christendom. When women
    passed I tried to frown.
Through landmarks famed in Holy Writ, Emmaus,
    Bethlehem … at last
We saw the walls of Zion lit blood-red by sunset and
    the past.
The conquest of another world unfurled beneath our
    feet, the land
Of miracle and mystery lay as a bauble in our hand.
The moat was wide; we feebly tried to stop its gape
    with pebbles, cried
'Fall, Jericho!' The blessed wall stood firm; but Christ
    was on our side.

107

The Church had saved Him from His wan repute and
thrust Him in our van,
Bronzed, scarred. Alas, the first crusade had made Him
out a fighting man!
He taught the Turks to mock Giaours! ... sent timely
Genoese to build
Wheeled wooden turrets. These we filled brimful.
Jerusalem was ours.
We entered, revent, barefoot; slew three livelong nights
and mornings through,
Then paused to sing a thanksgiving. We massacred the
morrow too.
Even I who was in love with Christ, I with the
conscience clean and cold
That hankered not for lands or gold, was wondering
how to clinch my hold
On reputation, while our chiefs, before we could
consolidate,
Rode a great wallop round the State and split it into
petty fiefs.
They vanished ... home ... to Sunflower-trees ... home,
where a man may die obscure!
Far off a carle of Albemarle trolled chanties like a
Siren's lure,
Sometimes qualms came. I looked askance on Bishop
Daimbert's schemes to enhance
His seat. The native Christians sighed, they missed the
Caliph's tolerance.

Time passed, and no one seemed to reck of Zenghi, the
first Atabek,
Though every year we failed to act the Saracens grew
more compact.
In vain I urged that we might fall, so slender was our
human wall,
So numberless the foe beside the Templars and the
Hospital.
The answer was that dyke and fosse were useless when
we had the Cross

108

With other relics by the score, to guard against defeat or
        loss.
I tortured every hour to find material things to prop
        behind —
Forgive me, God! — Your earthly realm. The need was
        great, for it was blind.

The mathematics of Abul Hassan, three hundred years
        at school
In Arabic philosophy, showed that the West was still a
        fool.
Nay, gently, call her still a babe. How should she know
        that I, the Great,
Had learned from savages to prate of compass and of
        astrolabe.
Our miracles were not so sure to heal as Rhazes'
        simplest cure.
His friends the moon and stars obeyed the rules that
        Abul Wafa made.

My stolen lore raised me above my fellows. Everything
        but love
Was mine, respect, authority. The jealous Church-men
        dared not move.
Our infant realm could not dispense with me, its shield
        and main defence.
I knew the Sarascene recipe for making steel, and made
        it cheap.
Nothing that I could do availed. My tongue grew bitter,
        girded, railed.
My labour only builded Me, but not the kingdom. So I
        failed.
Our Viscounts could but show their gums, while from
        Aleppo, Hama, Homs,
The foe crept onward like the months, culling our
        conquests like ripe plums.
For all response in Chastel Blanc and towering Markab-
        on-the-Sea
Some clerkly knight in red-crossed white recited magic
        formulae;

Then darkly hinted science, hell and I were leagued,
        because their spell
Would not or could not stave the blow that I foresaw.
        Edessa fell.
I prayed for help all night; and, warned by lost Edessa,
        Baldwin made
Great efforts to placate our God. The answer was a
        fresh crusade.

This was an answer none could doubt. We heard a
        preacher more devout
Than ours was quartering the west, and pulling true
        believers out.
He hight Saint Bernard of Clairvaux, the home of light
        and miracles.
The wives and mothers trembled so before his spirit's
        tentacles,
They hid their males – in vain. He swept the Emperor
        Conrad with him, kept
The collar of his pale adept, emasculated Louis Sept.
He cured King's Evils, raised the dead, he cast out devils
        by the gross.
'Twas said he promised us twelve legions of angels...
        From the darkest regions
Men flocked to Metz and Ratisbon. News came of more
        than half a million.
Not counting those that rode apillion. Our battle was as
        good as won.
Such glorious news might well inflame our hopes. We
        waited. Nothing came,
Not even light Turcopuli nor Conrad's Golden-footed
        Dame.

And nothing came ... no troops ... The Greek misled,
        starved, poisoned, murdered them,
Betrayed them to the Turk, whose bleak deserts went
        over them. Week by week
We waited. Nothing. Cadmus saw them cut to bits,
        Attalia's maw
Could not be sated with their ruck. King Louis' mind
        had just one flaw:

He would not hear of strategy, staked all on
                  supernatural help.
And nothing came, and nothing came. Our half-bred
                  curs began to yelp
'Good God, if truly God is good!' They kissed the
                  Cross. Gems hid the wood.
Had He forgotten? Was He deaf? Could such things be?
                  Who understood?
Louis and Conrad struggled through one day with some
                  small retinue.
I watched. Almost I could foretell what they and
                  Providence would do.
And I remember, as we fared, a Sufi — so the sect is
                  named —
Sat by the road as though he cared no jot for us, while
                  he declaimed:

    Her home is in the heart of spaciousness,
    In the mid-city of ideals. The site
    Is harmony, the walls are made of light.
    There with the mother-thoughts she stands to
      bless
    The godlike sons sent forth with her caress
    To make new worlds. I see them all unite
    Into the whole that our most starry flight
    Of worship knew far off, and strove to
      express.
    What can we do for her? We run to ask
    As restless children for a grown-up task,
    While wisdom in the porch, their kind old
      host,
    Smiles at nurse nature, and replies: The most,
    The least that we can do for Beauty is
    To love for love's sake and serve God for His.

But Conrad drove his lance in jest right through the
                  ragamuffin's chest,
Because his creed was not as ours; and on we rode, I
                  lost my zest.

111

To take Damascus was our plan, relying on a talisman.
I knew that this would not suffice, for I was still a
        fighting man.
It ended in repulse and shame. Saint Bernard proved we
        were to blame
For want of faith. Ah, some of us had had too much.
        We said the same
Of him. At our return, thick mobs of women filled the
        church with bobs
And bows, poor puppets, trying hard to sing between
        their stifled sobs:

> God, whose Son has fathomed sorrow,
> Give a mother strength to say:
> Mine has faced and found To-morrow.
> I will try to face To-day.

They turned to me. They thought me wise because I had
        been led by lies
To blind myself to them; and now I saw things through
        a woman's eyes.
And I went out. Not yet the end. Since innocence alone
        could save,
Saints hit on infant infantry, and fifty thousand found
        the grave.
The women kissed my feet, my horse; they clung to me
        like my remorse.
I that set out to make the world had made myself
        believe by force.
Fate cursed us with three minor kings, a leper then.
        Against these Things
Salah-ad-Din combined the entire orient. I wished our
        fate had wings;
The Moslems scorched us with Greek fire. As rain upon
        a funeral pyre
Their arrows hissed in sheets upon the smoking scrub.
        'Go on!' 'Retire!'
Our rabble cried, starting aside like broken bows; they
        tried to hide,
Split, fled for refuge to a hill, did nothing while the
        Templars died.

Perhaps in our appeal for ruth my wording stumbled on
the truth,
'One God that went by many names,' or else I knew
Him in my youth,
Or else that Sufi haunted me with something that I
could not see,
Something that only had not been because we would
not let it be.

Yet there remained the sharpest cup to drain: the moan
of us went up,
When from the topmost dome was hurled the Sign that
should have ruled the world.
Down, down it rumbled with our grand designs. All we
had built or planned,
Toiled, bled for, crumbled at a touch, was ruined like a
house of sand.
So soon we pass. The wind knows why. The efforts of a
century,
Three generations' handiwork failed in the twinkling of
an eye.
My soul had passed through every phase and, counting
forty thousand days,
Was farther off than at the start from comprehending
heaven's ways
The last remains of faith were shaken when I, the
oracle, was taken.
My pride was made to sleep in chains. I prayed that I
might never waken,
But woke. They gave me to a *rais* who wanted cattle,
not advice.
He flogged me down to Damietta. I was old and fetched
no price.
Nathless my battling heart was brave enough to work
me till I dropped.
I passed for twopence to a Copt who sold me as a
galley-slave

To Muscat. In the rhythmic stroke, old, undefeated,
gnarled as oak

113

I creaked and strained against my fate, until that Sufi-
                something broke.
'Twas not my heart. An inner morn put the dark age in
                me to scorn,
And in the light I found myself, a child at play with
                worlds unborn,
For all that I had thought and read, and fought and
                watched the world be led
By any who contrived to cut a know with that blunt
                tool, the head.
I laughed to think how sparrows might look down upon
                our highest flight,
While each succeeding age would have its oracle or
                stagyrite,
Would trace the good we never did, the evil that we
                never saw,
And out of our blind pyramid extract a stepping-stone
                to Law.
Here, where ambition had to cease in servitude, I tasted
                peace,
Free of illusion stretched and yawned. A fool would
                clamour for release.
I make the rowers' bench a throne to think, and thought
                implies Alone,
Of changing woods and endless streams. My happiness
                is all my own.
And often, when my mates deplore a brother who shall
                row no more,

I talk about my wolf-cub, Life. They think I speak in
                metaphor.
They gather round me all agog, they think a chronicle
                and log
Of Progress lies in withered hands. Their cry is for an
                epilogue.
Has aught been drafted yet? A blot, an echo void and
                polyglot.
Each century is written off as preface. Yes, most true ...
                Of what?

114

My gathered weight had held me bound to find for
        every fog a ground,
For every riddle a reply, an end to Being that goes
        round.
Now I can say, I do not know if there will be a book at
        all,
Or if the deepest chapters go beyond some writing on
        the wall,
Though wider worlds will yet embark, sworn to eclipse
        our sorry trades,
Succeed, and leave their little mark: a dynasty of
        thought that fades,
Fresh undergrowths of formulae. Through these no
        human eye can see
The open glade – the *last* crusade, in which Jerusalem
        might be
The symbol of all peopled space, and Time an emblem
        of the day

On which the nations march as one to liberate and not
        to slay.
A story has no finish when it leads to nowhere out of
        ken?
O friend, the lack of knowledge brings wisdom within
        the reach of men;
For whether hope can ever fit the future matters not a
        whit.
My duty is to tug my oar – so long as I am chained to
        it.

From *The Singing Caravan*, a Sufi Tale, by Robert Vansittart, London
(Heinemann) 1919.

Sufi Mystics of the West

Twelve men sit on sheepskin rugs, arranged in a circle on the floor of a large room in a country house in Sussex, England. It is Thursday night, and the meeting of Sufis is paralleled in a thousand lodges throughout Asia and Africa – and some in Europe and America as well.

The People of the Path believe, as the early anchorites of Arabia did, that a certain nobility of mind and purpose resides within every human being. This it is the task of the Sufi teacher to discover and develop in the individual. By the mental and physical methods of 'development' which are practised, it is believed that the human being finds his true place in life. It is rooted in the Persian and Arabic literature of the mystics who sought communion with an eternal principle through the cultivation of ecstatic states. But at the same time it is intensely practical. A Sufi is what a Westerner might call a hundred-per-center.

Yet the Sufis believe that if a person were to take their principles alone or piecemeal, this would result in an unbalanced personality. Sufism, they maintain, must be followed as a training system in its entirety.

How does one become a Sufi? This is extraordinarily difficult, Sufis are not allowed to seek converts. This is because the Sufi must obey every order of his superior, even unto death. If, the Sufis say, they were to recruit people by promising them worldly or even spiritual advancement, they would be accused of merely trying to get people into their power.

A candidate for initiation sits in an adjoining room, wondering what is in store for him. He has been introduced to the Path through what is considered to be the best of all ways of entry: through the desire to emulate. It is thought that a potential Sufi is destined for great things if he has noticed something unusual and impressive about a Sufi, and asks him how he developed this.

The way to initiation was devious. At more than one point the youth thought that his mentor was more than half mad. He took him for long walks ... sometimes he deliberately misconstrued something that the young man said and accused him of being stupid. Listening to the way in which he tested him — for patience, tact, moral probity and sheer endurance — one felt that there could be few who would stand the pace; in Britain today, at any rate.

Sufism enjoys a somewhat equivocal position in the countries of Islam, where it has its widest currency. This is because the orthodox religionists tend to frown upon a system which they believe is designed to set the individual free (after an appropriate period of training) from the restrictions of religion. At the same time, countless thousands of Sufi teachers' shrines are revered by the masses; innumerable classical books have been composed by Sufis; some of the greatest national heroes of Eastern lands belonged to one or other of the four main Orders of the Sufi Way.

That there is a supernatural element in Sufism cannot be denied. Members believe (and literature abounds with supposed examples of it) that the members of the higher degrees of initiation are capable of influencing the minds of men and even events in a totally inexplicable manner. And this belief is one which is as adamantly held by the Western members of the Orders.

It is more than likely that Sufism has influenced the modern schools of mysticism which are known in the West, as well as the monastic Orders of the Middle Ages. What do the Sufis themselves say about their history? To them, Sufism is the blending of mind-training with successful living which comes in association with what until recently has been considered to be religious ecstasy. Mankind, they say, has certain capabilities, certain ideas, certain capacities for experience. These things are all related. The goal is the Ideal Man, who shall use every aspect of his experience to be 'In the World and yet not Of the World'. These teachings have been passed down to the elect since the beginning of time.

The word 'secret' is used in a special sense. It refers to one or more of the inner experiences of the mind, and not to the mere possession of formal knowledge. In this way, Sufism differs from those schools of initiation which used to hold actual secrets, such as philosophy or how to work metals, or even how one could supposedly control spirits.

Sufis are to be found in every department of life, because few of them practise retirement from the world, except for short periods of reflection... There are military Sufis, commercial Sufis, teachers, travellers, contemplatives, healers and the rest. Some of them combine more than one attribute.

Some of them are women; and Rabiyya, one of the greatest ecstatics of the East, was a Sufi mystic. She, like others before and after her, stresses the fact that the stage of mystical illumination, release and understanding of the meaning of life, is only the first of two halves. The Sufis (unlike any other mystical school on record) say that, after reaching that stage the Sufi must 'return to the world' and must put his experiences into practice. This is the point at which his infallibility is first encountered. It is believed that he is now endowed with a perception far greater than that of ordinary men and women; and that he is 'rightly guided': will now always take the course, hold the opinion, or follow the path, which is for the best. This is because he is in harmony with the pattern of life which is almost all hidden to those who have not been through his training.

On the whole, the effect of Sufism upon society has been creative and wholesome. Sufis do not suffer from fanaticism, are not connected with magic (though they are thought to have special, extra-normal powers) and hold to the principle of honour and effort to an astonishing extent.

It is probable that the message is not susceptible to popularization on a theoretical basis alone; just as English translations of Sufi literature by erudite non-initiates are held by Sufis to be faulty to a degree. But the Path of the Sufi is likely to exercise a fascination over men's minds for many a year yet: and its influence in the West is undoubtedly increasing.

From *Secret Societies*, by Arkon Daraul, London (Frederick Muller Ltd.) 1961.

Dreams, Derivations

Dreams

Freudian analysis theories about dreams, etc., were advanced by Hakim Sanai of Ghazna (Afghanistan) ... years before Sigmund Freud was born.

Evolution

The claim that man is evolved and will continue to evolve is found in the works of Rumi, of Konia (Turkey) who died in 1273 ... years before Darwin.

Atomic Power

The claim that immense power resides in the atom was made by Shabistari, a Persian sage who died in the 13th century, in his *Secret Garden*.

Persian

Every English person knows a lot of Persian words. Examples are: *pyjamas, orange.*

Georgian Architecture

Anticipated at Naqsh-i-Rustam (Persian) tomb house of 6th century BC (Byron, R., *Road to Oxiana*, 1950, p.160 (illustrated)).

Arab Occult Writers: Their Effect on Europe

by *Hatim Janubi*

One of the greatest names in the history of Arabic arcane thought is that of Alkindi, who died about the middle of the ninth century A.D. He seems to have been a voluminous writer, translating the works of Aristotle and other Greeks into Arabic, but of his own personal compositions only a comparative few have descended to us. Of these by far the most important is *The Theory of the Magic Art* which is still to be found in Latin versions only.

The theory of this work is that of the astrological doctrine, of the radiation of occult influence from the stars; the Doctrine of Signatures, as it is known. Alkindi accounts for the diversity of objects in nature in two ways, first through the diversity of matter, and secondly by the varying influence exerted from the rays of the heavenly bodies. Each star, he tells us, has its own peculiar force, and certain objects are especially under its influence, for the movement of the stars to new positions and the counter-influence of their rays are productive of such an infinite variety of combinations that no two things in the world are ever found alike. But this Doctrine of Emanations is by no means confined to the stellar system, for every element in the world radiates force, even fire, colour and sound having their emanations. The power of the magnet and the reflection of an image in a mirror are symbolic of the occult interaction of remote objects. All such emanations, however, can be referred to the celestial harmony which governs the changes of the world.

Alkindi then proceeds to describe the magic power of words. He tells us that the imagination can form ideas and then emit rays which will affect outside objects, just as would the thing itself whose image the mind has conceived. If words are uttered in exact accordance with imagination and intention, and with faith, they are capable of exceeding potency, and this effect is heightened if they are uttered under favourable astrological conditions. Some magical utterances are most potent when uttered under the influence of certain planets. Some voices affect fire, some especially stir trees, some are even capable of making images to appear in mirrors or to produce flames and lightning.

Alkindi's principal work concludes by a discussion of the virtues of figures, characters and images. Figures and characters, he says, inscribed on certain materials with due solemnity of place and time, and with definite intention, have the effect of motion upon external objects. Every such figure emits rays having the peculiar virtue which has been impressed upon it by the stars and signs. Thus there are characters which can be used either to cure or bring about diseases, and certain images constructed in conformity with the constellations are capable of emitting rays holding the virtue of the celestial harmony.

This doctrine of the radiation of force had a strong influence upon the mediaeval learning of Europe, as had Alkindi's treatise *On Sleep and Visions*, which also is known in the West from a Latin translation in which he deals with clairvoyance and divination by dreams. He believes that the mind or soul has an innate natural knowledge and that the imaginative virtue of the mind is more active in sleep, a theory in which more than one great poet has found reason to agree with him.

The great majority of the works of Alkindi translated into Latin are of an astrological character. One of these was translated by Robert of Chester, an Englishman. But it is to be noticed that he employs Astrology in a strictly scientific manner, observing mathematical method and critical laws. In one of the few Arabic texts of his which is still available, is a piece of political prediction relating to the duration of the Arab Empire.

Albumasar was a pupil of Alkindi and died in 886. Like his master he lived at Baghdad. His writings are fairly numerous but are known to us chiefly through Latin translations of the fifteenth century. His chief work is *The Greater Introduction to Astronomy* and *The Flowers*, although *A Book of Experiments* is frequently quoted from by the mediaeval occultists. We also meet with citations from a work known as *Albumasar in Sadan*, or *Excerpts from the Secrets of Albumasar*. These works are almost entirely astrological.

Almost contemporary with these writers was Costa ben Luca, of Baalbek. His best-known treatise is *The Epistle Concerning Incantations and Adjurations*, which was a favourite among the mediaeval occultists and which seems to have been written to his son. Costa tells us that a perfect mind generally goes with a perfect body, and an imperfect mind with an imperfect body, as is seen in the case of children and old men, or in the inhabitants of intemperate countries such as Scotland and Scythia. He argues that if any one believes that an incantation will help him, he will at least be benefited by his own confidence, but if one is constantly afraid that incantations are directed against him he may easily develop serious illness, as modern observers will admit to be the case among the West African negroes, who are believers in the magical powers of *ju-ju*. It will be seen that this theory embodies sound psychological facts. He is, however, somewhat sceptical as regards the magician's ability to summon demons. He also considers the question of the validity of amulets in which he is not disposed to believe very strongly. At the same time he gives a long and valuable list of these, though he admits that he has not himself tested them.

Another valuable work by Costa is that *On the Difference between Soul and Spirit*. Spirit he believes to be a subtle yet material substance, unlike the soul which is incorporeal. It perishes when separated from the body, whose vital processes it nevertheless controls. The most subtle part of spirit is employed in the higher mental processes, such as imagination, memory and reason. He actually explains how this process takes place in the brain. There is an opening between the anterior and posterior ventricles of the brain, he says, which is closed by a sort of valve. When the man is in the act of recalling something to memory, this valve opens and the spirit passes from the anterior to the posterior cavity. The speed with which this valve works differs in different brains and this explains why some people are of slow memory and why others are more quickly respondent to a question. This theory caused a great deal of future discussion among the arcane thinkers of the Middle Ages of Europe.

Thabit ibn Kurrah was born at Harran in Mesopotamia about 836, spent much of his life at Baghdad and lived until about 901. Although he wrote in Arabic he was not a Mohammedan and seems to have been a Sabian. This particular cult had inherited much of the astrology of Babylonia and sacrificed to the spirits or genii of the planets. Indeed the entire corpus of Babylonian or Chaldean astrology seems to have been collected in their beliefs. Of his people, Thabit says, 'We are the heirs and posterity of heathenism'. He went to Baghdad, where he became one of the Caliph's astronomers. His writings were exceedingly numerous and included many translations from the Greek into Arabic or Syrian. Most of his treatises are short and philosophical in character, yet he had a definite tendency to the practice of astrology and the mystic power of letters. His most strictly occult work is his treatise on images of an astrological character. These images, to be efficacious, must be constructed under prescribed constellations, and frequently take a human form. The material of which they are made is not important, indeed any will serve so long as careful conformity to astrological conditions is recognised. The making of such images is, indeed, as other ancient writers on occult science have testified, the most important matter in astrology. At the same time after the image has been made, it is usually necessary to perform a purely magical ceremony. Precise instructions are given as to how the image should be used after they are manufactured. If it is desired to place a curse upon a man, the image is buried in his house, certain words being uttered during the ceremony. Other images are capable of driving off scorpions, laying waste a countryside, recovering stolen objects or conferring success in business or politics.

The famous Rasis was a Persian and appears to have died about 923. When about thirty years of age he came to Baghdad, where he served as a physician in the hospital. More than two hundred different works are ascribed to him, but although he had a wide knowledge of philosophy and alchemy, it is unlikely that all of them proceeded from his pen. The most notable of his books are the *Sayings of Almansor*, with which are associated ten subordinate treatises dealing with medicine and anatomy and the cure of diseases. He also wrote six books containing medical secrets and he was the first of the arcane writers to throw light on the practices of charlatans. He had a strong bias toward natural science, as is displayed in his treatise entitled *Opinions Concerning Natural Things*, and he wrote of the magnet's attraction for iron and of the nature of the vacuum.

Eight of his works deal with alchemy and make it plain that Rasis regarded the transmutation of metals as a possibility. One of these works was indeed an answer to Alkindi, who held that transmuation was chimerical. One of his treatises, *The Light of Lights* was translated into Latin by the Scottish astrologer Michael Scot, in the thirteenth century, and is principally devoted to the nature of salts and alums. Scot, as is well-known, came from the Scottish Borders and is probably buried at Melrose Abbey. He went to Spain where he studied in the Moorish schools, becoming most proficient in Arabic. But the connection of Rasis with alchemy seems to have been unfortunate, for the Caliph had him scourged because he failed to transmute metals into gold and there is a further story that when preparing the Elixir of Life, he almost lost his eyesight through the vapours raised by the experiment. He also seems to have been skilful in the cure of diseases by the magic art. But that he was a good Moslem is revealed by his work *On the Necessity of Prayer*.

The lessons of Arabic occultism, although employed by the Moors in Spain, were perhaps brought home more fully to Europe by a monk named Gerbert, who was attracted from his monastery in Auvergne to the North of Spain for the particular purpose of studying Arabic in the last quarter of the tenth century. Later he became tutor to Robert, King of France, a circumstance which naturally was most effectual in spreading his Arabic ideas. The mediaeval chroniclers have a great many stories to tell regarding his magical abilities.

William of Malmsbury, says that among the Saracens of Spain, he learned to read omens from the flight of birds and to bring spirits from the nether spheres, and Michael Scot tells us that he was the best necromancer in France, and that the demons obeyed him in all that he required of them, day and night because of the great sacrifices which he offered, and his prayers and fastings. Some early manuscripts actually say that he became Pope by the aid of the demons and that he had a spirit enclosed in a golden head who answered difficult questions on magical points.

The view that European learning was not affected by Arabic science until at least the twelfth century, cannot now be entertained. It is true that Robert of Chester stated that the West did not know what alchemy was, but the date of his treatise was misinterpreted. The fact is that the Arabic astrologers were being voluminously translated in the twelfth century; but in the eleventh, and even in the tenth centuries, there were numerous signs of Arabic influence in works on astronomy and astrology. Indeed it is known that a letter from Gerbert to a certain Lupitus of Barcelona in Spain, was written as early as 984, asking him to send the writer a book on astrology which he had translated. There is still extant at Munich, a manuscript on the use of the astrolabe, containing many Arabic names. But when Gerbert actually became Pope Sylvester II in 999 it cannot be doubted that the Arabic learning he had imbibed had an enormous influence on Latin Culture. If the *Book on the Planets* can really be ascribed to him, there can be little doubt that the good Pope Sylvester was in reality a thorough-going astrologer of the old Arabic school. It outlines the qualities of the twelve signs of the zodiac, discusses the origins of astrology and gives a description of the Sphere or Heavens. It states that human wealth and honours, poverty and obscurity, depend upon the stars, and adds that the sun and moon greatly affect human life. Saturn presides over reason and intelligence, while Jupiter has a practical aspect and represents the power of action. Mars signifies hatred, Venus love and Mercury interpretation, while the influence of the moon is proved by the circumstance that if men sleep out-of-doors at night they will find that more humour collects in their heads when they lie in the moonlight than when they do not. Some signs are masculine, others feminine and relate to the four cardinal points and the four elements. He provides certain Saracen names for the seven planets and gives the Arabic names for the twenty-eight houses into which the circle of the zodiac is subdivided.

A work ascribed to one Alcandrus, an astrologer, is found in two manuscripts of the eleventh century. This writer is mentioned in Michael Scot's *Introduction to Astrology* as the author of a book of fortune, which mentions the quality of the signs and the planets ruling in them, and Scot mentions that a similar method of divination is employed among the Arabs. The book of Alcandrus is almost certainly a translation from the Arabic; in any case it is full of Arabic expressions. It begins with a statement of the quality of the planets through these signs. Every planet, it tells us, is erect in some one sign and falls in its opposite, and any planet is friendly to another in whose house it is erect and hostile to that in whose house it declines.

The twelve signs are next related to the four elements and the opinion is expressed that since man, like the world, is composed of these four elements, it is reasonable to believe that human affairs are regulated by the celestial bodies. Twenty-eight principal constellations exist through which the fates of men are disposed and pronounced, future as well as present, and human affairs can be forecasted by the aid of these horoscopes. These twenty-eight parts are, of course, sub-divisions of the zodiac into houses of the sun or moon, and Arabic names are given for them, beginning with *Alnait*, the first part of the sign Aries. We can discover under which of them a man was born by a numerical calculation of his name and that of his mother and the kind of men who were born under each of these houses is described, their physical, mental and moral characteristics, and any particular marks upon the body. Directions are also given for the recovery of lost or stolen property and the manner of reading men's secret thoughts is described.

These are a few only of those early writers on the occult sciences who drew their inspiration from Arabic sources. Later, in the twelfth century, a very large number of translations were made from Arabic books on astrology and it is not too much to say that practically all later writers on arcane subjects were influenced by Arab learning. Moreover the travels of learned Europeans in the East assisted Arabic influence in the West. Thus Constantinus Africanus visited Baghdad about the middle of the eleventh century 'to improve his education', and is said to have learned necromancy there. He pursued his studies among the Arabs, Persians and Saracens and later became a monk. He seems to have translated certain works from the Arabic, indeed his *Pantegni* is merely an adaptation of the *Royal Art of Medicine* of Ali ibn Abbas, as Stephen of Pisa pointed out when he translated that work in 1127. He also adapted another Arabic book in his *Viaticum*, which was probably written by Abu Jafar Ahmed Ibn al-Jezzar, as Daremberg and others have established. These works are full of curious lore, but it remains to be said that many good authorities have given it as their opinion that the works of the Arabic arcane writers are much less prone to superstitious statement than those of much later European scientists.

If other 'well-known' Arabic writers on occultism have been omitted in this account it is because it deals almost entirely with material drawn from authentic sources and not, as is too often the case, with names and incidents drawn almost purely from tradition or legend. An extraordinary web of the fantastic has been spun concerning Arabic and Moorish early science, and if this has gilded and heightened European romance, only a very small proportion of it can be boiled down to actual hard fact. After a great deal of research on the subject the writer has here done his utmost to provide a useful summary of those writings of Islamic scientists which particularly affected European thought.

PSYCHOLOGY

Psychology

Cat and Mouse

There was once a king who asked his minister which was the stronger, innate character or training. 'Nature,' said the minister.

Now the king sent for some trained cats, which came into the room carrying lighted candles, and stood around. 'There you are,' said the king, 'training overcomes natural characteristics.'

The next time this happened, the minister had hidden a mouse in his sleeve, which he suddenly let loose. The cats immediately scattered, dropping the candles, scrambling for the mouse. This caused a fire, and the house in which they were was almost burnt down.

'Everything returns to its origins,' said the minister.

Nahfat Al Yaman.

Fatness and Medicine

A disciple went to a certain wise man and asked him all kinds of questions, hoping that he might gain wisdom or enter upon the Way of Truth by this method. The wise man knew, however, that the student's ignorance was such that he would not be able to benefit by any advice, exercises or teachings until he realised that something else than his own ideas about himself came first, to prepare him.

So the wise man, after hearing all the would-be Seeker-After-Truth's ideas and questions, said: 'I shall have to tell you a story – then we shall discover whether you are able to understand how to understand.'

And this was the story:

There was once a Persian king, who had become so fat that he could do very little other than roll about on cushions. One doctor after another was sent for, but none could help him, even though the king imagined from time to time that he was benefitting from these ministrations.

Ultimately a really wise doctor arrived at the Court, and the king asked him for medicine.

'First of all,' said the doctor, 'I have to spend three days in studying your case, by referring to your horoscope.' He said this because he knew that the king believed in astrology, though he himself did not.

When the three days were over, he returned to the Court and said:

'Your Majesty! There is no point in treating your obesity, for the stars say that you will be dead in forty days. If you do not believe me, put me in a dungeon for that period of time, and you will see ...'

The king had the man cast into prison, and began to dwell on his fate. Day after day he worried and fretted, lost his appetite and marched up and down the corridors of his palace, in an agony of fear.

When the forty days were over, the king was as thin as a rake from worry – and he sent for the doctor to explain himself.

'Your Majesty! I knew that worry and starvation were the only treatment for your fatness, and so I caused you to endure these. Now that your corpulence has gone, we can commence with the medicines which will cure you.'

When the sage had finished his tale, the would-be Seeker understood that the first problem of the teacher is to provide treatment for the disciple, irrespective of what the disciple himself thinks is the way in which he should learn.

But that disciple was unusual: as unusual as the king in the tale, who would probably have been more likely to have the physician's head struck from his body, and to have continued looking for medicines instead of mental and physical treatments.

Nahfat Al Yaman.

Pain in the Stomach

A man once went to see a miserly man, who was well-known for meanness. The miser was eating bread and honey. When his guest was announced, he put the bread away and left the honey on the table, thinking that nobody would want to eat honey on its own.

When the guest entered, the miser said: 'Of course you cannot eat honey without bread.'

'Yes I can,' said the other man, and he started to eat it.

This sight was too much for the miser, who could only think of saying, as he saw his honey disappear:

'My brother, I swear that eating like this will cause the heart to burn.'

'That is true,' said the guest, 'but it is *your* heart which will burn, not mine.'

Nahfat Al Yaman.

Psychotherapy of 700 Years Ago

It is related that Avicenna lived at Gurgan, and that his income became considerable and went on increasing day by day. Some time elapsed thus, until one of the relatives of Qabus, the King, fell sick. The physicians set themselves to treat him, striving and exerting themselves to the utmost, but the disease was not cured. Now Qabus was greatly attached to him. So one of the servants of Qabus did obeisance before him and said: 'Into such-and-such a caravanserai hath entered a young man who is a physician, and whose efforts are singularly blessed, so that several persons have been cured at his hands.' So Qabus bade them seek him out and bring him to the patient.

So they sought out Avicenna and brought him to the sick man. He saw a youth of comely countenance, whereon the hair had scarcely begun to show itself, and of symmetrical proportions. He sat down, felt his pulse, asked to see his urine, inspected it, and said, 'I want a man who knows all the districts and the quarters of this province.' So they brought one; and Avicenna placed his hand on the patient's pulse, and bade the other mention the names of the different quarters and districts of Gurgan. So the man began, and continued until he reached the name of a quarter at the mention of which, as he uttered it, the patient's pulse gave a strange flutter. Then Avicenna said, 'Now I must have someone who knows all the streets in the quarter.' They brought such an one. 'Repeat,' said Avicenna, 'the names of all the houses in this district.' So he repeated them till he reached the name of a house at the mention of which the patient's pulse gave the same flutter. 'Now,' said Avicenna, 'I want someone who knows all the households.' They brought such an one, and he

131

began to repeat them until he reached a name at the mention of which the same strange flutter was apparent.

Then said Avicenna, 'It is finished.' Thereupon he turned to the confidential advisers of Qabus, and said: 'This lad is in love with such-and-such a girl, in such-and-such a house, in such-and-such a street, in such-and-such a quarter; the girl's face is the patient's cure.' The patient, who was listening, heard what was said, and in shame hid his face beneath the clothes. When they made enquiries, it was even as Avicenna had said. Then they reported this matter to Qabus, who was amazed thereat and said, 'Bring him before me'. So Avicenna was brought before Qabus.

Now Qabus had a copy of Avicenna's portrait, which Yamin al-Dawla had sent to him. 'Why, here is Avicenna,' exclaimed he. 'Yes, O most puissant Prince,' replied the other. Then Qabus came down from his throne, advanced several paces to meet Avicenna, embraced him, conversed genially with him, sat down beside him, and said, 'O greatest and most accomplished philosopher of the world, explain to me the rationale of this treatment!' 'O Sire!' answered Avicenna, 'when I inspected his pulse and urine, I became convinced that his complaint was love, and that he had fallen thus sick through keeping his secret. Had I enquired of him, he would not have told me; so I placed my hand on his pulse while they repeated in succession the names of the different quarters, and when it came to the question of his beloved, love moved him, and his heart was stirred, so that I knew she was a dweller in that quarter. Then I enquired the streets, and when I reached the street in question that same movement occurred, and I knew she dwelt in that street. Then I enquired the names of the households in that street, and the same phenomenon occurred when the house of his beloved was named, so that I knew the house also. Then they made mention of the names of its inhabitants, and when he heard the name of his beloved, he was greatly affected, so that I knew the name of his sweetheart also. Then I told him my conclusion, and he could not deny it, but was compelled to confess the truth.'

Qabus was greatly astonished, and indeed there was good reason for astonishment. 'O most eminent and most excellent philosopher of the world,' said he, 'both the lover and the beloved are the children of my sisters, and are cousins to one another. Choose, then, an auspicious moment that I may unite them in marriage.' So the Master chose a fortunate hour, and in it they were united, and that prince was cured of the ailment which had brought him to death's door. And thereafter Qabus maintained Avicenna in the best manner possible, and thence he went to Rayy, and finally became minister to 'Ala al-Dawla, as is well known in history.

From *The Four Discourses*, 12th Cent., by Nidhami 'Arudi, translation by E.G. Browne.

The Hammam Name

Winsome Torment rose from slumber, rubbed his eyes,
                        and went his way
Down the street towards the Hammam. Goodness
                        gracious! people say,
What a handsome countenance! The sun has risen twice
                        today!
And as for the Undressing Room, it quivered in dismay.
With the glory of his presence see the window panes
                        perspire,
And the water in the basins boils and bubbles with
                        desire.

Now his lovely cap is treated like a lover: off it goes!
Next his belt the boy unbuckles; down it falls, and at
                        his toes
All the growing heap of garments buds and blossoms
                        like a rose.
Last of all his shirt came flying. Ah, I tremble to disclose
How the shell came off the almond, how the lily
                        showed its face,
How I saw a silver mirror taken flashing from its case.

He was gazed upon so hotly that his body grew too hot,
So that bathman seized the adorers and expelled them
                        on the spot;
Then the desperate shampooer his propriety forgot,
Stumbled when he brought the pattens, fumbled when
                        he tied a knot
And remarked when musky towels had obscured his
                        idol's hopes.
See Love's Plenilune, Mashallah, in a partial eclipse!

134

Psychology

Desperate the loofah wriggled: soap was melted
                  instantly:
All the bubble hearts were broken. Yes, for them as well
                  as me,
Bitterness was born of beauty; as for the shampooer, he
Fainted until a jug of water set the Captive Reason free.
Happy bath! The baths of heaven cannot wash their
                  spotted moon:
You are doing well with this one. Not a spot upon him
                  soon!

Now he leaves the luckless bath for fear of setting it
                  alight;
Seizes on a yellow towel growing yellower in fright.
Polishes the pearly surface till it burns disastrous bright,
And a bathroom window shatters in amazement at the
                  sight.
Like the fancies of a dreamer frail and soft his garments
                  shine
As he robes a mirror body shapely as a poet's line.

Now upon his cup of coffee see the lips of Beauty bent:
And they perfume him with incense and they sprinkle
                  him with scent,
Call him Bey and call him Pasha, and receive with deep
                  content
The gratuities he gives them smiling and indifferent.
Out he goes: the mirror strains to kiss her darling: out
                  he goes!
Since the flame is out, the water can but freeze.
The water froze.

James Elroy Flecker – from the 18th Century Turkish poet Baligh,
                  The Tale of the Bath, by a lady.

The Magic of Numbers
by *Edouard Chatelherault*

Finding your Magic Number

According to the age-old lore of Arabia, everyone has his or her lucky number. This is how to find yours:

Take your name, and add all the letters together, until you get a single number. If your name is, say, Rosita Martin, you will find that there are twelve letters in the name. This is a double number: 1 and 2. But because we concern ourselves only with single digits from 1 to 9, we need a single figure, so we add up again: $1 + 2 = 3$. Three is the personality-number of Miss Martin. It is as simple as that!

Things connected with the number three should be fortunate for this person. If the house is numbered three, or if any number connected with the person adds up to the personality number, there is a fortunate harmony with that thing.

Eight is favourable to three (see the table below); so the **Number Three** person also has a chance of success and happiness in anything connected with number eight as well.

This is the Table of Harmony and Disharmony:

Number	In Harmony with	Out of Harmony with
1	6	2
2	7	1
3	8	4
4	9	3
5	all numbers	no number
6	1	7
7	2	6
8	3	9
9	4	8

Work out the number of your fiancé. If his is even and yours is odd, you are well matched. If they both are odd, *you* will need more patience and understanding. If they are both even, *he* will have to get used to *your* ways!

Each number 'rules' a different type of character, and in this article I am going to give the natures and abilities of the people who come under the various numeral groups.

The Number One people are inclined to be self-assertive, and can always be relied upon to make the party go with a swing. The Number One girl may be secretive, but she knows when to say the right thing.

She has charm as well as ability, and thrives on criticism. Her strongest affinity is with number six, who alone can control her completely, for she may be very self-willed at times!

In her life she seeks companionship as well as a career, and she does not like working alone. At home, she can assume the role of peace-maker as quickly as that of the leading figure.

The Number One man, on the other hand, tends to be single-minded, and might become absorbed in only one activity unless he is provided with a mate who can 'take him out of himself'.

All Number One people can make a success of anything which would dismay anyone less strong-willed. They are willing and pleasant co-operators, but can be difficult as opponents.

Number One people thrive best to the north of the place of birth. They get ahead in occupations connected with liquids. They have saffron yellow as their fortunate colour, and their perfume is Jasmine. Their best day for new plans is Sunday, the first day of the week, or Friday, the sixth, with which they have a harmony.

In many Eastern countries, hardly any girl will do anything of any importance to her without first working out whether the numbers favour it or not. This is how it is often done:

Supposing George Smith has asked a girl to go out with him on Thursday. Her name is Rosita Martin, and her number is therefore three.

George Smith adds up to eleven, which equals 1 + 1, which is 2. The girl's name comes to three. Two plus three equals five, which is a number which harmonised with anything, as you will see in the table above. So far, so good.

But we can go further. Thursday is the fifth day of the week. Five is a fortunate number for this couple. Now we have:

Rosita Martin = 3
George Smith = 2
Thursday = 5
10 = 1 + 0 = 1

Where should they go? Anything which adds up to *one* is the answer; or *six*, which harmonises with it.

'Dance' adds up to 5, 'Film' equals 4, 'Dinner' 6, so the most harmonious part of their outing would be the dinner.

Simple enough, you may say. Millions of people believe in this system so much that a man may change his name to produce a harmony with the girl of his choice or with something that he decides is his ideal.

Numbers and Romance

Numbers are an expression of planetary forces. In no part of astrology is this more clearly seen than in the Number Two: the number of romance. From time immemorial, Two has stood for the affairs of women, and of love – even more than Venus, which seems to have been associated with matters of the heart much later.

The Number Two, therefore, stands for romance, love and court-ship. It also connects with all feminine affairs, and all luxury matters such as perfumes, jewellery and rich clothes.

First, then, is your name a romance-attracting one? If the sum of the letters adds up to 2, it is. Remember, when you are adding, that you must keep on adding and re-adding until you get a single figure. If your name is George Martin, for instance, this makes 12 letters. The number 12 is re-added: 1 + 2 = 3. This is the rule for obtaining the single romance-number.

Very well. If you want to attract the factors represented by the Number Two, you should have a name which adds up to 2. Many people, if their name does not add up to the required number, start using a name or nickname which does!

Number Two corresponds with the second day of the week, Monday, with the letter B, with twins and double things of all kinds – arms, legs and so on. So plans connected with love or other aspects of the Number Two should be carried out on Mondays, preferably at two o'clock. If they are connected with the letter B, so much the better. This is called the Law of Correspondences, and it is shared by all the mystical systems of the East.

I have a Persian charm, designed to attract love to the wearer, and it is a perfect example of this belief in the power of the Number Two to attract love.

It is drawn on paper and enclosed in a small leather case. In the centre of a circle is written a large 2. Under this is the name of the owner, which adds up to 2. Then there is a small crescent moon, which means that it was drawn on a Monday. On the other side is written the letter B, underneath which is written the name of a man. His name adds up to 7. Why not to 2? Because it was not in the power of the lady to change his name. But, according to the Table of Harmonious Numbers, Seven and Two are in harmony – so all was well, we expect!

Whether or not you are interested in attracting love, you may be a Number Two type of person. So if the letters of your name add up to 2, these are some of your characteristics:

You are modest and tidy, interested in matters of detail. You have a wide range of abilities, especially in the direction of personal appearance, clothes, perhaps precious stones.

Your temper will be steady, and you should find that things happen to you as a result of coincidences.

You would succeed best in partnerships with overseas interests, probably to the south-east of your place of birth.

Money should follow you when you make a change of residence.

The Number Two personality has a sense of intuition which enables him to guess with great accuracy what other people are thinking.

His affinity is with Number Seven, and with things connected with Saturday and the number 7 in general.

The Number Two should make sure that he has scope and plenty of room to manoeuvre. He is stifled in restricting circumstances, and he should not undertake long-term commitments which bind him to staying in one place too long. The people of Number Two should strive for progress in things of the mind, in places where they are not known, should use their mental qualities to advance their material interests.

If there are decisions to be made, the choice should always go to anything connected with number 7, because this is the harmony-number for number 2. But the number 1 is unfriendly to number 2. This means that loss or confusion could attend supporting things or ideas connected with number 1.

Number Two people have silver as their lucky metal, and white is a fortunate colour for them. The emerald stone is also said to bring them luck. Their perfume is poppy.

The time of the New Moon should be most favourable for all matters of ambition; but they should not carry out any important activity when the Moon is waning, but should postpone it until later.

The number 2 is used in divination sometimes for obtaining the answer to a question. This is how it is done:

The question is written down, and the number of letters in it are counted. They are added to themselves until there is only a single digit left. Then two is added to this number. If the resulting sum is an odd number, the answer is *yes*, if an even number, the answer is *no*. This must be done only once for each question, and it is not allowed to change the wording of the question to get another reading.

Questions are generally asked on the Day of Number Two (Monday) preferably at two o'clock.

The Marriage-Numbers

The number 3 'rules' marriage and things connected with the home, according to the traditional lore of figures.

If the numbers of your name add up to 3 (adding the letters, then re-adding the digits until you get a single number) you are more likely to get married than to stay single. The first thing that a person interested in his or her marriage outlook should do is to extract the marriage-number from his name and date of birth. The letters in the first Christian name are taken and added up first, thus: Mary = 4 letters = 4.

Now take the figures for the date of birth and add these together. Assume that you were born on January 1, 1935. This is expressed as 1 (first day) plus 1 (first month) plus 1 + 9 + 3 + 5. All added together = 20, re-added to get a single figure: 2 + 0 = 2.

The birth-number was 2, the name-number 4. Add together: 6.

Six is therefore the marriage-number of this individual. To find out what prospects there are for marriage with a certain person, the number 3 (which 'rules' marriage) is added to this: 6 + 3 = 9.

Look up the Table of Harmonies. You will see that 9 is in harmony with 4 and out of harmony with 8. This means that Mary will find her marriage affinity most strongly with a man whose name adds up to four. Of course, in making this calculation you have to take the man's marriage-number, which means knowing his date of birth.

Marriage with a person whose marriage-number is 8, however, would be less harmonious.

Suppose you want to know the number of children that can be expected from a given marriage. Seven is the number favouring children. So you take the marriage-numbers of the two people, add them and then subtract 7 from this number. If you get a *minus* number as a result, you should consider it to be a *plus* number.

Take an example. If the man's number is 1 and the girl's is 5, you have a total marriage-number of 6. Subtracting 7 from this gives us minus 1. The answer, then, is one child.

What are Number Three personalities like? They tend to be strong, faithful and militant. They come under the influence of the colour red, which is favourable to them. Luck follows if they make decisions and carry out plans on their day, Tuesday.

Number Three people should wear, for luck, a red topaz stone, and should seek their fortune to the west of their place of birth. They are often lucky in love, and can gain the ear of people in authority. Unfortunately, they often feel that they do not desire the support of others, and lose many chances in that way.

They succeed best when working with metals, through travel in a westerly direction and from things done on the spur on the moment.

In dealing with a Number Three subject, you may have to show a good deal of patience and understanding, because they are not likely to come half-way to meet you, and are inclined to be a little reserved.

The Number Three woman makes a fine career personality, and can organise far better than most of her sisters. The Number Three man often shows musical ability. He should not allow people to flatter him too much.

Your Money-Numbers

Money plays a large part in the lives of all of us. Even in the mystic East, where many people spend their entire lives in contemplation, money still makes the world go round, in a material sense.

Four is the mysterious number which is connected with your

141

money gains and losses. It is connected with movement and change, and the day which you should especially observe in all money planning is Wednesday, the fourth day of the week.

Talismans for attracting money luck to the wearer are frequently seen in some Oriental countries; and many of them are based upon the number four. They are square (four sides); they carry the name of the person written in four coloured inks on paper folded four times. Some talismans of this kind are made of an alloy composed of four metals: lead, silver, copper and tin.

The letter 'D' (fourth letter of the Roman, Arabic and Hebrew alphabets), is thought to have a mystical connection with money; and rich people write it somewhere in their houses, to safeguard their money. Poorer ones, on the other hand, write that letter on the flaps of their purses.

One of the most interesting ways of finding one's money destiny is contained in a method devised by a great Arabian sage.

First the name of the person seeking the information about his money fate is written in numerical form. The number of letters in his name are counted and the sum is written down.

Then the year of birth-numbers are written down, added up and compared with the name of the person for harmony. A typical piece of such divination might, therefore, look like this:

Name: Adam = 4 letters. Year of birth: 1938 (added) = $1 + 9 + 3 + 8 = 21$. Add the name-number and year-number: $4 + 21 (3) = 7$.

Seven is thus the money-number, which must be added to the mysterious general money-number of four: $7 + 4 = 11$. As we must always re-add when we have a double number, to get a single one, this now becomes $1 + 1 = 2$.

The sage will decide that every *two* years will be successful money years in this young man's life. Now he looks up the Table of Harmonies, to find that 2 is harmonious with 7. So any year which, when its figures are added up, makes a total of 7, will be exceptionally successful in the money sense for the inquirer. A special talisman might be made for this man, containing the numbers that affect him most favourably.

So much for the money fortune. How about the Number Four personality?

Number Four people are mercurial, restless, liable to change their opinions very quickly and completely. They are interesting companions, but they are a law unto themselves. Anyone who has to deal with them may have to adapt himself to their ways; it will not happen that the reverse will take place.

Any alloys of metals are favourable to them, and they should act in ambitious plans on Wednesdays. They make good doctors and also distinguish themselves in things connected with transport, travel and communications.

The Number Four man makes a good husband if he is given a good deal of freedom and allowed to follow his own personal interests or hobbies. The Number Four woman is demure, pleasant and charming, but can easily become very critical of others.

Number Four people get on very well with their harmonies – people whose number is nine. But they do not harmonise at all well with those whose number adds up to three. This is an important thing to remember. Harmonies and disharmonies can only be made favourable to one another if the number of one or the other of the parties can be made to change – by a person using a slightly different name, for instance, or a nickname.

Will You Travel?

Five is the number of travel, according to the age-old teaching of the numerologists of the East. It represents Thursday – the fifth day of the week – and has an affinity for tin and the colour blue. A talisman to keep a person safe on his journeys was always made on a Thursday. It contained, written on white paper in blue ink, the name of the person and the number five, drawn very large. Some of these amulets are actually made of pure tin.

How does a person know whether he will travel or not? The travel-number for each individual is first discovered. The first name is taken, and reduced to a single number, by adding the number of letters, then re-adding them if necessary, until a single number is obtained. Hence, if your name is Alexander (= 9 letters) your personal number is 9. To this is added the travel-number of Five: = 14 = 5. No wonder Alexander the Great travelled over most of the known world: his travel-number is the same as the mystical number of travel itself: 5!

Now, suppose that you want to travel to China. Will this be advantageous to you or not? Find your travel-number. Suppose that it is 6. Add the letters in the word 'China' – 5. This gives you the number 11, which can be reduced to $1 + 1 = 2$. In this form of divination, odd numbers mean *yes*, even ones *no* or *unlikely*. So you can see that China would not be the best destination.

Suppose you want to know how soon you may travel abroad. You take the letters in your name, add them to the number of letters in your parents' names. Reduce this to a single digit by re-adding if necessary. The answer gives you the number of *months* from now when the first opportunity should arise to make the journey of your choice.

Many people want to know whether travel would benefit them financially. Now, as we have seen earlier in this series, Number Four 'rules' money. So you should add the entire date of the proposed trip (day, month and year, as in 29.5.59) to the number of your whole name. Then add the money-number 4. Re-add until you have obtained a single digit. If the result is an odd number, the answer is *yes*. Otherwise, you should expect less success than you might have hoped for.

The Turkish system of travel-numbers includes this very interesting method: how to find out if one will marry and settle abroad.

The numbers of the inquirer's name and that of the country are added up. From this is subtracted the time of day when the question is asked. If the resultant figure is less than 5, it means *yes*; but more than 5 is a warning. Although the method is slightly different, the mystical travel-number Five is used by the Turks, as by the Persians and Arabs.

But what of the Number Five personality? You are a Number Five if your whole name adds up to 5. Fives are likely to be successful in things that they start on Thursdays – the fifth day of the week. They should wear as a mascot something dark blue and have social success far beyond the ordinary run of people. They may lack patience, especially if they are being made to do something that they do not really want to do.

As husbands, the Number Fives are pleasant and enterprising, though they expect their spouses to obey them! The Five woman is calm and interested in her husband's career more than in one of her own. She makes an ideal mother.

Either sex flourishes to the north-west of the place of birth, and agriculture or retail trade are among the ways in which they can find success. They excel in outdoor sports as well.

As an employer, the Number Five person is likely to be a little too easy-going at times, and as a result may have difficulty in maintaining discipline. But he can offset this by giving plenty of scope to senior employees.

The greatest lack of the Number Five individual comes through his own number and the harmony-number 14 – one of the few cases in which a double number is of importance.

Number Five people get on well with every other number, as they often get unexpected offers of help which can give them chances to fulfil lifelong ambitions.

They cannot be overcome by opponents if they plan their actions on Thursdays; or so, at any rate, goes the popular belief.

Numbers and Your Health

The health-number is 6; it is also connected with beauty and the way in which other people see one. In the Orient, the number 6 is not used so much to find out whether one is healthy and likely to remain so, as much as to increase the vitality and charm of the individual.

The lucky charm of Number Six consists of a square piece of cloth upon which is written the number. This is done on a Friday – the Day of Venus and Beauty – and the colour which is thought to correspond with it is green.

There are many superstitions and legends attached to Number Six and the colour green. Many Arab women believe that the Queen of Sheba charmed Solomon with a green handkerchief upon which was drawn the number 6. And there is a symbolic tale of six beautiful sisters, who became ugly when one of their number died and broke the 'six'.

Exercises for health and vitality are often associated with 6 and its multiples. Six, sixty and six hundred times are the stated repetitions for female health exercises among the tribes of the Arabian interior.

If the letters in your name add up to 6, you are likely to have greater physical vitality than most other people. For this reason some traditional physicians in the East recommend that the name of a child who is not thought to be strong should be changed to one with 6 letters.

The number 6 is also used in another interesting way. If a man wants to find out whether he will succeed in a competition or 'trial of strength' with another man, he takes his name-number (the sum of his name, counting all the letters and adding until there is only one single digit left), then adds 6 to this, and adds it to itself if necessary to produce a single number. Then the name of the opponent is taken, converted into numbers, and 6 is added to it. The two 'vitality-numbers' thus obtained are now compared. If one is larger than the other, this is the number of the person who will win. If one is 6, however, or a multiple of 6, this is the one who will win.

This method is also used to find out the relative strengths of opponents in any field of human activity, because it is believed that 6 connects with power in the general as well as the physical sense.

A Number Six person is one whose full names add up to 6. If a man, he is likely to have the power to influence others. He will be ambitious, and should succeed at anything which he tries in life – if he has the stamina to persevere. He may be fussy about food, but should have physical charm and some sort of inner 'magnetism' which attracts others to him.

The Number Six woman, on the other hand, may have to tone down her opinions, which are likely to be overpowering. She may be very beautiful; but even if she is not, she will never lack admirers. She has what people call personality – some sort of attraction that cannot be denied.

If the numbers of your birth add up to 6, you should always carry out important projects on Fridays, should follow this number and always associate yourself with it. People claim that once they have thus got into harmony with their numbers, their luck has changed for the better in a very dramatic way.

Number Six people should carry a piece of copper for luck, and should time important decisions and meetings for the sixth hour of the day. The sixth hour in this sense, it should be noted, means the sixth full hour after the person has risen from sleep, not six o'clock by the clock.

Six is also, oddly, the number of success in war. This may be a survival of the belief of the ancient Semites that Venus (Astarte) was a war-goddess and brought success. But it also ties in well with the notion of vitality.

The Numbers of Children

Seven, that mystical number of many peoples, is the lucky number of children of all ages up to sixteen. If your name, when the letters are added up, gives as sum the number 7, you will have most of the more endearing characteristics of a child. You will bring out the protective instinct in people, will be able to look upon all new experiences in your life with eyes of interest. You will find that people, especially those older than yourself, will help you.

Your lucky day is Saturday, which is the seventh day of the week, and dark colours should point a way to success.

To find your number, you must take the letters of your full name and add them up. If the result is a double number, you must add again, until you arrive at a single digit.

In some Eastern countries, where the number 7 is believed to protect children, this number is written with white ink on a black cloth. It is then sewn into a conical shape and suspended around the neck of the child. Many mothers believe that in this way their children will prosper and be saved from the evil eye of jealous people looking at them.

The luck of a child depends – so runs the belief – upon the relationship which the number 7 has to him. His seventh and fourteenth years are the most important. What happens to him, what he says, thinks and does, during these years, are carefully noted down, and his career is planned by the parents in accordance with the results they obtain.

When parents want to know whether to punish a child or not, they often take his name and the punishment, and write them both down. Then they add up the letters. If the result is 7, they do not punish. If it is any other number, they add 7 to it, then consult the Table of Harmonies. If the number they obtain in this way is a 2 (which harmonises with 7), they do not punish the child at all!

In the case of children, the full name is not taken. Most children throughout the world are known either by their first name only or by some pet name. This is the one which is used in calculating by the number 7.

What are Number Seven people like? They should do well in matters involving finance, land and property. Many Seven people are employed in Government service. They are attracted to those who like them – sometimes too much – and can be susceptible to flattery. As an emotional person, the Number Seven type is stimulating to friends and associates, but should be careful what he says in the heat of the moment.

Number Seven women are very likeable, sometimes a little naive. They find outlets for their very great energy in all sorts of activities, which often gain the admiration of their friends. They make excellent cooks.

Fortune, in a money sense, smiles upon Number Sevens throughout their lives. They are sometimes known to waste opportunities, as if they knew somewhere inside that they would have a chance of equal merit again. If they are ambitious, they should always make decisions and carry out plans on Saturdays, during the seventh hour after they rise in the morning, and should associate their hopes with dark colours, even black.

Seven is unfriendly towards six, which means that Friday is a bad day for the Seven people, who should attend only to routine tasks on this day.

They are among the best and most thoughtful of friends, and have the ability to command great co-operation and respect from all.

Numbers and Hidden Talent

How many times have you heard of people who have, perhaps after middle age, become successful through using a talent which has lain unsuspected for years?

In the nature of things today, few people can afford to change their jobs just at a whim. The result is that many remain in a rut, carrying on with a job which does not give them scope for their innate talents; they do so because, nine times out of ten, they lack the courage to exchange security for the unknown.

One of the few ways in which one can tell whether one has any hidden talent is through the use of numbers.

Suppose you are a clerk and you want to become a film star. Your friends have told you that your voice is wonderful, and your family think that you are more attractive than anyone in Hollywood. Who will tell you the truth? Consult the numbers.

The number 8 governs hidden talents of all kinds, and it is through the manipulation of this number that we can find out whether we need a change of career or not.

First take your personal-name number: the number of letters in your first name. From this sum, *deduct* the number 8. If the result is plus or minus, it does not matter; regard only the number itself. If that number is a 3, you should go ahead and change. You should seek the occupation that you have wanted to follow or for which you think you are fitted.

If the number is not 3, you must try again, adding the number corresponding to the profession that you want to adopt.

Let us take an example. Your name is George. This equals 6 letters. Deduct 8. The result is minus 2, which equals 2. Now you have to add the number of the profession. Supposing you have always wanted to be a journalist. This word contains 10 letters. You have 2 left over, and to this you add 10. The answer is 12. We cannot have double numbers, so you add the 1 and the 2. The answer is 3. Three means that journalism is favourable for you, that you have the talent. This is because 3 is the harmony of 8 in the Table of Harmonies.

If the answer had been 9, you would have been completely unsuitable, because 9 is hostile to 8 in the Table of Harmonies.

Suppose the answer is neither 8, 9 or 3? Then you have to add one more factor. This should be in all cases your date of birth. Suppose this to be 4.11.1940, which added together gives 2. Add to this your personal-name-number, which we will say is 5, making a total of 7. As this number is not 8, 9 or 3, the answer is that you have not the necessary talent.

What talents are indicated by what numbers? *Odd* numbers mean (in your personal-name's total) that you work best on your own, and that you have artistic or literary abilities. *Even* numbers in the personal-name total mean partnerships, employment, Government service.

If your name-number and birthday (date of birth) number are the same, you are likely to succeed in commerce or industry. If the name-number is larger, this speaks of help through elders and also a probability of setting up your own business. If the birth date is larger than the name-number, you should seek a steady career and gradual promotion. When the father's name and the name of the son or daughter have the same number of letters, the child usually has talents similar to those of the father; and the same goes for a correspondence of the names of the mother with the child.

Financiers, accountants and lawyers have numbers which are connected with three: 3, 6, 9. Military people, engineers and those who work with metals come in multiples of two: 2, 4, 6, 8. People who travel a lot and can benefit by changing their jobs at fairly frequent intervals are indicated by name-numbers which are multiples of four: 4 or 8.

In many cases when the career of a woman is cut short by marriage, so that she becomes a housewife instead of continuing work, the name-number is half that of the birth-number.

The Number Eight people (whose name adds up to 8) tend to be restless, and generally have a good many hidden talents. As you will have seen from a previous paragraph, 8 occurs in the names of such varied souls as engineers and 'those who benefit by changing their jobs'. This is typical of the Number Eight personality, because his abundance of talents makes him able to turn his hand to anything.

As a friend the Number Eight is loyal, but may be tempted to forget a kind action. As a husband or wife he or she cannot stand being tied down to the home. In business his talents always benefit those working with him just as much as they benefit him.

His best day is Sunday, and he is a great planner and schemer. Ancient manuscripts advise Number Eights to carry a piece of scented wood with them as a talisman of success.

How to Gain Powerful Friends

Number Nine people are those whose date of birth, when added to itself, makes a total of 9 if the name-number is added.

A person born, for instance, on 9.1.1931 would have: $9 + 1 + 1 + 9 + 3 + 1 = 24 = 2 + 4 = 6$. So 6 is the birth-number. If his name is Leo, this equals three letters: $6 + 3 = 9$. This person's number, *for the purposes of gaining friends and influence* (success number) is 9.

Suppose our friend Leo wants to influence another person in his favour. He takes the first and last names of the person in question, and adds all the letters up. Suppose that this gives him a result of 5.

Take the two numbers, subtract the lesser from the greater. In this case we get as a product 4. This stands for the fourth day of the Moon. Leo must make his approach to the person in authority on the fourth day of the New Moon. Suppose both his number and that of the other person are the same? Then they are *added*, and the resulting number taken to be the day of the Moon on which the approach is to be made. This is because 9 is a number of the Moon, and indicates the supposed power of the Moon.

If a Berber woman wants to attract the young man of her choice, she takes the numerical value of his name, adds it to her own, and spends half an hour concentrating her thoughts upon him on the night of the Moon which corresponds to the number she has obtained. It is believed that this charm never fails; and the only way in which a Berber youth can protect himself from these womanly wiles is to carry a small silver chain with nine links in his pocket!

There is only one difference between this method and those which I have already described. The numbers are not re-added to produce a single number. As there are only 28 days in the Moon's course from New to Full, if the number is over 28, any number above 28 is taken away from the end-total.

> *Example:*
> Name of the girl: 16 letters.
> Name of the man: 18 letters.
> Total: 34 letters.

34 exceeds 28 by 6 letters. Therefore discard 6, and concentrate upon the man on the 28th day of the Moon.

What happens to the extra 6, which we discarded? Well, this has a value too. This becomes the magical number for the *time* when the concentration is to take place. *Six* therefore stands for the sixth hour after moonrise.

The Number Nine personality is a complicated one. Depending upon his mood, he may be generous or irritable and, unless you know him very well, you can never be sure what kind of mood he *will* be in. There is one saving grace here: Number Nine people are always open to reason. They have logical minds when anything is presented to them in a cool and collected manner. But they become impatient if faced by indefinite suggestions; they are not fond of vague people.

They have powers of intuition, and can often guess the result of an event, or advise other people how they should act in matters which are baffling. They make good judges, clerks, travel agents and business representatives.

If you are a Number Nine personality, you should cultivate patience. Make sure that you do not overlook matters of detail. You may have too many plans going at once, and should finish one thing before moving on to another.

Your greatest strength is in making quick decisions correctly, and in so doing you can build up a considerable reputation of leadership for yourself.

The fortunate metal for Number Nine people is silver, and Sunday and Wednesday should be favourable. Lucky numbers are 4 and 9. These are also the hours in which the greatest successes are likely to come. Remember, however, that hours of the day in this system are counted from the time when the person rises in the morning, not from the first hour of the day. They are the 'hours of consciousness' – the hours dating from the time when the person becomes fully conscious after being asleep.

Numbers Applied to Ideas and Plans

The science of numerology states that people can find success in life through finding the 'nature' of a plan through numbers, and applying this knowledge. Your name and date of birth are associated with your fortune, and have to be linked in some way with the plan that you have in mind. This link is formed by means of numbers.

Add the letters in your name, not counting the vowels (A,E,I,O,U, or Y). The sum of these is your ideas-number. If it is the same as your birth-number (when the entire date of birth has been added and re-added to get a single digit) you are likely to succeed in giving ideas to others, and your ideas are likely to prove fruitful. Inventors have this kind of number. If the birth-number is larger than the ideas-number, you can benefit through the ideas of others. If the birth-number is smaller, you should think more about your life, and plan in great detail.

Now, suppose you have an idea. You want to know whether it will be successful. Take your ideas-number, and add it to the number of letters (excluding vowels) in the word which expresses the idea. If the result is *even*, the answer is *no*. If *odd*, you should succeed.

A favourite pastime to find ideas when one has none is also based upon this, and it goes back many centuries. It is called Bibliomancy. The person takes his ideas-number, and opens a book (any book will do) anywhere at random. Taking the left-hand page, he goes from one word to the next, until he finds a word with the same number of letters as his ideas-number. This word then becomes an *idea*, and he should act upon it.

I will give you an example now. My ideas-number is 12. I add the 1 and the 2, to get a single number, $1 + 2 = 3$. Three becomes my true ideas-number. Now I take a book at random from my shelves as I sit here; it is a dictionary. The first word of three letters that I find on the left-hand page where I open the book at random is 'try'. This is an answer to my question – because, of course, you have to have some sort of question in mind before you start this process. It is surprising how often you will get an interesting reply from this method.

If you have a plan which you want to make work, you can use this method to get advice as to what new element you should introduce into it. You can also work out plans by repeating this process *ten times*, because the number 10 is in direct relationship with ideas and plans. Suppose you have no plan at all. You find your ideas-number, open any book, look for a word with that number of letters. Remember to discard the vowels from your name, but not from the number of letters in the word which you obtain, just as I did above.

Repeat this *ten times*, writing down the word which you find each time. Then, from this collection of words, see whether you can find a plan, or a series of suggestions which will help you to make a plan.

I have a friend who tried this many years ago. The book (in this case a cheap novel) told him to travel, to go East, to deal in tea, to avoid partnerships. It all came true. He was poor at that time, with nothing to lose, so he could afford to go East. He got a job on a ship, went to Cairo, and started to buy tea there and offer it to firms in Europe. Tea is not grown in Egypt, and one would have wondered whether he could have been successful. But he was. But he forgot the advice about partnerships: for he thought that that applied only to his tea business. He lost a good deal of money in a printing business which he entered with a partner. Nevertheless, he is still a flourishing tea-merchant!

Your Career and Your Number

There are all sorts of interesting things that you can find out about your career through numbers. If, for instance, you take your full name, remove the vowels (E,A,I,O,U and Y) and compare it with your job, you can discover whether you will be promoted or not within a reasonable time. Here is an instance:

Full name: George Edward Smith. *Number of Letters (Consonants)* = 11. *Occupation* Bookseller, 6 consonants. Deduct the smaller from the greater: 6 from 11 = 5. This 5 tells you that five months from the date of asking the question, you have a chance of promotion. If the two numbers had been the same, the meaning would have been 'no change'.

In using this method, you have to concentrate upon the question, think hard about it before you ask the numbers. Otherwise, say the numerologists of the East, you may not get a true reply.

Careers which will suit you, if you list all the occupations you can think of, are those which contain the same *vowels* as your name.

Now take the consonants in your full name. Add them up. Add the date when you started your job. Keep adding all numbers over 9 until you obtain a single digit. If the result is under 6, you could work better on your own. If the result is over 6, you will have to wait that number of years, and half that number of months, before you get a chance to change your career, if you are seeking a change.

It is important in all cases to have a *harmony* between your name and your job. If the form of your name which you use is shorter than the name for your job, you should progress better at it. Thus, if your name is Alexander J. Smith, and you are a teacher, your name is too long. In order to obtain the harmony you need, you should become 'A.J. Smith', or 'A. Smith'. Of course, not all of us can change our names, or even be called by the form of the name that we wish; but the way in which you *sign* your name can be changed to apply this shortened form.

The date of birth, too, is important in a choice of career. Those who were born on the 1st to the 3rd of any month succeed best in things connected with land, mines, buildings and so on. The 4th to 6th are best for communicating ideas. The 7th to 10th people should buy and sell. People born between the 11th and 13th would succeed best in being in the public eye. Birthdays between the 14th and 16th are those of people with success to be found in writing, reading, teaching. Here are the remainder of the 'indications':

17th-19th: farming, countryside, dealing with animals;
20th-22nd: medical, research, large companies;
23rd-25th: metals, paper, wood;

26th-28th: athletic matters, war, diplomacy;
29th to end of month: advising others, secretaries, etc.

Numbers, Colours, Places and Ambition

The connection of numbers and colours, ideas and figures, places and calculations, run through the history and folklore of all the world's peoples. According to the Arabian system, there is an underlying harmony between all these; and they are also connected with human ambition and progress.

The purpose of this knowledge is to make numbers 'work for you'. This, too, is a human need all over the world. No sooner does a man discover something than he wants to know its practical application. Everything in human life and thought must 'work' — must perform a function. Even a work of art works by giving pleasure.

Certain numbers are connected with certain colours. This means that if the two are used together, a harmony, and hence a power, is formed or encouraged.

Take the letters of your favourite colour. Add them to the letters in your first name. The results will be a number which should point the way to progress for you in matters of the spirit, of the mind, of family success. When this number turns up, whether in a house number or anywhere else, it should benefit you in this way.

Now write down the number which expresses your individuality. This is composed of the day of birth, hour, first name of the person, and number of letters in the place of birth. Divide by two. This individuality-number gives you the letter of the alphabet which points towards personal success. Count the letters of the alphabet thus: A = 1, B = 2, and so on. You should 'adopt' this letter, and you will find that you have a harmony with people who have the same letter as the initial of their own first names. But remember that although there will be a harmony, it will be you who is the senior partner in such a friendship.

Money matters are connected, as we have seen earlier in this series, with the number 4. Four elements go to compose your successful destiny in the money sense. You should know the number of your home (the number of letters in its name or the house number), the number of letters in your first name, the number of letters in your secret wish and the number of letters in your favourite colour. Add these up and take away 4. If the number is composed of more than one figure, add the figures together until you get a single one.

The 'Mystical Number' is the one which should, according to the Cabbalists of the Sufi School, lead you to success throughout life. It should be written on paper of the colour you like best, and carried about with you in a sealed envelope, with your name written upon it.

The Sufis believe that this will bring prosperity through your main ambition in life, and the successful accomplishment of your secret desires.

Look up the Table of Harmonies to find out which of these numbers are in harmony with your own Mystical Number. Ignore those which are harmonious, but avoid the number which is given in the table as not in harmony: because this number can do your cause harm. Whenever you see it, try to avoid it. Do not take important steps of any kind on the day represented by that number.

CHIVALRY AND TEACHERS

Chivalry

Jaida the Beautiful

Born and bred in the desert, Mohammed, son of Saleh, directly descended from the Prophet, recited this story of his adventures in the Year 240, before the Caliph Al-Mutawakkil, reflecting the spirit of the Sons of the Prophet:

'The son of the Chief of the Tribe of Hilal was named Al-Ashtar, son of Abdullah. He was the most handsome man of all the Children of Hilal, and distinguished for his generosity.

'Al-Ashtar fell in love with a very beautiful girl, Jaida the Beautiful, and all knew of their love. Finally they were married, although their two families during the courtship, for another reason, became sworn enemies.

'Jaida was taken back into her family and was held in her father's tent. If she were to be rescued or to escape, the father said that he would punish her sisters, who were still with him.

'One day shortly after this, Al-Ashtar came to me and said:

'"Little Tiger (*Numair*) of the Family of the Lion (Ali) of the Hashimites! Wilt do me a favour?"

'"Gladly, if you invoke it in the name of the House (of the Prophet)," I said. He answered: "I do, and in the name of chivalry which is our common bond, and in the name of justice, as you are of the family of the most just."

'"Say on," I said, and he continued, "I am in love, as all men know, with Jaida the Beautiful, my wife, whom I am prevented from visiting or reclaiming, and she from joining me, for her sisters are held hostage. Before I can arrange her escape, such is the burning of my heart that I must visit her. What if she comes to believe that I have forgotten her, and left her to languish in hostile hands, even if they be those of her own kinsfolk?"

159

'"By God!" I said, "to aid justice and love, and also to perform an exploit is in the blood of the Sharifs."

'"The Sharifs," he said, "are the honoured of men, but they are the Elevated, while the spilling of blood is of the earth; and has your own grandsire not said, 'Not all the possessions in the world are worth the shedding of a single drop of blood in tyranny'?"

'"If the family of Jaida shed our blood, yours or mine," I said, "*there* will be the tyranny. For our part, honour and exploits, glory and satisfaction, the redress of wrongs, these are enjoined upon us, and in these I, Numair, join thee with this hand and heart."

'He took my hand in silence, and we rode our camels for a day and a night, and a day more, until we came upon her people, with their herds, when it was almost eventide.

'Behind the hills overlooking their camp we made our camels kneel in concealment, and then Al-Ashtar said:

'"You may go now and scout, for I am known to them and you are not. If anyone wants to know your business, say that you are looking for strayed cattle. My very name is poison to them, so speak it not until you can find a certain girl, maidservant of Jaida's, who will be watching the sheep."

'"Tell her that I am here; ask about Jaida's welfare. Tell her where we are concealed."

'Before long, creeping among the herds, I found the shepherdess, and gave her the message.

'She left me for a while, and then returned, and said;

'"It will be difficult, for her father does not let Jaida go far in case she escapes. At the time of the evening prayer, however, she will come out and stand over there under the trees behind our tents."

'I went back to Al-Ashtar, and we waited until it was dark. Then, as we heard the call to prayer, we led our camels silently to the meeting-place.

'Jaida appeared, and my friend stood up to receive her, and took her hand. I stood up to withdraw; but both protested. "By God," they said, "since there is nothing unbecoming between us, please stay and be with us."

'So we talked, and Al-Ashtar said, after a time: "O Jaida, have you an idea as to how we might spend the night together?"

'"By God!" she said, "there is no way, and I must return to the captivity which is known to you."

'"Though it means the splitting of the skies," he said, "I will somehow spend the night with thee!"

'Jaida now asked him, "Can you say that this comrade of ours, who has already taken risks for thee, is a man to be reckoned with in bad times?"

'"You speak," said Al-Ashtar, "of a son of the House of the Prophet: would such a one draw back, even in the face of Shaitan the Stoned?"

'"How say you?" asked Jaida of me.

'"I stand by the reputation of my family," I told her; and she said, "A word from such as thee is more binding than the oath of a king. I know you people. Say no more."

'So she put her clothes on me, and took mine to dress herself in.

'She said, "That tent over there is ours. Go into it and sit down, at the end where my curtain divides it. When my father comes in, he will ask you to hand him my milking-vessel. Do not give it to him, for I always refuse to deal with him. So he will take it and go to milk his camel. When he returns, he will offer it to you first, to drink from. Refuse to take it, as I always do. Only accept it when he places it upon the ground. After that, he will fold his cloak around him, and will not disturb you again until the morning, when I will have returned."

'I did all these things. When the father came I would not give him the vessel; then I would not take it; and then, as he was placing it upon the ground I reached for it, too soon; and together we spilt the milk, all of it.

'He said, "Now this is too much, you ill-mannered creature!" He came to my side of the tent with a whip, and threw me on the ground, giving me thirty lashes. I made not a sound, until Jaida's mother and sister came in and stopped him. Had the beating continued for a moment more, I feel, I would have thrown off my disguise and challenged him to combat. Then all three left the tent, while I nursed my wounds.

'After a long time, Jaida's mother came in to me and said, "O my daughter! Fear God and obey your father; do not give him cause to be angered. This will be better in the end."

'She continued, "I must go now, and I will send thy sister to keep thee company for the night, so do not be afraid."

'I lay down, and when the girl came and spoke to me, I refused to

161

say anything until she came and lay beside me. Then I placed my hand over her mouth and said:

'"Thy sister Jaida is with Al-Ashtar, her lawful husband. My back is in ribbons because of her, and you will be silent! Know, girl, that I am called Numair, and am the son of Saleh, of the Tribe of the Koresh and the Family of the Messenger, and so I cannot be unworthy of that lineage. Trust me, for I am he who carries his honour in his hand! If you decide to speak of this matter, now or later, your sister will suffer, and the blood of many will be spilt."

'She signalled to me to remove my hand, and she was trembling sorely with fright. But we talked all night, and she was a wonderful companion. Before light came, Jaida crept into the tent, terribly afraid, and asked me who I had with me.

'We explained, and she was reassured, while I dressed in my own clothes and gave hers back to her.

'When I made my way back to Al-Ashtar, he said:

'"Thou hast risked thy life for me, and I am in thy perpetual debt, and thou hast proved that service is the banner of the House, and that gallantry will ever be handed from father to son by its members: may we be worthy of this bequest which they are to us!"

'I said, "I have done what I undertook to do, and as much noise is now made about it as if I had failed in my duty! Is there no other topic of conversation possible between warriors?"

'He laughed and answered, "But I will reward thee. And this even if only because, as we see every day, those who do not honour and reward your people come upon some dreadful misery!"

'"That is not a matter within my control," I said; and after that we had many adventures, and Jaida was in the end rescued by our combined efforts, though it forms another tale, and to recite it would be to succumb to the temptations of boastfulness, near whose campfires we already sit.'

From *The Book of Virtues and their Contraries*, reputedly by Al-Jahiz (9th Century).

The Insight of Saladin

There was once a noted nobleman of France, the Count of Provence, who became convinced that, if he made a pilgrimage to the Holy Land, good fortune would attend him. He set forth, attended by a numerous retinue – but he was captured by the Saracen Sultan Saladin.

Because of his high repute and honourable disposition, Saladin treated the Count with great respect and consideration, and, although a prisoner, kept him at Court and allowed him a great deal of freedom under security of his word of honour not to try to escape.

Now, when the Count had departed France, he had left behind him a daughter who was little more than a child. As the years passed with her father in captivity, she grew to marriageable age, and her mother thought that something must be done to find her a husband.

There was no scarcity of suitors, of all kinds and conditions, for her fortune and noble lineage made her attractive, as did her beauty, to the flower of Western chivalry.

The Countess, however, felt that she must consult her husband, and letters were sent to him in Palestine, where the Sultan was campaigning, asking for his suggestions as to a bridegroom for the girl.

Of course, the Count had been away for so long that he had little knowledge and no details of the prospects and nature of the various suitors, and felt that he could offer few suggestions. So he went to the Sultan and asked him for his advice.

The Sultan received him kindly and proposed that his friend should seek a report containing the most minute details about all the potential suitors from the Countess, so that he could make a choice.

When his reply, with the Sultan's advice, arrived at their family home, the relatives were somewhat surprised that the Saracen King should be involved in the choice of a husband for their kinswoman, but they collected as much information as they could and forwarded it to their lord in his captivity.

When the letter and reports arrived, the Count took it to Saladin and said:

'My Lord! You have been so good to me and made me comfortable in honourable captivity here, so that I now feel like a kinsman of yours, and therefore ask a great favour. Examine these documents with me and give your advice upon who should be the husband of my daughter, so that our lineage and future shall be assured.'

Saladin agreed, and he and the Count sat down to examine the papers. Finally the Sultan said:

'Count, I have listed the good and bad things about all of these men. Every one of them has some flaw or drawback, whether of age, appearance, title or expectations, except one, this one, who seems to me to be the right man for your daughter. He has some fortune, but not too much; and, although he is not of your social rank, his record shows him to be a man of the greatest nobility of conduct: and, moreover, one of the most resolute in pursuing what he thinks to be right.'

The Count thanked the Sultan and fully agreed; so he sent word that this particular young man's proposal should be accepted. The family were greatly surprised at the choice, but they called the youth and told him what had happened. At first he thought that they were trifling with him, for he had not thought that a family of such illustrious ancestry would allow him to marry their most eligible lady. But the family council insisted that this was no joke, and, moreover, they added that the choice had been made by none other than Sultan Saladin himself, captor of their noble chief.

The young man said to himself: 'If such a man as Saladin has chosen me, from among so many, and done me such honour, then I must discharge the obligation of honourable conduct conferred by that act of confidence.'

The pair were married, and the young man immediately asked for the whole of the Count's property and estates to be handed over to him, together with all the rents which were paid by tenants. This meant that he had an immense amount of money at his disposal.

As soon as these arrangements had been made, the youth called a council of the family. He told them:

'As you have told me, I have been chosen from all the suitors of this lady, by the Count, on the recommendation of Sultan Saladin himself. As one who has received honours such as these, I must prove myself worthy of this trust. I shall, therefore, leave on a journey at once; putting the family estates in the hands of my wife, for I have a duty to perform.'

The young man made his way on horseback to the Near East, where he assembled a retinue and bought a large ship. He learned the language and found out all he could about the great Sultan Saladin.

Putting out from a secure harbour to one of the Sultan's seaside places, the young man took hunting dogs and hawks and filled his ship with servants and supporters. When he arrived at Saladin's camp, he presented himself to him, saying that he was a visitor who wanted to hunt with Saladin, but that he wanted nothing from him. He did not even kiss his hand or take food with him, contrary to accepted practice; but the Sultan liked the look of him, and welcomed him on a hunting party.

They went on the chase several more times and then, one day, the falcons pursued a crane towards the young man's ship where it lay moored in the harbour. The Sultan reined in just beside the ship, and the youth called his men-at-arms, who surrounded the leader of the Saracens.

'This, surely, is treachery!' exclaimed Saladin.

'Not at all,' said his captor, 'for I have neither kissed your hand nor taken salt at your table, nor have I accepted a single gift from you.'

Now he took the Sultan abroad his ship, and revealed himself as the son-in-law of the Count of Provence, chosen by the Sultan himself. 'Now, I beg of you,' he said, 'My Lord Saladin, yield up my father-in-law, and the whole world will know that you have chosen me well.'

The Sultan was at first amazed, then delighted, and he gave orders that the Count be brought to the ship, where everything was explained to him. The Count of Provence and his daughter's husband then sailed home, laden with the gifts which Saladin had bestowed on them, which included a sum of money equal to double the amount of all the rent of their lands which had accrued during his captivity.

Now this tale, used by Don Juan Manuel as the epitome of chivalry, in his famous romance 'Count Lucanor', is derived from the tales of the bards who promoted the theme, in the Christian and Saracen territories alike, that chivalry transcends enmity. It is recorded in the annals of the Sufi *Futuwwat* (Chivalric) organisations as having an added, inward, message: that, on a higher level, someone with greater insight can make choices which are, ultimately, right, and lead, in the end if not in the interim, to success and harmony.

The Loan

An ancient desert chieftain, in olden times, was approached in his tent by the son of a merchant. The young man said: 'I am the younger son of so-and-so, of such-and-such a place. I have several brothers, all of whom help our father in his commerce. But I do not want to spend my whole life in trade and counting money. I have decided to seek my fortune in the noble profession of arms. Please accept me as one of your fighting-men.'

The tribal chief agreed to train the youth in chivalry and the ways of the desert. When the time came to go to war, the young man was killed, to the great sorrow of the chief, who had come to love him like his own son.

He reflected, 'Although mourning is absurd, since we should rather exult in the knowledge that a meritorious warrior has reached a better world, there are pangs of suffering, personal deprivation, which people feel and which it is only humane to help assuage.' He set himself to thinking how he could soften the blow of the bereavement for the youth's father.

After long thought, the bedouin mounted his camel and rode to the city where the warrior's father lived. Entering his shop, he made the customary salutations and was invited to sit down.

The old chief said:

'I am a man of the saddle and the sword, and you are one of transactions and trust. I have come to ask you to answer a question.'

'Gladly,' said the merchant, who did not know who the visitor was.

'If,' continued the ancient, 'something precious is lent to you, and you look after it as best you can, aware that it is the property of another; and if the owner of that property eventually claims it back – do you let it go with a glad or sorry heart?'

'Is this a joke?' asked the merchant, 'surely any man of honour and humanity will know the answer. We should feel honoured at being trusted with something precious, and we should feel delight when it is safely claimed back by its owner.'

'I speak of the life of your youngest son,' said the old man.

Joha the Joker

Joha the Joker

The traditional gap between the Arabs and Persians, neighbours whose history has been linked for many centuries, is bridged by Islam and by common experiences. But nowhere is it more affectionately transcended than in the tales of Joha (to the Arabs), who is Mulla Nasrudin to the Iranians, Turks, Afghans and other Easterners as far away as Bangladesh.

The discussions about whether he was a fool or a wise man, a jester at court or a village schoolmaster, will perhaps always continue. As *Giufa*, our joker is well established in Europe as the clown of Sicily. It is likely that he has been known there since the island was a part of the Arab cultural area.

Joha was asked by his master to take care of the door of the shop in his absence. He did not fail to obey this order. When he wandered off to watch an actor performing, he carried the door strapped to his back. Exactly the same tale is told of Mulla Nasrudin in the tea-houses of Central Asia; and it appears in old English joke-books, like the ancient *Sacke Full of Newes*. Another time Joha (and Giufa) asked the apparently innocuous permission, from a judge, to kill flies wherever he could find them. Before he knew where he was, the judge who had granted this licence found the fist of the joker striking his nose.

According to the mood of the culture, we find the same tale used to illustrate teachings. The favourite contention that the law is an ass is the interpretation often given to this anecdote in the West. In the East it is sometimes invoked to support the assertion that rigid laws, especially in spiritual matters, have to be interpreted according to the prevailing context.

Literal obedience to instructions is certainly one side of the Joha figure's activities. His wife once went out and told him to feed the

167

hen so that she could keep the eggs warm. When the lady came back, she found that he had fed it continually so that it died, and was reduced to sitting on the eggs himself.

Joha Studies how to Learn

One day Joha's wife said to him, 'You really are disgracefully ignorant! You should find someone to teach you something, so that I need not be so ashamed of you...'

'Well,' said Joha, 'I am ready enough to learn, but I don't know how to go about it.'

'Then I shall tell you. Go to the middle of the market-place. There you will see a wise man sitting, reading from a book. Stand beside him and acquire some knowledge.'

Joha went off to the soukh and, sure enough, there was the learned man, with a book open in front of him, reciting tales of wisdom. Joha stopped and stood respectfully by.

At that moment, a prankster leapt onto Joha's shoulders, and sat there, laughing. Joha allowed him to stay where he was until the wise man took up his book and went on his way. Then the joker jumped to the ground and ran off.

When Joha arrived home, his wife asked him:

'Well, it wasn't very hard to learn, was it?'

'The learning was easy,' said Joha, 'but the weight on my shoulders was *terrible*!'

The Importance of Analogy

One day Joha was in a teahouse when a man knocked over his glass. 'You'll have to pay for that!' said Joha.

'Certainly not,' said the other man, 'for have you not heard the saying that "overturning the tea is not evil but a bringer of good luck"? This is an omen that something good will happen to you, and I am fortune's instrument!'

Joha was satisfied with this explanation until he discovered that the man was a tea-merchant. He never missed an opportunity of encouraging the use or waste of tea, so that he would be able to sell more.

A few days later, at the warehouse by the riverside, Joha was found emptying sack after sack of the tea-merchant's stock into the water. The infuriated owner took him to court.

'If one person can be allowed to "make luck", so can another,' said Joha.

'On the principle of *Adat* (application of local custom),' opined the judge, 'I have no alternative but to dismiss the case.'

Back to Front

> One Joha story, in which he appears as a wise fool, is not only current in the Arabian countries but can be found in the German jokebook of *Til Eulenspiegel*, Englished in about 1550 as *Owlglass*.

Joha borrowed a horse and a stable for the afternoon, from a friend, saying, 'I have need of money, and I can get it without deception, but through the self-deception of others.'

He stood outside the stable and charged one piece of silver from everyone who went in, after their curiosity had been aroused by his cry:

> 'Come in and see a horse with his head where his tail ought to be!'

One after another they paid their money and crowded into the exhibit.

When they came out, whether singly or together, the people were all strangely silent – which only encouraged more people to see the wonder – and many of them were shaking their heads in perplexity.

Because Joha had merely tied the horse up with its tail towards the eating-trough: where the head ought to be.

Indirect Teaching

The Wolf's Ear

> Among the Arabs, great store is placed on what is called 'indirect teaching', which is also considered to be the ability to see the reality behind appearances.

The story is told of the lion, the wolf and a fox, who went out hunting together.

They collected a donkey, a deer and a hare.

The lion said to the wolf:

'Divide the spoils between us.'

So the wolf said: 'The ass is for you, the deer is for me, and the hare is for the fox.'

The lion clawed him, tearing his ear.

Now the fox said:

'What a fool he is! That is no way to divide the product of the hunt.'

The lion said:

'Very well, then: you do the apportioning.'

The fox said:

'Nothing is simpler. The donkey is your breakfast, the deer is your dinner, and you can have the hare in between.'

'Bravo!' said the lion, 'but how did you learn such excellent judgment?'

'From the ear of the wolf,' said the fox.

Nahfat Al Yaman.

The Mice and the Money

According to Abu Bakr ibn Al Khazibah, he was sitting one night, when he was very poor, copying out some of the Traditions of the Prophet (Hadith).

A mouse came into the room and began running about. Soon it was joined by another, and they played a game. They came near to the lamp, and one of them approached quite near to Abu Bakr.

The man had a cup beside him, and he placed it over the mouse, so that it could not escape.

The second mouse then nosed around the inverted cup, and pushed against it. The man continued with his work.

The mouse went back into its hole, and after some time returned with a gold dinar in its mouth, and placed this before the man. But he only looked at the mouse and did nothing, and went on with his work.

The mouse looked at him for a time, and then it went back and brought another dinar, and again sat and watched.

This continued until the mouse had produced four or five dinars, when it sat and looked at the man for very much longer than previously. Finally, the mouse went to its hole and brought a leather bag, which it put on top of the dinars, making the man understand that it now had nothing more to give.

He lifted the cup and the two mice both ran to their hole. The dinars, when taken to the money-changer, were found to be of such good quality as to be worth a dinar and a quarter of the coin then current.

Abu Bakr ibn Al Khazibah, in *Nahfat Al Yaman*.

Armenian Lore

Contributed by *Amina Shah*

Say 'stew' – and the fly will appear from Baghdad.

* * * *

'Greetings, Friend,' smiled the wolf.
   'Brothers, fly for your lives,' cried the bell-wether.

* * * *

If he is asked to make a needle, he asks for a ton of steel.

* * * *

A prince was bitten by a flea. He was just about to squash it, when the flea cried, 'Do not kill me, I am too small.'
   'All the harm that was in your power to do, you did,' said the prince, and killed it.

* * * *

The eagle saw that the haft of the arrow which had brought him down from the sky was tipped with – eagle feathers.
   'Alas! we are the cause of our own destruction,' he said.

* * * *

Hump rocks with a wise man, by all means. But do not carry pebbles with a fool.

Eight Men who Deserve to be Slapped in the Face

He who despises one who has attained correct authority; he who goes into a house uninvited and unwelcomed; he who gives any order in a house not his own; he who seats himself above his position; he who speaks to one who does not listen to him; he who interrupts the conversation of others; he who seeks favours from the ungenerous; he who expects his enemies to love him.

From *The Book of Conduct*, tenth century.

Perfumes of the Imperial Treasury

There are yet (in the Sultan's treasure chambers) other Coffers filled with Amber-greece, Musk, the previous Wood call'd *Lignum Aloes*, and Sandal-wood. There is a certain sort of this *Lignum Aloes*, which is worth a thousand Crowns the Pound, according as it is Fat, or Oily, the most Oily being always the best, and the Turks are very expensive in this Aloes Wood. When some Persons come to visit them, and as soon as they are sate down, it is their custom to present them with a Pipe of Tobacco, with some *Lignum Aloes* in it, which is done after this manner. They take of that Wood, according to the Oilyness of it, and consequently its making a greater fumigation, the quantity of a Pea, or a small Bean, and after they have moisten'd it a little they put it over a few Coals in a Chafing-dish, in a kind of Perfuming-Pot, which they present one after another, to all the Company. There comes out a thick Stream or Exhalation, where-with everyone Perfumes his Head and his Beard, and sometimes the inside of his Turban, after which he lifts up his hands on high, crying *Elmendela* (al-hamdu lillah), that is to say, 'Thanks be to God'. But before they present them with the Perfuming-pot, there is some Rose-water brought in a Vessel of Gold, or Silver, according to the Quality of those who make the Visit. This Vessel is commonly a foot in height, the lower part of it being about the bigness of a man's fist, and from thence growing gradually smaller and smaller to the top of it, which is about the bigness of one's little finger. At the top of it there is a little hole, out of which comes the Rose-water, wherewith they wash their hands and faces, and then hold them over the suffumigation of the *Lignum Aloes*, which not only dries up the water, but also sticks so much the closer to the hair of the Head and Beard.

There are also in those Coffers abundance of Aromatical Simples, and precious Drugs, Bezoar-stones, and store of Mastick, where-with the Sultanesses, and the young Maids of the Seraglio pass away their time. They have of it perpetually in their Mouths, and this

Mastick sweetens the Breath, and cleanses the Teeth, upon which score they are the better belov'd.

From *The Six Voyages of John Baptista Tavernier, a Noble Man of France,* finished in the year 1670, made English by J. Phillips, 1678.

Yes, Your Highness

by *Richard Ellis*

The Arabs of the desert traditionally pride themselves on having no titles at all. The chief of a tribe, of course, was the Sheikh, and that is a title, sure enough. But it was limited by two factors: first, it simply means 'elder', secondly, there is no automatic inheritance of the title or of the position of tribal chief.

Arabs, in general, are much more concerned with their ancestry. Someone may nominate a relative to succeed him, even his son, but this must be confirmed by the assembly of the community. The noblest lineage in Arabia is that of the Quraish tribe, the ancestral line of the Prophet Mohammed. Watch for surnames: Qureshi, Hashimi and Al-Sayed are, strictly speaking, always applicable only to members of this family; so are some people surnamed Husseini and Fatemi (from Hussein, grandson of Mohammed, and his daughter, Fatima, to whom they trace their origins).

A Sheikh may be the headman of a village, the virtual king of a country, the head of a tribe, or merely a respected person. The usage varies from place to place just as a captain in the West is a relatively low rank in the officer cadre of the army, but a much higher one in the navy.

Emir, also spelt Amir, literally means 'commander', and our Western rank 'Admiral' is actually derived from the Arabic 'Amir-al-Bahr' – Sea-Commander. Descendants of the Prophet are also entitled to the rank of Emir. The style 'Commander of the Faithful', familiar to readers of the Arabian Nights, is a translation of 'Emir-al-Mominin'. *Amr* and *Umar*, however, are personal names. The letter 'i' on the end of a name means 'of or from'. Hence 'Emiri, Husseini, Fatemi'.

The very word *rank* in English is traceable to the Persian word *rang*, 'colour', referring to the colours borne on the arms of Saracenic nobility at the time of the Crusades, denoting – rank.

Malik means King, and is the title, for instance of the rulers of

Saudi Arabia. It is derived from the Arabic root-concept of 'owner'. Sultan, too, is a king. Both Maliks and Kings are referred to as 'Jalalatkum' – your Majesty. 'King ibn Saud' is incorrect. In Arabia he was always known as King Abdul-Aziz: just as Queen Elizabeth is not 'Queen Windsor'.

In Saudi Arabia it is becoming customary to refer to any respectable person or official of rank as 'Sheikh', virtually a courtesy title.

The word Saiyid (also spelt Sayed, Saiyid, Seyyed, etc.) is traditionally applied to descendants of the Prophet, and it means 'Prince'. Since, however, members of the Prophetic lineage have other titles at their disposal (Sharif, [Noble]) and can be distinguished by their family names, there is an increasing tendency to allot this style to ordinary people. This is why you will hear radio announcers and others saying: 'Saiyeds and Saiyedas' – Ladies and Gentlemen. In the non-Arab Islamic world, however, Saiyid still means a descendant of Mohammed, since such countries usually have their own style for 'Mr'. 'Shah' at the end of the name in such countries always means a descendant of the Prophet, except in cases where the bearer is not a Moslem: for instance among many Hindus of India. This stems from the habit of naming a sick child 'Shah' in the hope that it will recover from its illness, since people of the Prophetic lineage are widely believed, even among Hindus, to have healing powers.

The Turkish Empire's titles, such as *Bey* [roughly a knight], and *Pasha* [roughly a peer] and *Effendi* [Mr.], are dying out in most places.

The word for 'Chief' is *Ra'is* (also spelt Rayees, Rais, Raiyis, etc.). As in other languages, the status of a person with this appellation depends upon his position or job. *Ra'is* may be the President of the Republic, the Chief of Protocol, or the Chief clerk, just as 'chief' may mean many things in the West. Western newspapers regularly made the mistake of saying that President Nasser was known as 'The Boss' because he was the *Ra'is* [President] of the United Arab Republic. Perhaps they were more familiar with the numerous other kinds of *ra'ises* to be found in the Arab World.

It is a safe bet to call people of distinction *Hadrat*, which means 'Presence'. *Hadratkum* means 'Your Presence'; and people are addressed formally as 'Hadrat al-Amir' [His Presence the Amir] or 'Hadrat al-Sheikh' [His Presence the Sheikh].

It is always advisable to find out, by indirect enquiry, as to the correct name, style and title of anyone with whom you have transactions. Nothing grates on a person's ears in the Middle East more than being addressed by the equivalent of 'Mr. Sir', or 'Esquire Lord'. Such solecisms are very common indeed among foreigners.

One of the commonest is to write to someone, for example, as 'The Sheikh Abdullah... Dear Mr. Abdullah'; or 'The Sayed Ahmad... Dear Mr. Ahmad.' Letters are always addressed to: 'Hadrat al-Amir... Hadratkum [Your Presence]'. If in any doubt, always ask a secretary; but remember to fix it in your memory. You would never write a letter to 'Lord Smith' and then begin 'Dear Mr. Smith'.

The reason why some sovereigns will not take the title of King, Sultan or Malik is a belief that any Islamic state is administered only by a ruler of the rank of Amir, Commander, since Kingship is, strictly speaking, regarded as somewhat incompatible with the Moslem principle that all men are equal and they can therefore be ruled only by commanders. This is why the Caliphs (from Khalifa, Deputy) although more powerful than most contemporary emperors, only called themselves Commander of the Faithful.

To this day, some very religious people will only call even a king by his personal name but you should never imitate them.

There is also a host of other titles which belong to the tradition of the Islamic religion. Imams lead the prayers; Qadhis are judges, Muftis are legal experts, Qaris recite the Koran, Murshids are leaders of mystical brotherhoods, Mullas are religious men. There is, however, no ordained priesthood or order of monks. These are prohibited in Islam. They exist among Christian Arabs, however, who are always pleased to explain them, and constitute a completely separate system.

Arabic names, when given in full, can give you a great deal of information about the bearer. Take this one Sheikh Yusuf Abu-Hafidh ibn-Al-Ghazi al-Aneizi an-Najdi. It means: Sheikh Joseph, Father of he who knows the Koran by heart (Hafidh), son of the Holy Warrior (Ghazi), of the Aneizi tribe, of the country of Nejd (northern Saudi Arabia). After a certain amount of practice, one gets to know these names, and decodes them automatically. The full name, in such a form as this, is used by authors of books or on official documents. The author of the *Life of Saladin*, for example, is given on that book as 'The Learned Imam, Grand Qadhi of the Moslems, Bahauddin Abu-al-Mahasin Yusuf, ibn-Rafi, ibn-

Tamim, known by the name of Ibn-Shaddad, Qadhi of the Fortified City of Aleppo.'

If you have a Western title yourself, whether it is understood or used by Arabs will depend upon whether they are familiar with it. I have seen a knight referred to as 'Al-Faris' – the Cavalier, and 'Count' is translated as 'Qumis'. A Prince will generally be referred to as an 'Amir', but it is never wise to translate one's title from a dictionary. This is because the equivalent of 'Lord' is often given as 'Saiyid', which could confuse you with a Mister in the Sudan and a pretender to descent from the Prophet in some other places. 'Baron' has been translated as 'Baroon' and 'Marquis' as 'Markeez' or 'Amir' – but 'Duke' is also sometimes rendered as 'Amir', though it can be 'Douq'. In some dictionaries, 'Baroness' is translated as 'Baronet'.

The increasing tendency of Western visitors to ask to be addressed as 'Sheikh' is not to be imitated; nor is the tendency of knights and barons to style themselves 'Amir'. If you have a doctorate, you will be respected in Egypt, where there are many doctors of philosophy, letters and so on: but in some other countries, if you use your doctorate, you will be asked to prescribe medicines. 'Professor' has not a high rank in countries which have had French influence, as this is the term for all teachers: the Arabic word *Ustadh* is the equivalent to the English 'Professor'. Similarly, while 'doctor' may be anyone with a doctorate, *Tabib* means a medical man (feminine: *Tabiba*). All titles, virtually, are converted into the feminine by adding *a* to the end: Malika, Sheikha, Sharifa, and so on.

Finally, when you are dealing with Arabs and other Middle Easterners in Europe, you may find that they cease to use their titles, even if they are in the diplomatic corps. This is because they have tired of explaining exactly how their styles are used to people in the West. One consequence of this is that someone who may be listed as 'Mr. Yunus Hashimi' in the Diplomatic List may turn out, when you visit him in his own country, to be 'His Presence the Sharif Yunus of . . .' And I knew a man in a certain Middle Eastern country who was a baronet, with the abbreviation 'Bart.' after his name. He was almost reconciled to being known as 'Mr. Bart the Englishman'.

The Assemblies of Al-Hariri

The Assemblies of Al-Hariri (The *Makamat* in Arabic) was written around 1050 A.D. in Basra. This tale of the picaresque adventures of the wily Abu Zayd has been regarded for eight centuries as the greatest treasure in Arabic literature after the Koran.*

The Eleventh Assembly, called 'Of Saweh'

This and the following Assembly are justly reckoned among the masterpieces of the author. To pass suddenly from the most solemn subjects to pleasantry, to place in the mouth of a clever impostor the most serious warnings that can be addressed to mankind may be morally objectionable; but in the Moslem world, where religion is mixed up with all the concerns of life, and pious discourse and phrases abound, it excites little repugnance. The design of the author in the present composition was to produce an elaborate sermon in rhymed prose and in verse, and his genius takes a higher flight than usual.

The incident on which the Assembly is founded is simple. Harith, in a fit of religious zeal, betakes himself to the public burial ground of the city of Saweh, for the purpose of contemplation. He finds a funeral in progress, and when it is over, an old man, with his face muffled in a cloak, takes his stand on a hillock, and pours forth a discourse on the certainty of death and judgment; rebuking his hearers for their worldly selfishness, and warning them that wealth and power are of little avail against the general leveller. He then rises into poetry and declaims a piece, which is one of the noblest productions of Arabic literature. In lofty morality, in religious

* *The Assemblies of Al-Hariri* retold by Amina Shah (Octagon Press, 1980).

fervour, in beauty of language, in power and grace of metre, this magnificent hymn is unsurpassed.

From this, and other similar compositions of Hariri, a better idea of what is noblest and purest in Islam will be gained, than from the works of the most orthodox doctors. Harith, like the others who are present, is much affected; but he is indignant when he finds that the preacher is receiving abundant alms, and that beyond a doubt he is Abu Zayd. He taxes him with his hypocrisy, and receives an impudent reply. They then separate angrily.

In this Assembly a view of moral duties and future judgment is exhibited which differs little from that of Christians. The enlightened and polished man of letters of the fifth century was not likely to teach the coarse doctrines of a sensual paradise, to be secured by hard fighting, which roused the ignorant warriors of Arabia in the first days of Islam. In all the work of Hariri, there is not a trace of this theology, which the West erroneously attributes to every Moslem. Self-denial and benevolence are with him the duties of every man; and by them each may hope to obtain everlasting happiness, but on the nature of both future rewards and punishments he is discreetly silent.

The Twelfth Assembly, called 'Of Damascus'

Harith, being in affluence, crosses from Iraq to Damascus to enjoy the luxury of that city. After he has had his fill of pleasure he bethinks himself of returning homeward, and joins a caravan that is about to cross the Semaweh, the desert which lies between Syria and the Euphrates. The travellers are ready to depart, but are delayed by their inability to find an escort, which they think indispensable for their protection against robbers.

While they are consulting, they are watched by a dervish, who at last announces to them that he has the means of keeping them safe from harm; and, on their inquiring further, tells them that his safeguard is a magic form of words revealed to him in a dream. They are at first incredulous, but at length consent to take him with them, and to use his incantation. He then repeats it, and it proves to be a prayer full of assonances and rhymes, beseeching the general protection of the Almighty. They all learn it by heart and then set forth, repeating it twice a day on their journey.

As they are not molested on the road, they judge the charm to have been successful; and when they come in sight of 'Anah', the first town on the other side of the desert, they reward him richly with what he likes best, gold and jewels. When he has taken all he can get, he makes his escape, and the next thing they hear of him is that he is drinking in the taverns of 'Anah', a city celebrated for its wine. Harith, shocked at this enormity in a pious dervish, determines to seek him out, and soon finds him revelling amid wine and music in the guest chamber of a wine-shop. He taxes him with his wickedness, and then the old man improvises a Bacchanalian chant, which is one of the finest pieces in Hariri's work. In form, this poem resembles that which is introduced into the last Assembly, though the metre is more light and lively, as Hariri, no doubt, desired to display his genius by the contrast. Harith, charmed with the verses, asks who the old man is; and from his answer discovers that he is Abu Zayd. He makes an ineffectual attempt to reclaim him, and then quits the wine-shop, repentant at having set foot in such a place.

This Assembly is one of the most admired productions of the author, who has lavished on it all the resources of his marvellous rhetoric. It has been imitated with great skill by Ruckert; who, however, wanders very far from the original.

The Fiftieth Assembly, called 'Of Basra'

This last and crowning piece of Hariri's work is remarkable in two directions, which both bring it in close relation to the forty-eighth. In the latter the author extolled in eloquent strains the quarter of Basra, which was inhabited by him; here he out-soars the highest flights of his oratory in a magnificent encomium of his native town itself.

But the present Assembly is still more admirable as a counterpart of that of the Benu Haram with regard to the hero of the romance, who, having given there an account of an incident, which ominously inaugurated his questionable career, is now represented as redeeming, under the touch of divine grace, his life of venturesome expedients, frequently bordering on crime, by sincere repentance and transports of pure and unremitting devotion.

Middle East Facts and Fallacies : II

- The 'Moors' of Andalucia were overwhelmingly Spanish in blood, having been converted to Islam by the Arabs.
- Parnell's story 'The Merit' is taken from the Koran.
- The German poet, Goethe, was much influenced by the Persian, Hafiz.
- The oldest university in the world is Al-Azhar, in Cairo, dating to 970 of the Christian Era. European universities, mostly under Arabian influence, started to come into being in the twelfth century.
- European hospitals are believed to be imitated from the *Bimaristans* (places of the sick) established by the Seljuk Turkish ruler of Damascus and the Mamluks of Cairo, learned about by the Western Crusaders.
- Vaccination was introduced to the West from Turkey.
- The great Franciscan teacher, Roger Bacon, lecturing at the then new University of Oxford in the thirteenth century, wore an Arabian robe and taught from Arab textbooks on illuministic philosophy – mysticism – as well as Ptolemy and Euclid.
- In the Middle Ages, Europeans believed that Mohammed's coffin was suspended between heaven and earth; that the Arabs worshipped an idol called 'Baphomet'; and that they taught that women had no souls. In the twentieth century, an American professor noted that some of his students thought that Islam was a card game, that Mohammed wrote the *Arabian Nights*, and that Islam was an American organisation of Freemasons who wore strange costumes.
- An orange was originally called 'A norang' – Persian for 'free of care'.
- King Hassan of Morocco relates, in his autobiography, how President Roosevelt insisted on broadcasting, in French, to his people. His pronunciation was such that when he thought he was saying how much he liked the Moroccan farms (*fermes*) and towns

(*villes*) the amazed Moroccans found themselves hearing of his love for their wives (*femmes*) and daughters (*filles*).

● The 'Arab' invasion of Spain in 711 (the Muslims were expelled some seven hundred years later) was carried out by 300 Arabs and 7,000 Syrians, Copts and Berbers.

● The waltz is modelled on the movements of the Turkish 'Whirling Dervishes', introduced by them into the Balkans and thence to Vienna.

● The Greek 'Saint Charlambos' of the Christian Church has been discovered to be the Central Asian Dervish teacher, Haji Bektash; while the fifteenth-century Saint Therapion is in reality the Middle Eastern Sufi poet, Turabi.

● The star-and-crescent emblem is not an Islamic one: it was adopted by the Turks when they conquered Byzantium, from the Christians. They, in turn, took it from ancient Near-Eastern pagan religion.

● The first 'Arabian' university in Europe was headed by Abu-Bakr al-Riquti in the thirteenth century. It was sponsored by King Alfonso the Wise (1252 – 1281) and 'gave instruction in all the sciences to Christians, Jews and Muslims'.

● St. Thomas Aquinas (1225 – 1274) is regarded as one of the greatest of all Christian thinkers and divines. Yet parts of his thought are adopted from the Jewish thinkers; Maimonides of Cairo and Bahya ibn Pakuda. His use of doctrines of Islamic origin, too (especially from Ibn Rushd) in his *Summa* ('the very citadel of Western Christianity' says one scholar) has caused revision of the belief in his originality.

● Making a speech to Syrian troops, a French general was amazed to see them break ranks and charge him with fixed bayonets. He had said, in Arabic: 'I have a dog, and, that dog is you . . .', instead of 'I have a heart and that heart is you'. The difference between *qalb* and *kalb* is often difficult for many Western people.

RITUALS AND HUMAN NATURE

Strange Ritual in Tunisia

Surrounded by a number of small dumpy domes, as much of Africa as Arabia, the Zawiya of the Sheikh was sheltered by a row of very respectably sized trees, and there was an artesian well in the court-yard, where visiting dervishes refreshed themselves. Some wore little more than two jute sacks stitched together. Others looked for all the world like Oxford dons, with their hoods and dark sleeved robes, from which Western academic garb is said to be ultimately derived.

Beyond the courtyard a low doorway of Moorish horseshoe shape gave entrance to the Hall of Assembly, which served as school, gymnasium and prayer-hall for the community. Here the Sheikh sat, a small, neat figure in white turban and hooded robe, in the midst of his court. The mystics present sat in a circle with wide gaps in it, each on his small rug, all looking attentively towards their teacher. As we entered the room, he rose in token of great welcome.

Then the story which formed part of that day's teaching was resumed. It was intended to illustrate that, whereas all human beings might want to perform good actions, it was often impossible to foresee whether an action carried out in good faith would produce a good result. What was the way out of this dilemma? Through the *baraka* (spiritual force) of the Order, said the Sheikh, its members acquired a power known as *yakina*, which was an inner certainty that this or that action was for the real and ultimate good of mankind. The story was long, but it pointed the moral well enough.

Then came a pause for an incense-burner to be brought in by a novice, and we all in turn passed our hands over the smoke which poured from it. When mint tea was brought, the Sheikh turned to me, and asked me my mission. I told him that I was studying the teachings of the Sufis, and comparing what I heard, in each centre of

187

instruction, with a view to understanding exactly what this system was.

Sufism, he maintained, was the source of religion. All the religious teachers had been Sufis. 'Sufism is the milk, and religion is the butter, after it has been churned. You cannot taste the milk for the butter. We drink the milk.'

He was well read, in French as well as in Arabic and Persian, and had something to say about the relationship of his system with others. He did not believe that Sufism was an Islamic revolt against the austerity of the Prophet's creed, nor that it owed anything to India, to Buddhism or to neo-platonism.

'The superficial resemblances seized by scholars on the outside to account for our ways are not due to a cause-and-effect relationship,' he told me; 'rather are they due to the fact that the basis of our activity is to be found in all human minds. We alone, however, have systematised it, and can produce its full effect upon the human being. The goal is to make the Perfected Man.'

After a long conversation on these lines, the Sheikh told me that I was to be allowed to be present ('although you are of low rank in the Way') at one of the religious exercises – the *Dhikr* – of the dervishes. This was the first real *Dhikr* which I had attended; for the private exercises of this kind are not open to strangers. I was grateful for the opportunity.

The *Dhikr*, it was explained to me, is a dance or, more properly, a performance of a series of exercises in unison. The objective is to produce a state of ritual ecstasy and to accelerate the contact of the Sufi's mind with the world-mind of which he considers himself to be a part. In view of the recent wide-spread interest in ecstatic states in the West, in which drugs like Mescalin, LSD (lysergic acid) and hallucinogenetic toadstools were used, I felt that I might learn something that would be of abiding interest.

All dervishes, and not only the followers of Maulana Rumi (as most Orientalists erroneously believe) perform a dance. And a dance is defined as bodily movements linked to a thought and a sound or a series of sounds. The movements develop the body, the thought focuses the mind, and the sound fuses the two and orientates them towards a consciousness of divine contact which is called *hal* and means 'state or condition': the state or condition of being in ecstasy.

Armed with this information, I took my place in the double circle

188

which was being formed in the centre of the hall. The dervishes stood while the Sheikh intoned the opening part of this and every similar ceremony: the calling down of the blessing upon the congregation, and from the congregation upon the Masters of the 'past, present and future'. Outside the circles stood the Sheikh, a drummer and a flute player, together with two 'callers', the men who called the rhythm of the dance.

The drum began to beat, and the callers started to sing a high-pitched, flamenco-like tune, eerie and penetrating. Slowly the concentric circles began to revolve, each in the opposite direction, myself included, edging along, concentrating upon the sound.

The circles moved faster and faster, until I (moving in the outer circle) saw only a whirl of robes, and lost count of time. Now and then, with a grunt, or a sharp cry, one of the dervishes would drop out of the circle, and would be led away by an assistant, to lie on the ground in what seemed to be an hypnotic state. I began to be affected, and found that although I was not dizzy, my mind was functioning in a very strange and unfamiliar way. The sensation is difficult to describe, and is probably a complex one. One feeling was that of a lightening: as if I had no anxieties, no problems. Another was that I was a part of this moving circle, and that my individuality was gone, was delightfully merged in something larger.

Eventually, as the movements continued, I had the sensation that I must somehow tear myself away. And, oddly enough, as soon as the thought occurred to me, I found it easy to leave the group. As I stepped from the circle, I was taken by the elbow by the Sheikh, who looked at me closely, smiling.

It was only when I started to talk to him that I realised that it was impossible: the dervishes were producing such a penetrating buzz of sound that it would have been impossible to hear anything else. I looked at my watch. Two hours had passed in what seemed but a few minutes.

I went out into the courtyard, to assess my feelings. Something *had* happened. In the first place, the moon seemed immensely bright, and the little glowing lamps seemed surrounded by a whole spectrum of colours. My mind was working by a system of associations of some kind: because as soon as I thought of a thing, it was almost as if one thought bore another, until my mind lighted upon a logical consequence. An example may make this clearer. The lamps reminded me of a stained-glass window; and the window of an

189

argument I had had with a friend some months before, near a church. This, in turn, focused my attention upon this friend, and then, like a flash, I saw him in my mind shaking hands with a red-bearded man. Then the whole thing faded. This sort of experience remained with me for about a month, during which time I could reproduce it by thinking of the lamps.

When, later, I went to Paris and met this friend, I found that he had gone into partnership with a red-bearded man. This experience closely paralleled, therefore, one experienced a few years ago during a ritual by Mr. Wasson, the American authority on Mexican mushrooms. In his case there was a vision of his son in unfamiliar circumstances, which turned out to be correct.

The ritual continued, and the Sheikh took me into his private room, where we sat on cushions and talked about the meaning of the *Dhikr*.

Without the 'strange experience' we cannot become perfected. Take this analogy: all experience in the world is, in fact, strange. When it becomes habit or commonplace, one does not regard it as experience. But it is essential, is it not, to the learning process?

'I realise that you are not trying to impress me,' I said to Sheikh Arif, 'but I have a largely Western approach to such things as those which we have seen tonight. Would you allow me to test some of your dervishes to establish whether they are in any sort of a hypnotic state familiar to Westerners?'

'Gladly,' he said, 'though that would not invalidate anything, from our point of view; because what you call hypnosis is merely the beginning of something; the visible part of something that remains invisible to you.'

We returned to the meeting-hall, to find that several of the Sufis were still circling around. In order to be sure that I would be in a more objective frame of mind, I decided that I should postpone the test until another day. Most obligingly, the Sheikh told me to come when I liked.

The following morning the Sheikh sent word that he would be pleased to see us as soon as we liked. Hamid was not too sanguine about the success of an examination of dervishes in a state of *hal*, but came along to the assembly-room. Here we found the Sheikh eating a hearty breakfast from a bowl of meat and gravy. Pleading an indisposition, I refused the food, just in case it might have some hallucinogenic ingredient. Dervishes came in and out, shaking hands and saying 'Ishq' (Love) and then kissing their own hands. The Sheikh explained to them what we wanted, and though some did not seem to approve, we were left with eleven who might be termed the volunteers.

After a night's sleep, the Sheikh seemed completely won over to my idea, and rather peremptorily called the musicians and started the dance. I held my watch in my hand, timing the music and waiting for the first to pass into an ecstatic state. The first thing that I noticed was that the proceeding did not seem to affect those who did not take part in the dance. The music and rhythm seemed to be the same as on the previous night.

After six minutes the first dervish – a man of about forty – swayed and was led from the group. As soon as he sat down he seemed to lose consciousness. When prodded, he showed no sign of life, and he was breathing very shallowly. I opened his eyelid, but the eyeball was not turned up. The pupils were not dilated or contracted, neither did they react to light when I lit my cigarette lighter.

Out of the eleven participants, nine were in a state of *hal* after two hours. Unlike normally hypnotised people, they did not respond to words spoken to them; neither did they show the almost complete immobility which is one of the characteristics of the hypnotised person. Although anaesthesia of the nerves is normally produced only by suggestion to that effect, they did not seem to feel pinpricks or tickling applied without any suggestions. This did not seem to be a familiar form of hypnosis. Ordinary hypnosis normally passes into sleep. But these volunteers woke up direct into wakefulness without sleep supervening. What was more, there was no amnesia, and throughout they had been aware of what had been said and done to them; although in at least some cases (had this been normal hypnosis) partial amnesia could have been expected at this depth of hypnosis.

The next part of my test was to attempt to induce normal hypnosis. Only three out of the eleven passed into the lightest form of conventional hypnosis, which was the proportion which would be expected in a random sample of this size. None showed any evidence that they were conditioned: that is to say, that they were accustomed to passing into hypnosis of any kind, let alone a deep-trance state.

All this added up to the strong possibility that the trance into which these people threw themselves was not of a kind familiar to the West. In all cases they reported transcendental experiences during the trance: and two of them even purported to have read my thoughts. They claimed that they knew, when in trance, as to what I was going to try next, as a test.

None of this material, of course, is scientifically conclusive. What could be of paramount importance might be that the drumming and intonations contained a signal to which the subjects had been conditioned. I resolved to make tape-recordings of some future session, and replay them at intervals with similar volunteers, to see whether a later part of the proceedings would produce the trance more quickly when played back. This, however, would have to wait until I was better equipped.

The rest of my stay at the Zawiya was passed in taking notes of the methods of teaching and the theories which the Sufis passed on. In day-by-day instruction, two sessions were held. One was for younger initiates, who were passing through a thousand-and-one-days' novitiate. The other meeting was that to which 'Seekers' – adepts – were admitted. The disciples had to carry out memorising and meditative exercises, developing powers of concentration and reflection. The others, it seemed, were keeping up a sort of training of which thought and work, as well as exercises like the *Dhikr*, all formed a part.

After a few days, the air of mystery and strangeness which I had felt was replaced by a sensation that, however unfamiliar these practices might seem to the outsider, their devotees did not regard them as supernatural as we might use the term. As Sheikh Arif once said: 'We are doing something which is natural, which is the result of research and practice into the future development of mankind; we are producing a *new* man. And we do it for no material gain.' This, then, is their attitude.

From *Among the Dervishes*, by O.M. Burke, London 1973.

Human Nature

A story about the way in which *by bringing out the best in yourself you may bring out the worst in other people* . . .

The Pastry-Cook, The Customers and The Sufis

There was once a pastry-cook of the soukh at Damascus. He went to China to study rare and unusual confections, and became a master of the art, learning many new and highly delicious recipes.

He decided to specialise in coconut candy, which he offered, on his return, in his shop, to the delight of an ever-increasing and greatly appreciative clientele.

He responded to his customers' appreciation by constantly improving the shape, the flavour and the texture of his coconut sweet, and the people grew to expect that he would surpass himself, week after week.

Thus was his performance improved, and with it the appreciation and the expectation of his public until, suddenly and inexplicably, sales began to decline, people avoided him in the street – and not only his candies but all his products, all of the highest quality, found no market at all.

Now the pastry-cook was perplexed at this, because he could discern no reason for his sudden fall in popularity, or in that of his shop. Finally, when he had no customers left, he found himself ruined, and took to the road as a wandering mendicant, begging from town to town, and just keeping body and soul together, from the contributions of the Faithful.

One day he reached a caravanserai where three ancient dervishes sat in contemplation. The night was long and the weather was stormy, and the four men sheltered in the stables until they might be able to go on their way. When the dervishes had brought their awareness back to the lower world, the once-rich shopkeeper

193

saluted them respectfully and told them his tale, asking whether they might, in their wisdom, be able to unravel the mystery of his ruination, and to advise him how he might conduct himself in the future.

When he had finished, the grave-faced sages raised their heads and looked at one another, and then they laughed. The oldest bent upon the sweetmeat-seller a look of kindly compassion, and spoke:

'Know, O Friend of Man, that the appetite of the created being becomes insatiable. First, he knows about nothing, but still wants what he can get. This was the condition of your customers before there were any pastry-cooks at all on earth. Then, like your customers after they were offered the candies, they appreciate a taste of something and grow to expect it, and for it to improve. This, too, happened to you: and you fulfilled expectations. In the third stage, if no barriers of prudence are established, the created ones will allow expectation to run ahead of possibility. In your case, the people began to want even better candies than it was possible to produce. The result of this was the working of a certain strange but inevitable law. The appetite of the imagination actually made the people believe that your candies were getting worse, and that you were failing them. We smiled just now because, when we were in your own town some time ago, people told us how there was a certain deceitful former pastry-cook who had made, first, better and better coconut confections, and then made them worse and worse and worse until the people agreed that they were uneatable, and consequently shunned your shop.'

'We, of course, had realised that it was the people, not the products, which had changed: accustomed to better and better, they fantasised that things were worse and worse. They had compared imagination with actuality. Under these circumstances, actuality always appears worse and worse, because imagination makes things better and better.'

'Unwittingly, you had brought out the worst in people: and by bringing out the best in yourself. It is for this very same reason that the Sufis first make their 'clients', the Seekers, desire *less* so that they shall be able to perceive *more* – and better – when it is vouchsafed to them . . .'

Education and Knowledge

Once upon a time there was a king who had a foolish son. He put him into the charge of a clever teacher who insisted that there would be no difficulty in imparting knowledge and capacity to him. Naturally the king was so pleased that he gave the master many valuable presents.

The master taught the young prince everything he could, and the boy learnt a large number of remarkable abilities, some of them quite unusual.

The teacher brought the young man back to the king, who asked: 'If I were to take up an object and hold it in my hand, not visible, could you tell me what it is?'

'Yes,' said the prince, 'I have learned that art.'

The king took a ring off his finger and put it into his hand, with the fingers closed around it. 'What have I in my hand?' he asked.

'Father,' said the son, 'it is something which came from the mountains.'

The king thought, 'He must mean the gem in the setting.'

Now the boy continued with his psychometry: 'It is clearly round – so it must be a millstone!'

'Take him away,' roared the king, 'and try to teach him common sense as well as perceptions.'

From *The (Turkish) History of the Forty Viziers.*

Unity of the Arabs

Many years ago, when Abdalmalik, son of Marwan was fighting against Mus'ab, son of Al-Zubair, the leaders of the Greeks collected before their king. They said to him:

'By good fortune, the Arabs are fighting amongst themselves. This means that you can now attack and conquer them.'

The Greek king tried to argue them out of this frame of mind, but nothing would move them.

Now the King of the Greeks sent for two dogs, and they set about each other, fighting furiously. 'That is just like the Arabs,' said his nobles.

Then the King sent for a wolf. As soon as the dogs saw it, they left off fighting and both attacked the wolf as one, until they had killed it.

'This, too,' said the King, 'is just the same as the Arabs. They will fight one another: but when we appear, they will combine against us like one man.'

There was no further argument from the Greeks.

Nahfat Al Yaman.

Fools

The Schoolmaster in Love

I once saw a school where a teacher was hard at work, and went in. I found him a good-looking man, and well dressed. He stood up and asked me to sit beside him. I tested him on the Koran, in syntax and prosody and lexicography, and found that he was perfect in all that he should know; and I told him how excellent I found him.

After that, I used to see him often, and found many more good things about him, and I said to myself: 'This is certainly a wonderful teacher; for teachers, according to the wise, have learning but little intelligence.'

Then I saw him much less often; until one day I found the school shut, and asked the neighbours the reason. 'Someone has died,' they said. So I went to his servant and she told me that he was sitting alone, and mourning. I asked permission to join him to offer some consolation.

When he received me, I offered condolences, adding that it was necessary to be patient under such unfortunate circumstances. I asked him who had died. He said, 'One who was the dearest and most beloved.'

'Perhaps it was your father?'

'No.'

'Your brother?'

'No.'

'A relative?'

'No.'

'Then what relation was it?'

'My beloved.'

I said to myself, 'This is the first sign of his lack of sense.'

Then I said to him, 'Surely there will be others than she, and more beautiful?'

And he said, 'I never saw her, so that I couldn't tell.'

I said to myself, 'This is another proof positive.'

Then I said to him: 'And how could you fall in love with someone you had not seen?'

He replied, 'One day I was sitting at the window when a man passed, and he was singing this:

'Umm-'Amr, thy boons Allah repay!
Give back my heart, be it where it may!

And he continued, 'When I heard the man's words as he went by, I said to myself, "If this woman Umm-'Amr had not been without equal, she would not have been hailed like this by poets in poem and song". So I fell in love with her. But, two days afterwards, the same man passed by again. This time he sang;

'Aas and 'Umm-'Amr went their way.
Nor she nor 'Aas returned for aye.

'So I knew that she was dead, and mourned for her. That was three days ago, and I have been mourning ever since.'

So I left him and went away, having verified the absence of common sense in the pedant.

Richard Burton: *The Book of a Thousand Nights and a Night,*
adapted by Feroz Hafidh.

... And the Three Young Men

They tell the tale of the night that the Master of Police of Bassora went abroad to round up all vagrants and rogues and whomsoever he found wandering in an unfit state; and all were to be executed.

This was at the order of the famous El Helaj ben Yousef Al-Thekefi, governor of Irak under the fifth Kalif.

So, the sight of three young men, staggering along as if they had eaten and drunk to excess, enraged the Master of Police, and they were arrested.

'Who are you that transgress the law of the Commander of the Faithful?' they were asked, being brought before the Captain of the Watch.

'I am the son of he whose time does not descend, but returns each moment to its former height. There are many around him, you can see troops by the light of his fire, some sitting and some standing,' said the first youth.

So they refrained from slaying him as they said, 'He must be a kinsman of the Commander of the Faithful,' and they said to the second:

'Who are you who goes about at this hour of the night, disturbing the sleep of the Faithful?'

'I am the son of he to whom all necks are abased,' he answered proudly, 'they all come to my father and he takes their wealth and their blood!'

'He must be the son of a great man,' they said, and refrained from slaying him.

To the third they said then:

'And who might you be?'

The answer was, 'I am the son of he who plunges through the ranks with his might and corrects them with his sword, so that they stand straight and true. His feet are not loosed from the stirrup until the end of the day.'

So they said, 'He is the son of the champion of the Arabs!'

The three young men were led away to sleep off their carousing in the guardhouse, and next morning El Helaj inquired into their case.

Then he discovered that the first was the son of a hot-bean seller, the second was the son of a barber-surgeon, and the third the son of a weaver. The troops sitting round the fire were customers waiting for the hot beans; the barber, of course, was 'he to whom all necks were abased'. The stirrups are the loops of thread in which the weaver's foot rests; the correction by the sword meant the wooden shuttle used by carpetmakers. The ruler marvelled at their readiness of speech, and said to the courtiers around him:

'Teach your sons ready speech, and other ways of saying things, otherwise they may lose their heads!

'For, by Allah, but for their deportment, I would have smitten off their heads!'

From the Breslau Text of the *Alif Leyla Wa Leyla*, translated into English by John Payne.

The Qadi who was an Ass

There was once a poor and simple fisherman who was passing a schoolhouse when he heard the teacher addressing his pupils:

'You are still asses, though I have worked so hard to make you rational humans. You must try harder; and eventually you will be transformed into real people ...'

So, thought the fisherman, this is what happens in schools. Then he remembered that he had a young donkey and, having no child, he might as well send it to school to be transformed by the method which the teacher obviously knew.

He accordingly went the following day with the ass and a sum of money, and, explaining himself, asked the teacher to accept a new pupil.

Now this schoolmaster was something of a rogue, and – having thought of a plan – took the donkey and the money, telling the fisherman to come back in three years.

As is natural, this simpleton became more and more impatient as the time to receive his educated and humanised ass approached, and he called several times at the school: only to be told that he must be patient. Finally the teacher, continuing his deep-laid plan, told the man to present himself at the school at a certain time on a certain day, and not to be a minute earlier or later, or the spell might not work properly.

He was a day late, for fishermen are not famous for punctuality.

'Alas,' said the master, 'you have just missed your new son. But never fear, he has set off for the great city, to take up his new appointment as Qadi – judge – there.'

At first the fisherman was annoyed at losing the services of a useful boat-hand; but then he realised that a Qadi for a son might be even more useful. So he and his wife set off for the city to meet their lad.

When they arrived at the court, the fisherman went in and saw the fine and distinguished figure of the judge presiding over the proceedings. Walking up to him with a handful of hay and the ass's old bridle, he called him loudly:

'Hey, ass! My little donkey, what a great man you have become, son!'

The judge endured this for the whole of the day, supposing that the fisherman was an unfortunate lunatic and no more. After the court closed he went up to the fisherman and asked him kindly, what he could do for him.

'So, you don't recognise me? Have you forgotten that you were my ass, transformed into a man and educated by the mullah of our village, at enormous expense?'

When the judge realised what had happened he ordered an investigation, and the mullah was heavily fined.

It is said that this story should be kept in mind by people who believe that learning is always accompanied by honesty; and those who have not realised that they may get money easily from someone more foolish than themselves, but that future developments can unmask them ...

Middle Eastern tale retold by Jabir Siddiqi.

Who He Really Was

There was once a Governor of Iraq, who went out with his companions, and then felt that he would like to be by himself for a time.

He sent everyone away, and sat thinking. Before long an old man of the 'Ijl tribe came along, and the Governor asked him where he came from.

'From that nearby village,' said the ancient.

'And what of your rulers?'

'God remove them from all good, and also those who appointed them!'

'Do you know who I am?'

'No.'

'I am the Governor!'

The old man said: 'And do you know who *I* am?'

'No,' said the Governor.

'I am the well-known lunatic of the 'Ijl, and do not know what I am saying twice a day!'

The Governor laughed, and gave him a present.

Nahfat Al Yaman.

Charms and Pearls

The Origin of the Evil Eye Averter

Throughout the ages man has used charms and magic to avert the influence of the malevolent 'evil eye' which exists in some form in every culture, from Lilith, the night hag of the Hebrews, to the oldest mentions of the Evil Eye which are found in Sumerian, Babylonian and Assyrian texts dating from the third millenium B.C. The Arabs have believed in its influence in all periods of their history and one of their commonest names for it is the 'eye of envy', *ain al-hasad*. It seems to be a consistently held view amongst all the early races of mankind that envy, jealousy and the Evil Eye were one and the same thing. Mohammed the Prophet was a firm believer in the Evil Eye, and Asma bint Umais states that when she asked him if she might use spells on behalf of the family of Ja'far he replied, 'Yes, for if there were anything in the world which would overcome fate it would be an evil eye' (*Hughes, Dict. of Islam*, p.112).

Bacon, in his Ninth essay, states that, 'of envy there be none of the affections which have been noted to fascinate or bewitch, but love and envy; they both have vehement wishes, they frame themselves readily into imaginations and suggestions, and they come early into the eye, especially upon the presence of the objects which are the points that conduce to fascination if any such there be. We see likewise the Scripture calleth envy an evil eye. Of all other affections, it is the most important and continual ... for it is ever working upon some or other. It is also the vilest affection and the most depraved; for which cause it is the proper attribute of the Devil, who is called "The envious man that soweth tares among the wheat by night."' (Matt. xiii, 25).

The amulet most familiar to us in the West as an evil eye averter is the small blue glass bead we bring back from Mediterranean holidays by the sackful. These beads are attached to the harness of every camel before setting out on a journey and usually every man of the caravan carries an amulet either in his clothes, turban or attached to his body. The interesting origin of this particular amulet is Persian. During pilgrimages to Mecca when immense amounts of sheep were slaughtered the pilgrims would imbed turquoises into the eyes of their sacrificial victims. Since the name of the turquoise in Persian means 'Victorious' or 'Courage which leads to fulfilment and success' perhaps the idea was that the negative and debilitating influence of the 'eye' was overcome and vanquished by the positive quality of the stone.

Aminu'sh and the Jinns

In this connection, it may not be out of place to give the experiences of another experimenter in the occult sciences, who, although at the time sufficiently alarmed by the results he obtained, subsequently became convinced that they were merely due to an excited imagination. My informant in this case was a philosopher of Isfahan, entitled Aminu'sh-Shari'at, who came to Teheran in the company of his friend and patron, the Bananu'l-Mulk, one of the chief ministers of the Zillu's-Sultan. I saw him on several occasions, and had long discussions with him on religion and philosophy. He spoke somewhat bitterly of the vanity of all systems. 'I have tried most of them,' he said. 'I have been in turn Musulman, Sufi, Sheykhi, and even Babi.'

'At one time of my life I devoted myself to the occult sciences, and made an attempt to obtain control over the Jinnis (*Tashkir-i-jinn*), with what results I will tell you. You must know, in the first place, that the *modus operandi* is as follows: The Seeker after this power chooses some solitary and dismal spot, such as the Hazar-Dere at Isfahan (the place selected by me). There he must remain for forty days, which period of retirement we call *chille*. He spends the greater part of this time in incantations in the Arabic language, which he recites within the area of the *mandal*, a geometrical figure, which he must describe in a certain way on the ground. Besides this, he must eat very little food, and diminish the amount daily. If he has faithfully observed all these details, on the twenty-first day a lion will appear, and will enter the magic circle. The operator must not allow himself to be terrified by this apparition, and, above all, must on no account quit the *mandal*, else he will lose the results of all his pains. If he resists the lion, other terrible forms will come to him on subsequent days – tigers, dragons, and the like – which he must similarly withstand. If he holds his ground till the fortieth day, he has attained his object, and the *jinnis*, having been unable to get the mastery over him, will have to become his servants and obey all his behests.

'Well, I faithfully observed all the necessary conditions, and on the twenty-first day, sure enough, a lion appeared and entered the circle. I was horribly frightened, but all the same stood my ground, although I came near to fainting with terror. Next day a tiger came, and still I succeeded in resisting the impulse which urged me to flee. But when, on the following day, a most hideous and frightful dragon appeared, I could no longer control my terror, and rushed from the circle, renouncing all further attempts at obtaining the mastery over the *jinnis*.

'When some time had elapsed after this, and I had pursued my studies in philosophy further, I came to the conclusion that I had been the victim of hallucinations excited by expectation, solitude, hunger, and long vigils; and, with a view to testing the truth of this hypothesis, I again repeated the same process which I had before practised, this time in a spirit of philosophical incredulity. My expectations were justified; I saw absolutely nothing. And there is another fact which proves to my mind that the phantoms I saw on the first occasion had no existence outside my own brain. I had never seen a real lion then, and my ideas about the appearance of that animal were entirely derived from the pictures which may be seen over the doors of baths in this country. Now the lion which I saw in the magic circle was exactly like the latter in form and colouring, and therefore, as I need hardly say, differed considerably in aspect from a real lion.'

From *A Year amongst the Persians*, by E.G. Browne, (1893).

The Pearl in Arab Literature

The Arab proverb states that, 'The rain of the month of Nisan brings forth pearls in the sea and wheat on the land'. This proverb underlines the belief that the growth of pearls in the pearl oyster is due to rain drops falling into the shell, which rises to the surface of the sea and opens to receive the rain drop. The month of Nisan, the beginning of spring, was the period when pearl fishing began in the Orient.

The Persian poet, Saadi, uses this analogy in the following poem:

> A drop which fell from a rain cloud
> Was disturbed by the extent of the sea:
> Who am I in the ocean's vastness?
> If IT is, then indeed I am *not*!
> While it saw itself with the eye of contempt,
> A shell nurtured it in its bosom.
> The heavens so fostered things
> That it became a celebrated, a royal Pearl,
> Becoming high from being low
> It knocked on the door of nothingness
> Until being came about.

Interestingly, the form *farada* of the Arabic farid (meaning pearl) translates as 'to become single, sole, one and no more'.

Two Arab travellers, Hasan ibn Vazid and Sulaiman, who visited India in the 9th century relate the following amusing story of the discovery of a pearl under very singular conditions.

'An Arab came to Bassora with a very fine pearl. He took it to a druggist whom he knew and asked the latter how much it was worth. The merchant estimated it at a hundred pieces of silver, to the great surprise of the Arab, who demanded whether anyone could be found willing to pay so much. Without hesitation the merchant declared that he was ready to give the price himself, and immediately paid over the money. He then took his purchase to Baghdad, where he secured a large profit on his investment. On concluding his sale the Arab told the Bassora druggist how he had secured his pearl. One day, while walking along the Bahrein coast, he saw on the sands a dead fox, whose mouth was tightly compressed by a strange object. On closer observation this proved to be an enormous pearl-oyster shell. Evidently the fox had thrust his snout into the shell while the valves were open so that he might devour the soft contents, but the valves suddenly closed upon him and he had died of suffocation. On prising open the shell, the Arab found therein the pearl which was destined to bring him what he regarded as a fabulous sum.'

Another tale current in Venice in the sixteenth century tells of a Jew, who after long and perilous wanderings in the East, succeeded in bringing with him to Venice a great number of fine pearls. These he disposed of there at satisfactory prices, with the exception of one pearl of immense size and extraordinary beauty, upon which he set a price so high that no-one was willing to pay it. Finally the Jew invited all the leading gem-dealers to meet him on the Rialto, and when as many of them as answered his call had assembled, he once more, and for the last time, offered his peerless pearl for sale, detailing all its perfections in eloquent terms. However, he made no concession about the price, and the dealers unanimously refused to purchase it, probably expecting that the Jew would at last be forced to make a reduction, but to their amazement instead of doing this, he threw his pearl before their very eyes into the water of the canal, preferring rather to lose it than to cheapen it.

From *The Magic of Jewels and Charms*, George F. Kunz, (J. Lippincott Co.) 1915.

On the Procession of the Caravan to Mecca

> This description of a caravan on its way from Cairo to Mecca was recorded by Richard Pococke in 1743 during his travels in the East.

The procession was in this manner:

1. One iron cannon and six brass cannon on neat carriages, each of them drawn by two horses.
2. Four frames in embroidered cases, I suppose of leather, for holding powder and ball, drawn by men on foot.
3. Seven camels with the provision of the Emir Hadge, or Prince of Pilgrims.
4. Four camels with persons on them that played on some musical instrument.
5. A caravan or litter, carried by four mules.
6. Eight light litters of the Emir Hadge each carried by two camels.
7. Seventy camels loaded with biscuit.
8. Fourteen with oil and butter.
9. Fifty with corn, and one with two long boxes of large wax candles for the service of the house of Mecca.
10. Ten with sugar, coffee and the like.
11. Four with kitchen utensils.
12. Nine with plates.

13. Eight with kitchen tent, and tables for the cooks.
14. Eighty-six camels of the Emir Hadge not loaded.
15. Twelve others in the same manner, very finely caparisoned.
16. Sixty camels of the Emir Hadge not loaded.
17. Fifty-four camels loaded with water.
18. Ten loaded with tents.
19. Eight camels loaded with water.
20. Twelve with a sort of boxes on each side to carry the sick; two of the boxes being covered, in which if I mistake not, were medicines for the sick, and on one were two boards, with holes in them, for washing the dead on. All these are said to have been from some private benefactor.
21. Two camels on which were the persons that take care of the sick.
22. Men on camels, beating kettle drums, as almost at the end of every string of camels.

Nearly half an hour after these, the rest proceeded in the following order:

23. Six camels loaded with iron frames in which they make fires.
24. A litter.
25. Four loaded camels.
26. One camel with kettle drums on it and two men each beating a drum.
27. Twenty camels without loads.
28. Two cases for ball and powder.
29. Six camels loaded with tents and other things.
30. Five cases for ball and powder.
31. Ten camels loaded with water.
32. One camel with kettle drums.
33. Two cases with ball and powder.
34. A litter.
35. Two camels loaded.
36. One with music.
37. Thirty-one camels not loaded.
38. Ten overseers of camels to carry water given by some Califs and Sultans of Egypt and others.
39. Three camels without music.
40. Twenty camels with loads.
41. Two camels with water.
42. Sixteen overseers of the water on horses.

43. Three men on camels.
44. Twenty unloaded camels.
45. Four cases for ball and powder.
46. Two camels loaded with water.
47. The Imam, or Head Sheikh, on a camel, who is chaplain of the caravan and offers up the prayers at the place of Abraham's sacrifice. His outward garment of ceremony was white; he carried a green flag and blessed the people with his right hand, by holding it out, and moving it gently as they do when they salute, but not bringing it to his breast.
48. Eleven camels not loaded.
49. Three with pilgrims on them.
50. Two camels with music.
51. Twenty-two without loads.
52. Two camels with Sheikhs on them who lead the way on the road.
53. Twenty camels loaded with water, one with drums.
54. Ten without loads.
55. Five loaded with water.
56. The banner of the body of Saphis, called Cherkes.
57. Thirty of their body.
58. Twenty Ikiars of that body, each having a pike carried before him.
59. The Sardar of the Cherkes, and his lieutenant.
60. Three or four led horses.
61. Two Seraches, who are servants under him.
62. Twelve slaves on horses.
63. Sixty of the body called Tuphekjees.
64. Thirty Ikiars, or elders of them.
65. Four slaves on horseback in coats of mail made of wire.
66. One and twenty slaves.
67. Twenty men on camels, most of them slaves of the Sardar.
68. Two led camels for the Sardar.
69. Two camels without loads.
70. Two camels with kettle drums.
71. Seven with baggage.
72. Fifty of the body of Gjurnelves.
73. Their Sardar.
74. Twenty soldiers and ten slaves with bows and arrows.
75. Thirteen camels with men on them.

76. Two camels with kettle drums.
77. Four loaded camels.
78. Two officers, called Oda Bafhas.
79. Two led horses.
80. Two Sabederiks in Caftans.
81. Seven camels saddled.
82. Two led horses.
83. Two Oda Bafhas.
84. One camel.
85. Thirty-four Charfes, or messengers of the divan.
86. Other officers.
87. Then came the officers of the Emir Hadge, particularly these that follow:
88. A Chous, or messenger in black.
89. Three standards.
90. Five saddle camels.
91. Eight led horses.
92. Two Seraches.
93. Two janizaries.
94. Two Caias of the Emir Hadge.
95. The Hasnadar or treasurer of the Emir Hadge.
96. Twenty-six saddle camels.
97. Five horses.
98. One saddle camel.
99. Twenty-eight men on camels; two of them playing on musical instruments.
100. Five loaded camels.
101. Next came the body of the Azabs.
102. Their two Sabederiks.
103. Odabashas.
104. The standard of the Azabs.
105. Three in Caftans who walked.
106. Three Azabs in dress of ceremony.
107. The Sardar and his lieutenant.
108. Saddle camels.
109. Man on loaded camels.
110. Music.
111. A body of Azabs.
112. Then followed the janizaries.
113. Two Sabederiks of that body.

114. Two janizaries.
115. Two Seraches.
116. A standard.
117. Three men walking in Caftans.
118. Three janizaries.
119. The Sardar of the janizaries and
120. His lieutenant.
121. Two janizaries.
122. Two saddle camels.
123. Thirty-four men on camels.
124. Eight loaded camels.
125. A body of janizaries.
126. One standard bearer.
127. Another dressed in a leopard skin.
128. One and twenty Chouses.
129. The Agas of seven military bodies with silver chains hanging from their bridles to their breast plates.
130. Twelve beys.
131. Before each of them two Shatirs with black velvet turbans.
132. The Trucheman Aga.
133. The Muteferrica Bashee.
134. The Muteferrica guards.
135. The Chousler Caia.
136. The guard of Chaoufes.
137. Then followed the immediate attendants of the Emir Hadge.
138. Eighteen janizaries in their dress of ceremony.
139. Four officers of the Pasha.
140. Four janizaries.
141. A standard.
142. Two standards.
143. Four Arab Sheikhs.
144. Two mad Sheikhs, bare headed in white shirts.
145. The Emir Hadge in a rich Caftan and on a beautiful horse, adorned with the richest trappings.
146. About forty soldiers.
147. Two janizaries.
148. The Caia of the divan.
149. Sixty slaves with bows and arrows.
150. Two Imams.
151. Four led horses.

152. A band of mules.
153. Four led camels.
154. Twenty six camels, loaded.
155. Two men on camels.
156. Then came the Sheikhs of the mosques and the several companies of tradesmen with their standards as in the procession of the hangings from the castle to the mosque; some of them dancing in the same manner. The fisherman carrying fish like serpents, probably eels, tied to the ends of long fishing rods.
157. Four Chouses of the divan.
158. Sixteen janizaries in their high dress.
159. The Sheikh called Caffani.
160. The great standard, carried by the proper office on a camel.
161. Five camels; three of them having tappings of very fine embroidery.
162. The covering, as in the other procession.

Richard Pococke goes on to describe the procession in more detail:-

All camels in this procession were painted yellow and had some ornaments on them, especially the first of every company had on its head and nose a fine plume of red ostrich feathers and a small flag on each side, the staff of which is crowned likewise with ostrich feathers and the trappings adorned with shells; the second and third had a bell on each side about a foot long and all of them some ornaments. Under the saddle of each of them was a coarse carpet to cover them by night. As soon as they are out of town, they go without any order to Sibil-allam, three or four miles off, where they encamp for three days; afterwards they encamp at the lake, the Emir Hadge not returning to town. The encampment at the lake is very fine, all the great men pitching their tents and staying there and passing the time in feasting, the whole city pouring out to see this extraordinary sight and to join in keeping the festival: in the evenings they have bonfires and fireworks. It is said forty thousand people go in this caravan. They begin their journey in a week after the procession.

There is a story among the people, that those of Barbary are obliged to be a day behind the others when they arrive at Mecca, and to leave it a day before them, on account of a prophecy they talk of, that those people shall one time or other take the country of Mecca. A great trade is carried on by the caravan as they always return laden with the rich goods of Persia and India, brought to

211

Geda on the Red Sea near Mecca. Another caravan sets out from Damascus and, if I mistake not, carries the same presents and the old hangings which I think belong to the Emir Hadge, are cut in pieces and given about among the great people, as the most sacred relick. It is looked upon almost as an indispensible duty to go once to Mecca and those that cannot go, it is said, think they gain merit by bearing the charges of another person to go in their places.

From *A Description of the East and Some Other Countries*,
by Richard Pococke, 1743.

More East/West Encounters: Idries Shah

What is a Basin?

I once went on a journey in India with a talented medical man. We stopped at one village, remote from most towns, where the people were unusually poor and ignorant. One man had a broken arm which had been wrongly set, and it was giving him a good deal of pain.

I said, 'My friend is a doctor, he will help you ...'

'I don't care who or what he is,' said the man, 'just do something about my arm.'

At another place, we handed out simple remedies to crowds of villagers who clamoured for medicine.

I said to one of them, 'How can you trust us to be useful? You do not know us.'

The man replied, 'Trust and mistrust, knowing and not knowing, only exist where there are doubt and fear. We are too poor to afford either. If we doubt, we lose the chance that these medicines may help us. People who fear are those who fear loss. Once that you see that you have nothing, how can you fear its loss?'

After much more travelling, we arrived in a more sophisticated, medium-sized town, and went to a poor resthouse to stay. A woman was lying on the earth of the yard, with people standing around her and a wound in her arm, crying.

My doctor friend knelt beside her and said to the people, 'Get me a quantity of cloth and some water in a shallow container ... whatever you call it ...'

The woman stopped sobbing and shouted: 'Get him out of here! He has no idea what to do! How can I have confidence in a man who cannot even remember the word *chilamche* (basin)? He is more ignorant than anyone else here!'

You do not need much knowledge – only a certain attitude – to be an 'intellectual'.

We were driven out of that town almost at once.

Encounter with an Afghan Frontiersman

'Where have you been living?'

'In England.'

'Is it as noisy there as they say?'

'It can be rather noisy, yes.'

'But houses are well away from the roads?'

'Unfortunately many of them line the roads, but one soon gets used to the noise.'

'How soon?'

'A few weeks.'

'But you do not live in a road?'

'No. How did you know?'

'It would be a discourtesy to your guests to subject them to noise, wouldn't it?'

Kent

We were living in Kent, not far from a village where the taxi-driver was a Pakistani; my children went to school with some Vietnamese infants, where several Iranians and their families could be heard speaking their Farsi language in the streets, and one or two Jamaicans and a Trinidadian could be seen, from time to time, going their various ways.

Our frequent overseas visitors were convinced that this was a typically English place, and such is the nature of the British at home that I am sure that everyone around here really feels that this is as English as you can get. Many of them have Dutch names, having immigrated from the Continent; and my driving instructor had German parents; our nursemaid, though from a Kentish village, was of Jewish extraction, and the headmaster of the locally most important school was an Armenian.

London, I had always imagined when I lived there, was the really cosmopolitan part of the Kingdom, but really East Kent, to me, was far more exotic. This was underlined for me one day when a very distinguished lady, a world-famous writer, 'came down' all the way from London, to do a story on me for some magazine. From the moment she entered the house she seemed ill at ease. 'You don't sit on the floor?' she said, as I ushered her to a chair. 'Do you eat, er, foreign food?' I told her that I sometimes did – there are Chinese, Austrian and Indian restaurants nearby. But when she met my wife, she could not hide her disappointment: 'Why are you not in seclusion?' she asked. She never did do that article for her magazine.

Kings, Crooks and Caliphs

Richard the Lionheart and Saladin

The King of England was powerful, brave and full of resolution. As regards his kingdom and rank he was inferior to the King of France, but outstripped him in wealth, in valour and fame as a soldier. He conquered Cyprus and arrived at the Crusaders' camp on 8th June, 1191, with twenty-five ships.

An ambassador was sent by the King to the Sultan, asking for an interview, and this was agreed. But a message came later that Richard was ill; and the report was that the Frankish princes had prevented him. But he wrote denying these rumours and stating that he was master of his own actions.

After much fighting, increased by the arrival of the King, he met El Malik El Adil (Saladin's brother) and suggested peace, with the Saracens withdrawing from the territory. El Adil refused, and negotiations were suspended.

After more fighting, the English King again sent embassies to El Adil, referring to him as 'my brother', asking for the True Cross, the land to the other bank of the Jordan, and Jerusalem. Saladin sent back his message of refusal.

Next El Adil informed a council of Richard's proposal to marry his sister to El Adil. She was to live in Jerusalem, and her brother would give to her the coastal cities under his occupation (Acre, Jaffa, Ascalon). El Adil would be proclaimed King of the coast by Saladin, the Cross was to be given to the Franks, all prisoners would be released, and the English King would go home.

Sultan Saladin gave his consent. But Richard sent a message that the princess now refused to marry a Muslim: but if El Malik El Adil would become a Christian, the marriage could take place.

After further negotiations and fighting, Richard proposed that he should seek the Pope's permission for the marriage; and that, if this

216

Rituals and Human Nature

was not forthcoming, he would betroth his niece to El Adil, which did not need leave from the Pope.

Nothing further is recorded on this subject, and the war and negotiations continued for a division of the Holy Land. Peace was ultimately concluded, the Franks gaining permission to perform pilgrimages to the Christian shrines.

Saladin remained in Jerusalem until the King of England had embarked for his own country, which he did on 1 Shawal (10th October, 1192. On 27 Safar 589 (4th March, 1193) Sultan Saladin Ayyubi died.

From *The Life of Saladin*, by Imam Grand Qadi of the Muslims Bahauddin Abu El Mahasan Yusuf, known as Ibn Sheddad, of Aleppo. With the Permission of the Commander of the Faithful. (English translation: London 1897).

The King and the Alchemist

There was once a man who decided that he would become rich by posing as an alchemist, capable of turning base metals into gold, by playing on the credulity and greed of a certain notorious king. He laid his plans well.

He first obtained a quantity of gold filings and melted them down with a very much larger quantity of lead. Out of this alloy, he made a large number of lumps of metal, all in about the same size, shape and appearance, which looked unlike anything else. Then he took the lumps and travelled to the country of an avaricious king. When he got to the capital city, he toured all the shops in various heavy disguises, and sold the lumps of alloy for next to nothing to their owners.

The shopmen asked him what these strange items were. 'These are things used in the making of gold, though they are worth little by themselves,' he said, 'from time to time people may ask for them. They are called *Tabarrat*.' Now this word in Arabic means 'ruin-ation', but he pronounced it to sound somewhat like *Tibrat*, signifying 'gold particles'.

Now the swindler set himself up in a fine house and dressed gorgeously, spreading the story that he was a successful alchemist. Before long the king came to hear of him.

The king, of course, sent for him and asked if he could make gold. 'Indeed I can; though, of course, I need the necessary materials.'

The king supposed that these would be very expensive.

'I do not know how much the stuff costs in your country,' said the alchemist, 'but it is cheap in mine, for it is the secret which is rare. If you care to send some of your minions to the market, they could enquire how much lumps of Tabarrat cost in these parts.'

Within a very short time the lumps of alloy had been procured, and the alchemist mixed them with various other substances, and then separated the gold which they contained from the base metal by adding acid. The king was delighted, and asked how much the alchemist wanted for his secret. 'You can have it free of charge,' said the alchemist, 'for what do I want with money when I can make gold?'

So the alchemist went back to his house, and the king continued to 'make gold' from the Tabarrat. He was far too covetous to notice that the alchemist, in his own private joke, now openly referred to the stuff as *Tabarrat*, 'ruination'.

Before very long, as the alchemist knew would happen, the shops all ran out of the essential ingredient. 'Various wanderers brought it in at different times – we get a lot of things like that,' said the shopkeepers, unable to supply more.

But the king had only made a limited quantity of gold, and he sent for the alchemist again.

'I need fresh supplies of Tabarrat. Where can I get it?' shouted the king.

'Well,' said the alchemist, 'for all I know you can buy it every-where. But there is plenty of it where I come from, and I suppose I could go and get some for you, if you really are keen.'

The king, overcome with greed, offered to pay all the alchemist's expenses, if he would only go and buy the precious material and bring great quantities back to him.

The alchemist agreed, working out the expenses at a few thou-sand gold pieces, which he got from the treasury and decamped.

The king was furious when he was told that some idle wags were circulating a paper with a list of all the greatest fools in the country on it. His name led them all. He called the chief joker, a privileged member of the Court, and said: 'Supposing the alchemist returns with the Tabarrat, after all? Will you then take my name off the list? He may come back you know!'

The languid and insolent courtier replied:

'I shall not only take off your name, Sire: I shall put in its place the name of the alchemist!'

Nobility

King Bahram was known for his nobility of mind.

One day he was out hunting when he became separated from his companions.

Seeing a herdsman under a tree, he stopped to answer a call of nature, and handed the man the bridle of his horse.

The man took the bridle, which was richly decorated with gold, and cut a piece off, which he hid beneath his cloak.

Bahram saw this, and felt ashamed for the man, that anyone could do such a thing.

He said nothing, but thanked the herdsman and mounted his horse again.

When he returned to the royal stables, he said to the Master of the Horse:

'You will note that the end of my bridle is missing. I have presented it to someone, so make sure that nobody is blamed for its loss.'

Nahfat Al Yaman.

The Great King Anushirwan

The great King Anushirwan, known throughout the East for his justice, was also remarkable for his generosity, a quality which many Arabs prize almost above any other.

One day this king was celebrating the Persian New Year, and a splendid banquet had been laid, with gold and silver vessels on the table.

One of the nobles at the feast took a valuable golden cup and hid it in his robe. Now the cup-bearer, counting the items under his care, called out that it was to be returned, and that none should leave the hall until it had been found.

The King said:

'There is one who has taken it and will not return it; and there is One who has seen him take it and will not tell anyone. Therefore let nobody be searched.'

The man who had stolen the cup took it home and had a sword-decoration and a belt made from it. When it was time for him to appear in public before Anushirwan again, the King called him and said:

'Does this come from that?'

219

'Yes,' said the courtier, kissing the ground, 'may Almighty God bless thee.'

Nahfat al Yaman.

Music and Other Diversions

Influence of Music and Song in Moslem History

The Medieval Rulers of Muslim Spain had at their Courts many singers and music-makers whose names have been preserved with their instruments, such as the reed-pipe and the tambourine, and the rhythmic wavering note of music which began life in Spain from the call of the Muezzin to prayer. Many instruments have found their way to Europe by way of Spanish Muslims: the lute, the guitar, and an ancient musical instrument known to Elizabethan England as the *ribible*, which was one of Chaucer's favourites. This is somewhat like a violin, and the word in use for it in Portugal today is the same, deriving from the Arabic *rabab*.

The tambourine comes from the word *tambour*; and the Persian *song*, meaning 'jangling' or 'tinkling' still applies to the small metal circles let into the sides of the frame to clash together when the taut parchment is struck in time to other music, or as an accompaniment to dancing.

The famous Persian scholar, Ibn Sina of Hamadan, whose medical works have been most useful to the science of healing, has also left us a remarkable treatise on music; and much ground on this subject has also been covered by two other Muslims, Al Farabi, and Al Kindi.

As early as the 8th century, what later became known as 'measured' music (supposedly invented by a Frenchman), was already in existence, and mentioned by Al Khalil. Northern musicians later wrote in glowing terms of Oriental music and by means of this theory, music could be written down, instead of having to be remembered and taught by ear alone.

In Iranian Courts, in order to keep recited sagas at a certain level of entertainment, music had to accompany most of the ancient Persian storytellers or reciters, when the pipe, small drum and cymbals were used to emphasise points of the story, or the rising tension of a culminating tempo, stimulating the leaders doubly; by the pounding of war drums or high, shrill piping, as a lull came in the proceedings; and by the teller stopping with histrionic and dramatic suddenness to let the musicians take charge for a few moments.

The lay of the Arabic minstrel and the wandering French troubadour had the same idea in common – they both entertained the King and ignorant peasant alike. They themselves must have been men of exceptional ability to captivate such different audiences. Sometimes they worked in unison with musicians, sometimes they had only their own voices upon which to rely, but their work has come down to us through the ages by virtue of the simplicity and power of some magic mystery the King or peasant wished to learn, yet somehow failed to grasp without the singing poet's aid.

Duff was the word which meant any sort of tambourine, but in reality it stood for the species of this instrument which was square-shaped.

The organ of the present day derives from the hydraulically-driven original in Arabia, and the Italian organ-grinder with his barrel organ can trace his machine's ancestry back to the *dutab*.

Inventions and improvements were greatly accelerated by the Muslims in Spain, and manuscripts have been discovered to prove that Al Hakim, who died in the year 976, improved the reed-blown *Buq*; the range of the lute was added to by Ziryab, and Al Zunam (in the 9th Century) designed an extraordinary woodwind instrument known as the *Nay Zunami*.

Many old time troubadours are supposed to have been inspired by Jinns or spirits. There is a wonderful book, poetically entitled *Meadows of Gold* (written about the year 949) in which the author, Al Masudi, dwells on the earliest practice of music in Arabia. Al Isphani, the Persian who dedicated his whole life to music, has left us his monumental work *The Great Book of Songs* (comprising twenty-one volumes). The value of such outpourings can only be appreciated by music lovers as dedicated as was this master. Both India and Turkey borrowed largely from the Arab treatises and traces of the Islamic legacy are to be found to this day in Spain and France.

Under the influence of Persian singers, the lyrics of old Arabia become welded into a strange wilfulness of style: and have remained so ever since. The love-poem took the place of the martial saga, and the language of ancient legends became more and more romantically inclined, emphasising the stories of hapless lovers and wandering genii-brides rather than the Rustum or Alexander-like historical dramas of earlier times.

The origin of the word *music* itself is interesting – it comes from the word *musiqi*, adapted from Greek, and later made into *musiqa*, applied to the whole of music. This leaves the Arabic word, *ghina*, which usually does double duty for both music and song, entirely out of it, except in usage signifying the practical art.

Saladin was a great patron of the Arts and he caused poets and musicians to blend airs and sagas together to inspire his men in battle. In peacetime, he instituted rallies of visiting troubadours and dancers, giving valuable prizes to the winners. He caused an unknown poet's mouth to be filled with gold and jewels, so pleased was he with the young man's immediate response to a line of his own construction, which needed another two to convey the meaning of a subtle paradox well known at Court.

Thus the finger of Islamic culture traces a note of music through the dust of centuries, and it is well worth the modern musician's while to listen carefully to the monumental works of the last hundred years, thereby to recognise in them the golden strains of the age-old rhythm of Muslim Music.

The Work of Al-Hakim (The Al-Buq)

There is a Spanish proverb, 'The Work of Al-Hakim', when something really constitutes a worthwhile act, referring to the Moorish king in Andalucia more than a thousand years ago. Now, the 'Moors' have not been in Spain for almost five hundred years, and the Spaniards are Catholics for the most part: yet the worthwhile work done by Al-Hakim was the building of the great Mosque of Cordoba.

The Sufi teachers have commented on this proverb; but before we look at their impressions, we can look at the background of the saying.

Reference books show that the ruler Al-Hakim improved the musical wind instrument *Al-Buq*, making its range greater through the addition of an extra perforation at the bottom of the horn.

Tradition says that Al-Hakim was very proud of this

achievement, being a man of culture and refinement; but the more he caused word of his development of the horn to be spread around, the more the people spoke, derisively, of 'The Work of Al-Hakim'.

The Sultan asked his advisers why something which was a positive advantage should thus be turned, in the mouths of the people, into a joke, and one describing any useless activity. They told him that it was a matter of priorities. Things which the aesthete might pride himself upon, do not always recommend themselves to the people at large.

So Al-Hakim thought and thought. Eventually he diverted all his energies to work on the Great Mosque of Cordoba, whose building took a hundred years. So identified with this task was he, and so wonderful was his contribution, in the eyes of the populace, that this, and not the improvement of the note of the horn, became known as 'The Work of Al-Hakim'.

Now Al-Hakim had achieved his desire: to be respected by the people for something which they valued. His name is honoured in proverb.

The Sufi sages, however, have taken this history in a slightly different sense. They point out that there are three things to remember. First, if you want to please yourself, do not expect other people to appreciate what you are doing. Then you can 'improve the Buq'. Second, if you want to be remembered, choose something which the people at large consider to be an achievement: 'build the Great Mosque'. Third, ask yourself if you are following an interest in personal frivolity – Al-Buq – or public renown – the Mosque – or something which lies beyond these things. The first seems real to you, and others do not agree. The second seems real to them, but not to others. Think of the third, which actually *is* reality, and which is not dependent upon what you imagine or upon public opinion.

The Invention of Chess and Backgammon

Sincere in his religious belief and virtuous in his conduct, Al-Suli merited the confidence which was always placed in his word. As a chess-player he was without an equal, and, even to the present day, it is said as a proverb of a player, whose skill one wishes to extol, that his game is like that of Al-Suli. I have met many people who believe Al-Suli to have been the inventor of chess, but this is an erroneous opinion, that game having been imagined by Sissa the son of Dahir, an Indian, for the amusement of King Shihram.

Ardeshir, the son of Babek, the ancestor of the last royal house of Persia, invented the game of *nard* or backgammon ... He designed it as an image of the world and its inhabitants, and therefore divided the board into twelve squares to represent the months of the year; the thirty pieces (or men) represented the days of the month, and the dice were emblems of Fate and the vicissitudes thereof, with which it conducts the people of the world. But to expatiate on these points would lead us too far and cause us to digress from the subject in which we are now engaged. As for the game of *nard*, the Persians count it as one of the inventions which does honour to their nation.

It is said that, when Sissa invented the game of chess and presented it to Shihram, the King was struck with admiration and filled with joy; he had chess-boards placed in the temples, and he expressed the opinion that the game was the best thing man could study, inasmuch as it served as an introduction to the art of war, and that it was an honour to the Faith and the World, as well as the foundation of all justice.

The King also manifested his gratitude and satisfaction for the favour which Heaven had granted him in shedding lustre on his reign by such an invention, and he said to Sissa, 'Ask for whatever you desire.' 'I then demand,' replied Sissa, 'that a grain of wheat be placed in the first square of the chess-board, two in the second, and that the number of grains be progressively doubled till the last square is reached: whatever this quantity of wheat may be, I ask you to bestow on me.'

The King who intended to make him a worthy present exclaimed, that such a recompense would be too little, and he reproached Sissa for asking so inadequate a reward. Sissa declared that he desired no other gift and, heedless of the King's remonstrances, he persisted in his request. The King at last consented, and gave orders that the required quantity of grain be given to him. When the chiefs of the royal office received their orders they calculated the amount, and answered that they did not possess near as much wheat as was required. When these words were reported to the King, he was unable to credit them and had the chiefs brought before him; when questioned on the subject they declared that all the wheat in the world would be insufficient to make up that quantity. They were asked to prove the truth of their contention, and by a series of multiplications and reckonings they demonstrated that such was indeed the case. The King then said to Sissa, 'Your ingenuity in imagining such a request is even more admirable than your talent in inventing the game of chess.'

The way in which the doubling of the grains of wheat is to be done consists in the calculator placing one grain in the first square, two in the second, four in the third, eight in the fourth, and so on, until he comes to the last square, placing in each square double the number contained in the preceding one. I was doubtful of the contention that the final amount could be as great as was said, but when I met one of the accountants employed at Alexandria, I received from him a demonstration which convinced me that their statement was true: he placed before me a sheet of paper, on which he had calculated the amount up to the sixteenth square, obtaining the result 32,768. 'Now,' said he, 'let us consider this number of grains to be the contents of a pint measure, and this I know by experiment to be true,' – these are the accountant's words, so let him bear the responsibility – 'then let the pint be doubled in the seventeenth square, and so on progressively. In the twentieth square it will become a *wayba*, the *waybas* will then become an *ardeb*, and in the fortieth square we shall have 174,762 *ardebs*; let us consider this to be the contents of a corn-store, and no corn-store contains more than that; then, in the fiftieth square we shall have the contents of 1,024 stores; suppose these to be situated in one city – and no city can have more than that number of granaries or even so many – we shall then find that the number required for the sixty-fourth and last square corresponds to the contents of the granaries of 16,384 cities; but you know that there is not in the whole world a greater number of cities than that ... This demonstration is decisive and indubitable.'

From Ibn Khallikan's biography of Abu-Bakr Al-Suli *Eminent Men* (13th Century), by Baron de Slane.

Customs and Social Habits

Middle Eastern Dress

In Islamic countries, although there are variations in clothes, the example of the Prophet Mohammed is followed in many aspects of dress. These include the turban (the Prophet was not a Bedouin, and did not wear the headscarf and fillet often associated with 'the Arabs'), the shirt (*qamis*), the drawers or trousers and sandals.

The Prophet declared that it was unlawful for Moslem men to wear silk or gold, though women could adorn themselves with them. He himself generally wore white, but was also known to wear green, red, yellow or black wool.

Although it is widely believed that it is an Islamic tradition to remove the footwear when entering houses or mosques, there are very numerous traditions of the Prophet attesting to the fact that he frequently prayed with his sandals on.*

In many Moslem communities, only *Sharifs* (descendants of the Prophet) are allowed to wear green turbans or robes. This is considered to be a legal requirement; but in fact the custom dates only to the Egyptian Sultan Al Malik Al Ashraf (1362-1376) and was spread elsewhere by the Turks.

Similarly, the wearing of various colours by sectarians and adherants of dynasties has no religious sanction, and is now largely abandoned.

The turban, or any headgear, is respected, and should not be insulted. The story is told (by Lane) of a religious sheikh who was thrown from his donkey, when he rolled one way and his turban the

---

* 'The number of traditions which prove that Mohammad allowed his followers to worship with their feet covered is very numerous, and they are held to be *Ahadis* [Prophetic Traditions] of good authority and supported by *Fatwas* [legal rulings] of eminent doctors of law'. (Hughes, *Dictionary of Islam*, s.v. *Shoes*, quoting Abu Sa'id Al Khudri, *Mishkat*, the *Hidaya* and the Companion Amr ibn Shu'aib, etc.).

other. People began to run after the turban, calling out, 'Lift up the crown of Islam!' At this the unfortunate man of learning, whom nobody was helping, cried out, 'Lift up the *Sheikh* of Islam!'

From Hughes, *Dictionary of Islam*, and Lane, *Manners and Customs of the Modern Egyptians*.

Dress of the Bedouin

In summer, men wear a coarse cotton shirt, over which the wealthy put a *kombar*, a long gown of silk or cotton. Most, however, do not wear the kombar, but simply put on over their shirt, a woollen mantle.

There are different kinds of mantles: one is very thin, light and of wool, made in Baghdad and called the *masumi*. A coarser and heavier kind, striped white and brown and worn over the masumi, is called the *abba*. The most esteemed are the Baghdad abbas; those made at Hama are called *boush* and have short wide sleeves.

In the northern parts of Syria, every kind of woollen mantle, whether white or brown, black or white and blue, are called *mishlah*.

All bedouins wear on the head, instead of a fez or turban, a square kerchief of cotton or cotton and silk mixed, called the *kaffieh*. This they fold about the head so that one corner falls backward and the other two corners hang over the two shoulders. With these two corners they cover their faces to protect them from the sun's rays or hot wind or rain, or to conceal their features if they wish to be unknown.

Over the kaffieh a cord of camel's hair is tied, called the *aqal*. Under the kaffieh they may wear a small skullcap: the *araqia*.

In winter, the bedouins wear over the shirt a *pelisse*, made of several sheepskins stitched together; many wear them even in the summer, because experience has taught them that the more warmly a person is clothed the less he suffers from the sun.

The ladies' dress is a wide cotton gown of a dark colour: blue, brown or black. On their heads they wear a kerchief called *shauber* or *makrun*, the young females having it of a red colour, the old of black. All the Ranalla ladies wear black silk kerchiefs, two yards square; these are made at Damascus. The bedouin women half cover their faces with a dark-coloured veil, called a *nekia*, which is so tied as to conceal the chin and mouth.

From *Notes on the Bedouins and Wahabys*, by Burckhardt.

The Mosque

With Islam the largest religious denomination in Britain after Christianity, the number of mosques listed as such in the country had risen to 183 by 1978, with 29 in London alone and a further 263 at the planning stage. Thirteen thousand people prayed at the Birmingham mosque at the festival of the *Breaking of the Fast* in September, 1978.

In spite of this enormous expansion, the mosque remains more than a little mysterious to most Western people.

The dome and minaret, long considered basic mosque features, are innovations in the sense that neither had appeared during the Prophet Mohammed's lifetime: the minaret of Medina, for instance, was built by order of Omar ibn Abdul-Aziz, eighty-six years after the Prophet entered that city. The oldest minaret extant is the square one at Qayrawan, Tunisia, and is over twelve hundred years old.

Other aspects of the mosque, such as the ablutions fountain and prayer-niche, are also innovations. The pulpit (*Mimbar*) from which the sermon is delivered, was introduced at Fustat (Cairo) in the year 642, and after this came the niche, indicating the direction of Mecca, towards which all prayers are said.

Fundamentally, therefore, the mosque (derived from *masjid*, place of prostration) is a prayer-house without embellishments or altars or other religious objects. Prayers were originally said towards Jerusalem, and the first mosque of Islam was built on the instructions of the Prophet, at Medina, in 622. Two years later the direction of prayer was changed to Mecca.

Mosques, palaces and castles are the most important of the Islamic architectural heritage and, together with some colleges, are the structures which most influenced later European building. The prototype of the 'Gothic' pointed arch is found in Iraq, at Ikhaidr, while minarets were the models for many Western bell-towers now familiar throughout Europe and the Americas. A well-known Western use of the Eastern dome and towers motif is that of Sir Christopher Wren, in St. Paul's Cathedral in London. The Arabic monumental script has its parallels in decorative, especially 'Gothic' writing noted on buildings from Cairo to London, Norfolk and Yorkshire. Military, 'Gothic', Renaissance and Tudor architectural forms have been traced by Western scholars to Middle Eastern forms, through the Saracenic contact.

Westerners often imagine that some of the famous Middle Eastern and Islamic buildings are mosques when they are intended for other purposes. The Taj Mahal, for instance, is a tomb; the Dome of the Rock in Jerusalem is a *mashshad*, or place of pilgrimage, covering the spot from which Mohammed travelled on his famous Night Journey; the Alhambra of Moorish Spain is a palace; and the Mosque of Aya Sofia in Istanbul was originally a church, and is now a museum. The mosques which Moslems of the time of the Prophet – were they to return – would most readily recognise as such are not the amazing edifices of Cordoba, Delhi or Cairo, but the ones built on the plan of the first mosque, at Quba, near Medina; which are found in the villages of Afghanistan.

As there is no clergy in Islam, anyone may lead the prayers, and mosques have no appointed officials. The *Muazzin* [Caller to Prayer] is, like the Imam [Prayer Leader] a voluntary position; though mosques usually have a trustee who superintends it under the deed which governs the building.

In many parts of the Islamic world, non-Moslems are allowed to visit mosques as sightseers. But in others, visitors are not admitted, in accordance with the admonition of the Koran, Chapter 9, Verse 18:

'The mosques of God
Shall be visited and maintained
By such as believe in God
And the Last Day:
Who establish regular prayer
And practise regular charity
And who fear none (at all) except God.
It is they who are expected to be on true guidance.'

Allama Yusuf Ali's translation.

The Toothpick

The toothpick plays an important part in the life of most Mohammedan nations. According to Wiedeman, who wrote extensively on the subject, there are two main types of toothpick. The *siwak* or *miswak* is a small staff with which the teeth are rubbed and cleaned, the end of which becomes rather like a brush after much chewing. The *chalil* is the toothpick as we know it in the West which is used to remove food particles from between the teeth.

The *siwak* is made of various different and often fragrant woods, including arak, sugar-cane, roots of the lily, wood of mahlab, roots of idchis and knots of dracuncula and its use seems to be governed by fairly rigid convention. It may be used in the morning and the evening, at noon, before breakfast, after prayers, at bedtime, and when the stomach is empty. It should not be used while standing or leaning against something or in bed, or when somebody is watching. Neither should it be used while speaking. It should definitely not be used in closet or bathhouse, nor in the street or where people assemble. The more wealthy use beautiful containers of ebony and bamboo to carry their toothpicks and they are wrapped in silk to keep them clean.

They are traditionally given as presents and considered to be a keepsake or pledge.

There are numerous quotations stated by the Prophet on the toothpick including the following:

> 'A prayer which is preceded by the use of the toothpick is more worth than seventy-five common prayers.'

> 'You shall clean your mouth for this is a means of praising God.'

> 'God has advised me to use the siwak so impressively that I almost feared he might prescribe it to me as a revealed law.'

> 'If it were not too great a burden for the believers I would prescribe that they use the toothpick before each prayer.'

Apparently he also jokingly said that the angel Gabriel had commended the toothpick to him so often that he was afraid he might lose his teeth because of their frequent rubbing with it.

According to a report in 'True Traditions' the Prophet advised the use of the siwak, perfume, and henna in marriage.

There is a story related by the Arabian philosopher Gazzali in *The Beginning of the Leading* that the Prophet went to a bush and cut two siwaks, one curved and the other straight. Giving his companion the straight one, he kept the crooked one for himself. 'O envoy of the Lord,' said the man, 'thou hast more right to keep the straight one than I have.'

Toothpicks made of aloe wood were dipped in the sacred well, Zamzan in Mecca, and pilgrims took them home as reminders of their great pilgrimage.

There is an amusing story of an explorer, travelling in Arabia who would tell the Mohammedans that his toothbrush bristles were made of the hair of wild horses since, if they had known that the brush was made of hogs hair, they would have refused to speak to him.

Omar Khayyam, it is said, used to clean his teeth with a golden toothpick while poring over the metaphysical work of Avicenna, the '*Shifa*'. When he reached the chapter 'On the One and the Many' he placed the toothpick between two pages and said: 'Call the almoner, I wish to make my testament'. And having made his will, stood up, prayed, and ate and drank no more – and died.

From *Folklore of the Teeth*, Leo Kanner, MacMillan, 1928.

The Turkish Bath
by *Lady Mary Wortley Montague*

In one of these covered wagons, I went to the *bagnio* about ten o'clock. It was already full of women. It is built of stone, in the shape of a dome, with no windows but in the roof, which gives light enough. There were five of these domes joined together, the outmost being less than the rest, and serving only as a hall, where the portress stood at the door. Ladies of quality usually give this woman a crown or ten shillings; and I did not forget that ceremony. The next room is a very large one paved with marble, and all round it are two raised sofas of marble, one above another. There were four fountains of cold water in this room, falling first into marble basins, and then running on the floor in little channels made for that purpose, which carried the streams into the next room, something less than this, with the same sort of marble sofas, but so hot with steams of sulphur proceeding from the baths joining to it, it was impossible to stay there with one's clothes on. The two other domes were the hot baths, one of which had cocks of cold water turning into it, to temper it to what degree of warmth the bathers pleased to have.

I was in my travelling habit, which is a riding dress, and certainly appeared very extraordinary to them. Yet there was not one that showed the least surprise or impertinent curiosity, but received me with all the obliging civility possible. I know no European court

232

where the ladies would have behaved in so polite a manner to such a stranger. I believe, upon the whole, there were two hundred women, and yet none of those disdainful smiles, and satirical whispers, that never fail in our assemblies when any body appears that is not dressed exactly in the fashion. They repeated over and over to me: '*Guzel, pek guzel*,' which is nothing but '*Charming, very charming*'. The first sofas were covered with cushions and rich carpets, on which sat the ladies; and on the second, their slaves behind them, but without any distinction of rank by their dress, all being in the state of nature, that is, in plain English, stark naked, without any beauty or defect concealed. Yet there was not the least wanton smile or immodest gesture amongst them. They walked and moved with the same majestic grace which Milton describes our general mother with. There were many amongst them as exactly proportioned as ever any goddess was drawn by the pencil of a Guido or Titian, – and most of their skins shiningly white, only adorned by their beautiful hair divided into many tresses, hanging on their shoulders, braided either with pearl or ribbon, perfectly representing the figures of the Graces.

I was here convinced of the truth of a reflection I have often made, *that if it were the fashion to go naked, the face would hardly be observed*. I perceived that the ladies of the most delicate skins and finest shapes had the greatest share of my admiration, though their faces were sometimes less beautiful than those of their companions. To tell the truth I had wickedness enough to wish secretly that Mr. Jervas could have been there invisible. I fancy it would have very much improved his art, to see so many fine women naked, in different postures, some in conversation, some working, others drinking coffee or sherbet, and many negligently lying on their cushions, while their slaves (generally pretty girls of seventeen or eighteen) were employed in braiding their hair in several pretty fancies. In short, it is the Women's Coffee-house, where all the news of the town is told, scandal invented, etc. They generally take this diversion once a week, and stay there at least for four or five hours, without getting cold by immediately coming out of the hot bath into the cold room, which was very surprising to me. The lady that seemed the most considerable among them, entreated me to sit by her, and would fain have undressed me for the bath. I excused myself with some difficulty. They being, however, all so earnest in persuading me, I was at last forced to open my shirt, and show them

233

my stays; which satisfied them very well; for, I saw, they believed I was locked up in that machine, and that it was not in my power to open it, which contrivance they attributed to my husband.

Afterwards a Sherbet

Eating Customs among the Turks and Arabs

When the Turks eat, a little round or octagonal stool is set on the sopha, or a coloured cloth laid on the ground. Round it they throw a long cloth to be put in the laps of the guests; and with those of condition a napkin is given to everyone when he washes, as they always do before they eat. This they likewise lay before them, and wipe with it when they wash after dinner. On the stool they put a copper dish tinned over, from three to six feet in diameter, which is as a table; all their dishes and vessels being copper tinned over, inside and out. Round this dish they put bread, small dishes of pickles, salads and the like; and then they bring two or three large dishes, in two or three courses.

None but the common people eat beef, and the flesh of the buffalo, as they have a notion that it is not easy of digestion. It is said in the hot Hamzeen season in the month of April and May, they eat for the most part nothing but dishes made of pulses and herbs and also fish as being easy of digestion; and the great heats taking away their appetites for all sorts of meat. The most vulgar people make a sort of beer of barley, without being malted, and they put something in it to make it intoxicate and call it *Bouzy*; they make it ferment, 'tis thick and sour, and will not keep longer than three or four days. It appears from Herodotus, that the Egyptians used some sort of beer in his time, which he calls wine, made of barley. If they do not drink wine, they seldom drink whilst they are eating. They either sit cross-legged, or kneel, and make use only of the right hand, not using knives and forks, but tear the meat with the hand; and the master of the house often takes pieces in his hand, and throws them to his guests, that he would pay an extraordinary compliment to. Immediately after eating, coffee is brought. This is the Turkish manner. Their dishes consisting of Pilaw, soups, Dulma, which is

235

any vegetable stuffed with forced meat, as cucumbers, onions, cawl leaves, stewed dishes, sweet tagoos, pieces of meat cut small and roasted, and several other things. All is taken out and eaten by the inferior servants, not by the slaves who have a dinner prepared for them of more ordinary dishes in another room.

With the Arabs and people of the country, either a round skin is laid on the ground for a small company, or large coarse woollen cloths for a great number, spread all over the room and about ten dishes repeated six or seven times over laid round at a great feast and whole sheeps and lambs boiled and roasted in the middle. When one company has done, another sits round, even to the meanest, till all is consumed. And an Arab prince will often dine in the street, before his door and call to all that pass, even beggars, in the usual expression, *Bissimallah*, that is, 'In the name of God', who come and sit down, and when they have done, give their *Hamdellilah*, that is, 'God be praised'. For the Arabs are great levellers, put everybody on a footing with them; and it is by such generosity and hospitality that they maintain their interest, but the middling people among them, and the Coptis, live but poorly.

I have often sat down with them, only to bread, raw onions, and a feed pounded and put in oil, which they call *Serich*, produced by a herb called *Simsim*, into which they dip their bread, that is made as often as they eat, in very thin cakes, baked on an iron plate, heated. They have a very good dish for one who has a good appetite, which is these cakes broken all to pieces, and mixed with a sort of syrup made of the sugar cane when it is green. This cane is a great desert with them, by sucking the sweet juice out of it. They also eat a sour milk turned with seeds. They have a dish among the Moors called Cuscasow, which is made with flower tempered with water, and rolled in the hands into small pieces, and being put in a cullender, over a boiling pot stopped close round it is dressed with the steam, and then they put butter to it. They also sometimes dress dates with butter. Their great meal is generally at night taking a light collation in the morning of fried eggs, cheese, and, at great tables, olives and honey. And this is also usual with the Turks, especially if they go out to do business, or for diversion to stay abroad most part of the day, otherwise they dine rather before noon, and sup early in the evening. They probably choose to eat early in the morning before the heat takes away their appetite, and eat again soon in the evening when it begins to cool. When they have no company, they commonly go into the harem, or women's apartments, at the time of eating, to a wife in her separate apartment, who either prepares the dinner or inspects it, though they are great persons, having their offices adjoining to their rooms.

And a great man who has four wives, has five kitchens, one for each of them, managed by their slaves or servants, and one great one for public entertainments for the master, when he dines out of the harem, and for the slaves and servants. At a Turkish visit a pipe is immediately brought and coffee, and if it is a visit of ceremony, sweet-meats with the coffee, and afterwards a sherbet, and then according to the dignity of the person, incense and rosewater to perfume which is a gentle way of dismissing the company.

Friends who visit, especially women, stay a night or two or more carrying their beds with them, though in the same town, and coffee or sweet water boiled on cinnamon are brought at least once in an hour. And I have been told that it is a mark of great respect among them, often to change their garments during the visit. If anyone goes to the house of an Arab or his tent, bread is immediately made, and they serve sour milk and cucumbers in it when in season, fried eggs and oil to dip the bread in, a fat cheese like curds and such like. They do not take it well if you do not stay and eat, and think it such a favour to come to their houses and put yourself as it were under their protection, that where there have been any enmities if one goes to the other's house and eats with him all is forgot. And I have seen them sometimes show resentment by refusing to take coffee or anything offered, like the janizaries, who when they mutiny, will not eat the Grand Signor's Pilaw, but if pressed to eat and they comply, it is a sign the resentment is past.

They generally rise early at break of day and often go at that time to the mosques, the common people at least. Thence they resort to the coffee houses, and having taken their collations, go pretty late to their shops and shut them about four in the afternoons. The great people either visit or are visited. In Cairo on Sundays, Tuesdays and Thursdays, they go to the Pashas Divine, and these are the general days of business. Fridays they stay at home, and go to their mosques at noon, and though with them it is their day of devotion yet they never abstain from their business. The three other days of the week they call *Benish* days, from the garment of that name, which is not a habit of ceremony. They then go out early with their slaves, to public places out of town, commonly called *Meidans*, or Places, where they have a sort of open summer house and see their slaves ride, shoot and throw the dart and regale themselves with their pipe and coffee.

The Way of Ordering the Pilau

The Turks, and generally all the Inhabitants of the Eastern Parts, make the Pilau after this manner. According to the quality of the persons who are to be entertained, and the quantity which is to be made of it, you either take a piece of Mutton alone, or together with that some Pullets or Pidgeons, which are to be boyl'd in a Pot, till they are half done, or somewhat more. When you think them so far boyl'd then pour out both Meat and Broath into a Basin, and the Pot being washed, put it on the Fire Again with Butter on it, which they suffer to melt, till such time as it is very hot. Then they chop the meat which had been half-boyl'd, into little pieces, the Pullets into quarters, and the Pidgeons into halves, and so they cast it into the Butter, they fricass it till it be of a very brown colour. The Rice being well wash'd they put some into the Pot over the meat, as much as they think fitting, and the Broath which had been pour'd into the Basin, they also put into the Pot Ladle-ful after Ladle-ful, over the Rice, till such time as it stands two fingers breadth above it. Then is the Pot immediately cover'd, there is a clear Fire made under it, and they ever and anon take out some grains of the Rice, to see if it be softened, as also whether it be not requisite to put in some more of the Broath to compleat the stewing of it. For it is not like the Rice brought into our parts, which presently breaks asunder, but their Rice is of such a kind, that it must be fully boyl'd and yet the Grain entire, as well as the whole Pepper wherewith they season it. As soon as it is come to that condition, they cover the Pot with a Cloth three or four times doubled, and set the Pot-lid upon that, and sometime after they make another melting of Butter, till it be very red; to be cast into the holes, which are made in the Rice with the handle of the Ladle, after which they cover it again of a sudden, and so let it stand soaking a while, and then serve it up. It is put into large Dishes with the Meat, handsomely disposed upon it, and some part will be white, that is, continued in its natural colour, some part yellow, occasioned by a little mixture of Saffron, and a third part of a Carnacion-colour, done by the tincture of the juice of Pomegranate. Nay, though the meat be as fat as is requisite for the ordering of this Dish, yet to make the Pilau more delicate and palatable to them, they bestow three pounds of Butter on six pounds of Rice, which makes it so extraordinary fat, that it disgusts, and is nauseous to those who are not accustomed thereto, and accordingly would rather have the Rice itself simply boyl'd with Water and Salt. There are always two or three Dishes served up after that manner, to the Grandees of the Port, who for the most part keep open Table, and instead of Flesh they cover them with a great Aumelet or Omelet, made with good Herbs, and about three fingers thick, or with some poached Eggs, which are neatly disposed about it. A man is never incommoded by this kind of Rice, but the other, which is too fat, is not fit for those who drink Wine, and will not excite in them a desire to Eat of it often.

From *The Six Voyages of John Baptiste Tavernier* by Tavernier (1670).

Moorish Food – The National Dish

The typical dish of Morocco is the famous *kesk'soo*, of the name of which an able writer on the gastronomy of Morocco* has declared that 'the mere sound of the syllables is musical, with a sweet sibilance suggestive of twin kisses united to the coo of the turtle-dove and the note of the cuckoo'. But without indulging in such rapture over its name – only to be explained by the qualities of the dish described – I do unhesitatingly assert, from an exceptionally wide and appreciative acquaintance with native cookery the world round, that I do not know a dish at the same time more nutritive, more wholesome, more simple and more tasty. Its basis is the nourishing granular nodule or germ found only in wheat grown in comparatively poor, dry soils, which from the difficulty of grinding it is known as *semolina*, i.e. 'half-ground'. On the Continent this is used in the form of macaroni and other pastes, and in England it is advertised as 'Vitos' or 'Hovis' and kindred prepared breads. The Moors, who call it *smeedh*, make also from it a delicious white or macaroni-coloured bread. For the preparation of kesk'soo or, as the country-folk pronounce it, *siksoo*, the grains of *smeedh* are moistened and rolled in fine flour till they form pellets about the size of buck-shot, the smaller being considered the best. After being steamed and dried in the sun, it will keep good in a bag for many years, and a few days since I partook of some which I procured from

* G.D. Cowan in *Moorish Lotus Leaves*.

Fez eight years ago. For eating, the kesk'soo is again steamed, this time over a bowl of rice stew which is served on top of it, heaped in the centre of a big basin, sometimes with the addition of stewed quince or other fruit. But before serving the grains are carefully separated by rubbing in butter, some portion of which, called *smeen*, has been preserved till it has acquired a sort of Gorgonzola flavour. Too strong a dose of this at first is apt to repel the novice, but if tested gradually, this, more than anything else, renders Moorish dishes attractive, for it whets one's appetite, as assafoetida does in an Indian curry or 'Yorkshire relish'.

Not that the Moroccan cuisine depends on its green-streaked smeen, which has perhaps been buried in an earthen jar for twelve months – a little of which then goes a long way, – for with a liberal use of capsicums ('red peppers') and the usual Oriental spices, coriander, cummin, sesame, fenugreek, cinnamon, carraway, cloves and nutmeg, there is no lack of flavour, but the Moors are not fond of 'hot' things. A speciality of their kitchens is rather the use made of raisins, dates, etc., in their meat stews, with most excellent results. After kesk'soo, their stews are their strong point, and right tasty and tender they are, whatever the age of the creature supplying the meat, as they needs must be, when they have to be carved with the fingers and thumb of one hand.

Koumiss: Fermented Mare's Milk

A passable imitation of the Tatar *Kumiz* – fermented mare's milk – called Kumis in Russian, can be made with cows' milk.

Take:
12.5 g. dextrose
1.1 g. yeast
100 ml. cows' milk
100 ml. water.

Preparation:
Dissolve the dextrose in the water and add the yeast and milk. Pour into a champagne or other strong bottle and fit with wired cork. Keep in a cool place for four days, shaking several times a day.

Recipe contributed by the Assembly of Western Tatars, by courtesy of Qizil Yunus
Abdurrauf Beg.

Eight Recipes

Roast Fowl

Boil 1 lb. oil in a stew-pan till it smokes, then add 1/2 lb. butter, and put a fowl in, ready trussed and stuffed, with a little salt rubbed into it. Turn it occasionally, over a moderate fire, till it is brown and tender.

The latter point can be ascertained by touching with the finger, but beware of a scald! An excellent stuffing is made with chopped almonds, raisins, bread-crumbs, eggs and spices.

Joint of Mutton or Beef

Beef or mutton may be cooked like the fowl, with spices to taste added to the gravy. When the meat has absorbed most of the oil, add water, hot or cold, to make the required quantity of gravy. Keep close covered, and turn, taking care that the fire is not fierce enough to burn it. If onions or other vegetables are fancied with the meat, some of the gravy is poured into a separate vessel to stew them, and they are served round the joint in the same dish. Chopped carrots, etc., may be poured out over it, stewed in this way.

This is often accompanied by salad on a separate plate, and with mutton – of which the breast and shoulder are the favourite portions – a plate of pounded cummin and salt mixed forms a most agreeable relish into which to dip the meat as it is plucked from the joint. Olives are often added to the gravy, or apples, and are delicious thus.

Stew (*Tajin*)

For a stew, boil oil till it smokes, and add two tablespoonfuls of pounded capsicum. When boiling add half a pint of water. When cold pour off the clear oil from the top into a stew-pan. Add two or three heads of garlic, and when boiling put in the meat, cut up. Stew till tender.

When nearly ready add the vegetables, leaving them long enough to cook, according to what they are, any sort being suitable, but potatoes least of all so.

Fowl and Olives

Stew a fowl (cut up) in butter and oil, with pepper, salt and allspice (all in powder), the butter to be put in first, and the oil poured on when melted.* The meat should be first rubbed with salt, and left so ten minutes, after which the salt is washed off, just before putting it into the pot. Cook a quarter of an hour. Then replace the lid for ten minutes, after which put in the onions, cut up, and pour on a pint of water: boil till nearly all this has evaporated. Stew till no moisture comes out when a fork is stuck into the meat. Now add the raisins, and in five minutes add the olives and grated nutmeg, as much as a pea of the latter. Leave it near the fire for a quarter of an hour. Serve with plain boiled rice, like a curry. It should take altogether an hour and a half to cook.

Egg and Coriander Soup (*Harirah, Hawuwah*, or *F'toor*)

The following recipe will make good soup for four persons. Chop up the onions very fine, with pepper, salt, and green coriander. Put into a pan with 1 oz. *smeen*, and add half a pound meat, cut into dice. Leave all to simmer about half an hour, watching that it does not burn. Then fill up with a pint and a half of water. Leave it to stew slowly till the meat is tender. Then add 2 oz. vermicelli. Mix water, and pour it in. Boil a quarter of an hour longer, and remove from the fire; at that moment pour in two eggs well-beaten up and serve. Parsley may be substituted for coriander if the latter is unobtainable, but it is not so good.

Fish in Garlic

Half a dozen mackerel or large herrings, or an equal quantity of any fish, when seasoned with garlic according to taste, form a favourite dish, especially among the Jews.

Boil 4 oz. oil in a frying-pan over a slow fire. When bubbling, add 1/2 oz. sweet red pepper powder and a little water. The fish being prepared on the bottom of a stew-pan, be careful not to wash off the breadcrumbs, etc. Do not pour out the red pepper sediment; throw it away. The dish will be ready in twenty minutes to half an hour, if kept covered up. See that it does not burn. A slow fire is preferable.

---

* For one fowl use: Olives, 3 doz.; butter, 2 oz.; onions, 3; Spanish Oil, 3 tablespoonfuls; Raisins, 2 oz.

Sponge Fritters (*Sfinjes*)*

Knead 1 lb. flour with warm water and 1 oz. leaven into a stiff dough for half an hour, keeping on till it bubbles; then commence to thin down by adding warm water in small quantities, and kneading well till it is reduced to a thick paste, sufficiently stiff to remain in a long thread from the finger to the trough when a piece is pulled up with the hand. Leave it to ferment for a quarter of an hour, or more if necessary, till bubbles rise freely. It is then ready to fry.

Take hold of a piece in the hand, and break off a ball the size of a hen's egg. Pierce this with the fore-fingers and thumbs of each hand, and drawing it into a ring, drop it into *boiling* oil, turning it over when one side is browned. These are deliciously light and appetizing and may be eaten either alone or with salt, sugar, honey, etc.

Pikelets (**Hartaitahs**)

Prepare dough as for *sfinjes*. Clean an earthen pan by well rubbing with soft soap and drying. Place it on a slow fire till very hot. Then drop in a spoonful of the thin dough. When the face is set, turn the pikelet thus formed, being careful that the fire is not fierce enough to burn it to the bottom. In case it does, scrape the pan well, butter and soap as before.

Serve very hot, and eat with butter, or butter before serving. More or less salt should be added to the dough, according as they are intended to be eaten with fresh butter or sugar or honey.

From *A Description of the East and Some Other Countries*,
by Richard Pococke, 1743.

* Evidently the Greek word (spongos) a sponge.

WISDOM AND HONOUR

Words of the Sages

The Tale of the Gleaner
by *Sheikh Al Bashihi*

One night Harun-ar-Rashid was quite sleepless, and said to his vizier, Jaafar, the son of Yahya, the Barmecide: 'I cannot sleep this night; I feel oppressed, and do not know what to do'. The servant Masrur, who happened to be standing near, burst out laughing at these words, and the Khalif continued: 'What are you laughing for? Do you mock me or wish to show your levity?'

Masrur said: 'I swear by your relationship to the Prince of Apostles that I have done this unwittingly; but last evening I was near the castle, and walked to the bank of the Tigris, where I saw many persons assembled around a man who made them laugh, and just now I recollected some of his words, which caused me to smile; his name is Ben Almugazeli, and I crave pardon from the Commander of the Faithful.'

Then Rashid said: 'Bring him here this moment.'

Accordingly Masrur went to Ben Almugazeli and said to him: 'The Commander of the Faithful wants you.'

He replied: 'To hear is to obey!'

And Masrur continued: 'But on the condition that, if he presents you with anything, one-fourth of it will belong to you, and the rest to me.'

The man rejoined: 'No, I must have one-third of it and you the other two-thirds.' Masrur would not agree to this proposal, but at last consented after a great deal of haggling.

When he was admitted and had made his salutations, the Khalif said: 'If you make me laugh I shall give you five hundred dinars, but if not I shall give you three blows with this sock.'

Now Ben Almugazeli said to himself: 'What are the odds if I get three strokes with the sock?' because he thought it was empty.

247

Accordingly he began to jest and to play tricks at which low people might have laughed, but not Rashid, who did not even smile. The man was first astonished, then grieved, and at last frightened when Rashid said: 'Now you have deserved the blows.' He then took up the sock and twisted it, but at the bottom there were some balls, each of which weighed two drachms.

When he had struck Ben Almugazeli once, the latter yelled pitifully, but recollecting the condition Masrur had imposed upon him, he exclaimed: 'Mercy, O Commander of the Faithful, listen to two words of mine.'

He said: 'Speak what you like.'

The man continued: 'I have promised Masrur to let him have two-thirds of the bounty I might receive, and to keep one-third for myself, and to this he agreed only after much bargaining. Now the Commander of the Faithful has decided that the bounty shall consist of three blows, of which my share would be one, and Masrur's two. I have received mine, and now is his turn to take his.'

Rashid laughed, called for Masrur, and struck him; Masrur groaned from pain, and said: 'I present him with the remainder.'

The Khalif laughed and ordered them to be presented with one thousand dinars, of which each received five hundred, and Ben Almugazeli went away grateful.

Razi

Ibn Faris ar-Razi, the philologist, is the author of these verses:

> Well, some things succeed and some fail: when my heart is filled with cares I say: 'One day perhaps they may be dispelled'. A cat is my companion; books the friends of my heart; and a lamp my beloved consort.
>
> From Ibn Khallikan's celebrated *Biographical Dictionary*.

Al-Kadi

Abu Wathila Iyas Al-Kadi was renowned for his excessive acuteness of mind, observation, and penetration. Many stories are told about him in connection with these qualities, which are really astonishing. It is related of him that he said: 'I was never worsted in penetration but by one man: I had taken my seat in the court of judgment at Busra, when a person came before me and gave testimony that a certain garden, of which he mentioned the boundaries, belonged to a man whom he named. As I had some doubts of his veracity, I asked him how many trees were in that garden, and he said to me, after a long silence: "How long is it since our lord the Kadi has been giving judgment in this hall?" I told him the time. "How many beams," said he, "are there in the roof?" On which I acknowledged that he was in the right, and I received his testimony.'

It is a curious circumstance that Homer the Greek poet, Radaki the Persian poet, and Bashshar bin Burd the Arabian poet, were all blind. Here is a specimen of one of the verses of the last-named:

> Yes, my friends! My ear is charmed by a person in that tribe; for the ear is sometimes enamoured sooner than the eye. You say that I am led by one whom I never saw; know that the ear as well as the eye can inform the mind of facts.

He composed also the following verse, which is the most gallant of any made by the poets of that epoch:

> Yes, by Allah! I love the magic of your eyes, and yet I dread the weapons by which so many lovers fell.

From Ibn Khallikan's celebrated *Biographical Dictionary*.

Sari Al-Saqati

It is related of Sari al-Saqati, the celebrated Sufi, that he said that for twenty years he never ceased imploring Divine pardon for having once exclaimed, 'Praise be to God!' and on being asked the reason he said: 'A fire broke out in Baghdad, and a person came up to me and told me that my shop had escaped, on which I uttered these words; and even to this moment I repent of having said so, because it showed that I wished better to myself than to others'.

From Ibn Khallikan's celebrated *Biographical Dictionary*.

Shahabuddin

Shidab Ad-Din (Flambeau of the Faith) as-Suhrawardi was a pious and holy Shaikh, most assiduous in his spiritual exercises, and the practice of devotion, and successfully guided a great number of Sufis in their efforts to obtain perfection. Many persons wrote to him for his opinion on circumstances which concerned themselves, and one wrote as follows: 'My lord, if I cease to work I shall remain in idleness, and if I work I am filled with self-satisfaction; which is best?' To this the Shaikh replied: 'Work, and ask Almighty God to pardon thy self-satisfaction.'

The following is one of his verses:

> If I contemplate you, I am all eyes; and if I think of you I
> am all heart.

From Ibn Khallikan's celebrated *Biographical Dictionary*.

The Barmecide

Abu Ali Yahya, the Vizier of Harun-ar-Rashid, was the son of Khalid, and the grandson of Barmek. Yahya was highly distinguished for wisdom, nobleness of mind, and elegance of language. One of his sayings was: 'Three things indicate the degree of intelligence possessed by him who does them: the bestowing of gifts, the drawing up of letters, and the acting as ambassador'. He used to say to his sons: 'Write down the best things which you hear; learn by heart the best things which you write down; and in speaking utter the best things which you have learned by heart.'

From Ibn Khallikan's celebrated *Biographical Dictionary*.

Honour

Not Worth the Money

Ibn Al Kharif relates that his father once gave to a broker, Ahmad ibn Al Sabb, a robe. He told him: 'If anyone wants to buy this, point out that it has a defect, a tear, so that he shall not buy it while thinking that it is intact.'

That same evening the merchant returned and gave him some money, saying, 'A foreigner, a stranger, bought the robe from me for these dinars.'

'Did you show him the fault in the robe, so that he might know about it?' asked the owner.

'No, I completely forgot to do that.'

Ibn Al Kharif's father continued the tale:

'I said to him, "May God not give you a good reward! Come now with me to him."

'And we went together to his house, but the man had gone. We were told that he had left for Mecca with the caravan of pilgrims.

'I got a description of the man and followed the caravan on a hired horse, and eventually I caught up with it.

'Finding the man, I said to him: "Yesterday you bought a robe from such and such a person, at this price. It had a slit in it, so take back the money, and give me back the robe."

'Now the man got up and looked for the garment and found the rent. Then he said: "Old man, bring out the money, and let me look at it."

'I had not examined or tested the gold. When I brought it out he said: "That is my gold. Examine it, O Sheikh".

'I looked at the gold and saw that it was counterfeit and worthless.

'Then the man took the money and threw it away. He said to me:

"I will now buy your robe with its defect, for the same amount of real gold."

'And he paid me, this time in good money, and I came back with it.'

Nahfat Al Yaman.

Abbas and Haroun-Al-Rashid

Abbas, the chief of the police of the Khalif Mamun, said: 'One day I was present in an assembly of the Prince of the Faithful, before whom a man was standing heavily fettered with chains of iron. As soon as the Khalif perceived me, he said, "Abbas, take good care of this man, and produce him again tomorrow."

'Accordingly I called for some of my people, and they carried him away, because he was so heavily shackled that he could scarcely move. Considering that I had been ordered to take every care of this prisoner, I concluded that I had better keep him in my own house, in a chamber of which I then confined him. I asked him what place he had come from, and on his replying that it was Damascus, I expressed my best wishes for the prosperity of that town, whereat he was astonished. I told him that I had been there, and asked him about a certain man; he said that he would like to know how I could be acquainted with him, and on my replying that I had had some business with him, he promised to satisfy my curiosity if I gave him first some information. Accordingly I made the following statement:

> When I was with some other officials at Damascus the population rebelled against us, and even the governor was under the necessity of escaping by getting himself let down in a basket from his palace. I also fled, and whilst doing so the mob pursued me, and I ran into the house of the above-mentioned man, who was sitting at the door of it. I said to him: 'Help me and Allah will help you!'
>
> He received me kindly, and told his wife to put me into a certain room, whilst he remained sitting at the door. I had scarcely gone in when my pursuers likewise rushed in and insisted on searching the house, which they actually did, and would certainly have discovered me had not the man's wife kept them off from the room in which I sat trembling for my life. When the people at last dispersed, the man and his wife

comforted me as much as they could, and hospitably entertained me in their house for four months, till every danger had
passed away.

When I was bold enough to go out and see what had become
of my slaves, I found that they had all dispersed, and I asked my
kind host to allow me to depart to Baghdad. He consented, but
when the caravan was starting he insisted on presenting me
with a horse, a slave, and all the provisions required for the
journey. All these were surprises thrust upon me when I was
about to start, and was wondering how I could possibly travel
without any of these things. Moreover, during my whole so-
journ this kind man had never asked me my name for fear that I
might thereby be compromised. After I had safely arrived in
Baghdad I desired many a time to show my gratitude to this
man, but could obtain no information about him. I still desired
to requite his services, and this is the reason why I was so
anxious to learn something about him from you.

'After the man had listened to the above statement he said: "Verily,
Allah has enabled you to requite the kindness of that man." I asked:
"How can that be?" and he replied: "I am that man, but the trouble
in which you see me has hindered you from recognising me." Then
he reminded me of various circumstances, and so established his
identity that I was perfectly convinced of it, and could not restrain
myself from embracing him most fervently. To my inquiries how he
had fallen into the calamity which had overtaken him, he replied:

"A disturbance arose in Damascus similar to the rebellion
which had broken out when you were there; the Prince of the
Believers sent troops and suppressed it, but I, having been
suspected as one of the ringleaders thereof, was captured by his
command, brought as a prisoner to Baghdad, and considered
to have forfeited my life, which I shall certainly lose. I left my
family without taking leave, but a slave of mine has followed
me here, and will carry back information about me. He is to be
found at such and such a place, and if you will send for him I
will give him the necessary instructions. I shall consider it a
high favour, and as a reward for all the obligations under
which you were to me."

'I told him to put his trust in Allah, and got a smith to relieve him first of his irons, then I made him enter the bath, provided him with good clothes, and sent for his slave, to whom he gave, with tears in his eyes, the message for his family. I then ordered my people to get ready several horses and mules, which I loaded with baggage and provisions, gave the man a bag of ten thousand dirhems, with another of five thousand dinars, and ordered my lieutenant to escort him on his journey to Damascus as far as Anbar.

'But the man replied: "The Prince of the Believers considers that I have committed high treason, and will send troops to pursue me; I shall be recaptured and executed, and by allowing me to escape you will endanger your own life."

'I said: "Never mind what will become of me, but save your life, and I shall afterwards endeavour to save mine."

'He rejoined: "That shall not be, and I cannot leave Baghdad without knowing what has become of you."

'Seeing him determined in his purpose, I ordered my lieutenant to take him to a certain place in the town where he could remain in concealment till the next day, when he might be informed as to whether I had extricated myself from the difficulty, or had lost my life, in which latter case I should only have repaid him for having risked his in Damascus to save mine, and after that he could depart.

'The lieutenant had taken the man away, and I made preparations for my death, getting ready my winding-sheet in which my corpse was to be shrouded, when an official on the part of Mamun arrived with this message: "The Prince of the Faithful orders you to bring the man with you." Accordingly I hastened to the palace, where I found the Khalif sitting and expecting me. The first words he said to me were these: "I want to see the man!" I remained silent, and on his uttering them more emphatically, replied: "Will you please listen to me, O Commander of the Believers?" He continued: "I am determined to strike your head off if the man has fled." I said: "O Prince of the Faithful, the man has not escaped, but listen to what I have to say about him, and then you may act as you deem fit."

'He continued: "Speak!" Accordingly I narrated everything, and said that I was anxious to requite the man in some measure for all the good he had done to me, that I was desirous to save his life even at the cost of my own, if need be, and finished my explanation by showing the winding-sheet I had brought with me.

'After the Khalif had patiently listened, he exclaimed: "His merit is superior to yours, because he has treated you nobly without knowing you; whereas you only do so after having enjoyed his beneficence. I desire to reward him myself."

'"The man is here, and would not leave until apprised of my fate; I can produce him at once."

'The Khalif said: "This trait of his character is even more noble; go, comfort the man, and bring him here."

'Accordingly I departed, and when I introduced the man to the Khalif, he received him kindly, offered him a seat, conversed with him till dinner was brought in, of which he made him partake in his own company. Lastly, the Khalif invested him with a robe of honour, and wished to appoint him Governor of Damascus, but this he humbly refused. Accordingly, Mamun presented him with ten horses saddled and bridled, ten mules caparisoned, and ten bags, each of which contained ten thousand dinars; he also gave him ten slaves, with animals to ride upon, and a letter to the Governor of Damascus to absolve him from the payment of taxes. This man afterwards corresponded with Mamun and when a courier arrived from Damascus, the Khalif used to say to me, "Abbas! a letter from your friend has arrived".'

From *The Gleaner* by Sheikh Muhammad ben Ahmad al Bashihi.

Sayings of the Prophet Mohammed: II

Islam

I asked the Prophet: 'What is Islam?'
  He answered: 'Islam is purity of speech and hospitality.'
  I asked: 'What is faith?'

  He said: 'Faith is patience and generosity.'

I asked: 'Who is the best Moslem?'

  He said: 'The one from whose tongue and hands the Moslems are safe.'

I asked: 'What is the best part of faith?'

  He said: 'Kindness.'

Amru ibn Abasah, in Shaybani's Collection.

The Five Opportunities

The Prophet said:

  'Seize the Five Opportunities:
  Your youth before the feebleness of age;
  Your health before your sickness;
  Your riches before your poverty;
  Your leisure before your work;
  Your life before your wealth.'

Amr ibn Maimun al Audi, in Tirmidhi's Collection.

Knowledge

The Prophet said:

  'Whoever seeks knowledge, it will be an atonement for what he has done previously.'

Anas, in Tirmidhi's *and* Darimi's Collections.

Behaviour

The Prophet said:

> 'The most beloved of mine among you is whoever has the best manners.'

Ibn Amru, in *Bukhari's and Muslim's Collections*.

The Parable of Wisdom

The Prophet said:

> 'When God created Wisdom, he said to it, "Stand up."
>
> 'It stood up, and he then said to it, "Turn around," and it turned around.
>
> 'Then God said to Wisdom: "Come to me." It came to him, and he said to it, "Sit down," and it sat down.
>
> 'Then he said to it, "I have not made in all creation anything better than you, nor anything more excellent than you, nor more beautiful than you. By means of you, I take; by means of you, I give. I am known by you, and by you I punish. By you comes success, and by you punishment".'

Abu Huraira, in *Baihaqi's Collection*.

Refreshment of the Teaching

The Prophet said:

> 'Truly, God will raise up at the beginning of every century, for this people, one who will renew their religion for them.'

Abu Huraira, in *Abu Daud al Sajistani's Collection*.

Lying

The Prophet said:

> 'It is lying enough if anyone is to repeat whatever he hears.'

Abu Huraira, in *Muslim's Collection*.

Forgiveness

The Prophet said:

'Truly, it is better that a leader should err in the direction of forgiveness than that he should err in punishing.'

Aisha, in *Tirmidhi's Collection*.

Education

The Prophet said:

'No gift or present, out of all the gifts and presents given to a child, is superior to a good liberal education.'

Sa'id ibn al As, in the *Collections of Tirmidhi and Baihaqi*.

Disposition

The Prophet said:

'Whoever has a good disposition attains through it the status of one who carries out prayer and fasting.'

Abu Darda, in *Tirmidhi's Collection*.

Prayers which are Answered

The Prophet said:

'There is no doubt that three kinds of prayer are answered:
  The prayer of a parent:
  The prayer of a wayfarer:
  The prayer of someone who is oppressed.'

Abu Huraira, in the *Collections of Tirmidhi, Sajistani and Ibn Maja al Qazwini*.

Word

The Prophet said:

'Nobody has ever eaten anything better than what has come from the work of his own hands.'

Miqdam ibn Ma'dikarib, in *Bukhari's Collection*.

258

Trust and Promise

The Prophet said:

'He who does not fulfil his trust has no faith: and he who does not fulfil his promise has no religion.'

Anas, in Baihaqi's Collection.

The Strong

The Prophet said:

'He who overthrows people is not strong and has no power. 'The strong among us is he who controls himself when he is angry.'

Abu Huraira, in the Collections of Bukhari and Muslim.

The Stages

'Verily,' said the Prophet, 'the grave is the first stage of the stages of the hereafter.'

Uthman, in Tirmidhi's Collection.

Grave-Worship

'Beware!' said the Prophet, 'For those who were before you took the burial places of their prophets and men of truth as places of worship. Beware! Do not make graves into places of worship. I forbid that to you.'

Jundub, in Muslim's Collection.

Alms

The Prophet said:

'It is better that a man should give one silver piece during his lifetime in charity than that he should bequeath a hundred at his death.'

Abu Sa'id in Sajistani's Collection.

Abstinence

'Wearing rough clothes,' said the Prophet, 'and eating coarse food is not abstinence from the world. Abstinence from this world is only in lessening desire.'

Sufian al Thauri, quoted in *Baghawi's Collection*.

The Dead and the Living

The Prophet said:

'Do not abuse the dead, for in so doing you will hurt the living.'

Mughira, in *Tirmidhi's Collection*.

Animals

'If anyone kills a sparrow for no reason,' said the Prophet, 'it will cry out on the Day of Requital, and it will say: "O my Lord! Such and such a man killed me for nothing; he did not kill me for any good reason!"'

Shuryad ibn Suwaid, in *Nasai's Collection*.

The Prophet said:

'One of the great prophets of old was bitten by an ant, and he ordered the nest to be burnt. Upon this, God sent a revelation to him, saying:

"An ant has bitten thee, and thou hast burnt a people who affirmed the glory of their Lord!"'

Abu Huraira, in the *Collections of Bukhari, Muslim*, and elsewhere.

It is related that the Prophet was once sitting in a garden when a camel came up to him, sobbing bitterly, with tears streaming from its eyes.

The Prophet took its head, and stroked its head. Then he asked:

'Who is the owner of this camel?'

One of the Helpers said: 'It belongs to me, O Messenger of Allah!'

260

Then the Prophet said:

'Have you no fear of God about this animal which God has given you? It complains that you are its oppressor, and that you make him exhausted.'

Reported by Abdullah ibn Ja'far, in Sajistani's Collection.

Charity

'Charity,' said the Prophet, 'is smiling upon your brother. It is also encouraging good and opposing wrong. It is charity to put a man in a strange land onto the road. Helping someone with defective eyesight is charity. To remove harmful objects from the road is charity. Emptying your bucket into the container of your brother is charity.'

Abu Dharr, in Tirmidhi's Collection.

Fear God

One of the followers of Mohammed said: 'O Messenger of Allah! I have heard so many things from you that I fear that I shall forget their purpose and object. So tell me in a word something which shall contain everything.'
The Prophet said:

'Fear God in accordance with what you know, and act accordingly.'

Yazid ibn Salama, in Tirmidhi's Collection.

Cursing

'Do not curse,' said the Prophet, 'with the name of God or with the wrath of God, or with the fire of Hell.'

Samura ibn Jundab, in Muslim's Collection.

Envy

'Envy and jealousy, the twin maladies of those who came before you,' said the Prophet, 'are creeping into you.

'These will shave you smooth. They will not shave your hair, but will shave away religion in you.

'By Him in whose hand stands my life! You shall never enter paradise unless you love one another.'

Zubair, in *Tirmidhi's Collection*.

Excess

'The Prophet,' reports Abu Sa'd, 'saw to it that we knew that none of us had a right to anything which we had in excess. He said:

'"Let him who has an excess give it to him who has it not".'

Muslim and Sajistani.

Revenge

The Prophet said:

'Moses asked God: "O my Lord! Who, in thy sight, is the most honoured of thy servants?"

'God answered:

'"He who forgives when he is able to avenge".'

Abu Huraira, in *Baihaqi's Collection*.

Greed

'There are two kinds of greedy people who are never satisfied,' said the Prophet.

'The man of avarice who devotes himself to knowledge is never content, and the avaricious man devoted to the world is never satisfied with it.'

Anas ibn Malik, in *Baihaqi's Collection*.

Knowledge

'The calamity of knowledge,' the Prophet said, 'is forgetting;

262

and the wasting of it is to speak of it to whomever is not fit for it.'

A'mash, in Darimi's Collection.

Nature and Nurture

The Prophet said:

'Everyone is born with a certain nature, the constitution of God wherewith he has designed men. But his parents make him a Jew, a Christian or a Majian ... Do you see anyone mutilated among you unless you have yourselves mutilated it ... ?'

Abu Huraira, in Bukhari, Muslim and elsewhere.

Of Us

The Prophet said:

'He is not one of us who is unmerciful to the young, who honours not age, who encourages not justice and does not oppose wrong.'

Ibn Abbas, in Tirmidhi's Collection.

Teaching

The Prophet said:

'Whoever shows (a way) to good, he shall have a reward equal to that of whoever does good.'

Abu Mas'ud al Ansari, in Muslim's Collection.

The Warner

The Prophet said:

'The analogy of me and of what God has sent me is as that of a man who goes to his people and says:

'"Verily, I have come to warn you that I have seen a large army, so save yourselves". And some of his people obeyed him. They arrived at a place of safety, and were saved. A number of them called it a lie, and they awoke in the morning as the army came upon them and destroyed them.'

Abu Musa Abdullah ibn Qais al Ashari, in the *Collections of Bukhari and Muslim*.

Evil Speaking

Aisha reports:

> 'Whenever the Prophet heard anyone saying anything evil of a man, he did not say, "What will be the state of such-and-such a man?" But he said: "What will be the [future] state of a people who say such things?"'

Sajistani's Collection.

Manners

The Prophet said:

> 'Assuredly, the believer attains by good manners, the stage of the man who stands in prayer all night and who fasts throughout the day.'

Aisha, in *Sajistani's Collection.*

The Moslem and the Believer

The Prophet said:

> 'A Moslem is he from whose tongue and hands the Moslems are safe. A Mumin (Believer) is he in whom mankind have a refuge for their blood and their possessions.'

Abu Huraira, in the *Collections of Tirmidhi and Nasai.*

Tongue and Prayer

Someone said: 'O Messenger of God! There is a woman who is famous for her prayer, fasting and charity. But she gives offence to her neighbours in her speech.'
    The Prophet said:

> 'She will be in the Fire.'

The man continued: 'Another woman is less distinguished for her fasting, alms and prayer, and she gives little in charity. But she does not cause offence with her tongue.'
    The Prophet said:

> 'She will be in Paradise.'

Abu Huraira, in the *Collections of Shaibani and Baihaqi.*

War and Flight

The Prophet said:

'A Holy Warrior is he who carries on the Holy War with his own Self; and a Refugee is he who flees from crime and sins.'

Fudala, in *Bahaqi's Collection.*

Places of Prayer

The Prophet said:

'All the earth is made a place of prayer for me and pure. Any one of my people may pray anywhere he finds the occasion of prayer.'

Jabir, in *Nasai's Collection.*

Prayer of Mohammed

'O God! Purify my heart from hypocrisy, and my work from ostentation, and my tongue from lies, and my eyes from deception.'

Ummi Ma'bad, in *Baihaqi's Collection.*

Pride

A handsome man came to the Prophet, and said:
    'I love beauty and, as you see, I have been given it. So I do not like to have shortcomings even in the thong of my sandals. O Prophet of God! Is that pride?'
    The Prophet said:

'No. But to reject the truth and to despise men, that is pride.'

Abu Huraira, in *Sajistani's Collection.*

The Koran

The Prophet said:

'The Koran descended in five categories:

'The lawful, the unlawful, the obvious, the figurative and the parables.

'Therefore observe the lawful and forbid the unlawful, act upon the evident and believe in the figurative, and take the parables as examples.'

Abu Huraira, in *Baihaqi's Collection*.

Polytheism

The Prophet said:

'Even the smallest display of piety is associating (something else) with God.'

Umar ibn al Khattab, in *Ibn Majah and Baihaqi's Collection*.

Wisdom, Abstinence and Distinction

The Prophet said to Abu Dharr:

'There is no wisdom like organizing, no abstinence like self-restraint, no distinction like good manners.'

Baihaqi's Collection.

Time

The Prophet said:

'God says: "The Son of Man aggrieves me when he abuses time, for I am time – all matters are in my hand; I change the night and the day".'

Abu Huraira, in the *Collections of Bukhari and Muslim*.

Wealth

The Prophet said:

'There is a trial for every people, and the trial for my people is the trial by wealth.'

Ka'b ibn Iyad, in *Tirmidhi's Collection*.

How the Prophet Lived

Aisha said:

'Many a month would pass when we never lit the fire in the

hearth. Our food would be only dates and water, unless some-one gave us some meat.'

Bukhari, Muslim, Tirmidhi.

How the Prophet Taught

Mu'awia ibn al Hakam said:

> 'By my father and mother! I have never seen a teacher, either before him or after him, who taught better than the Prophet. 'By God! He never looked severe, neither did he chastise anyone, nor revile them.'

Muslim, Sajistani and Nasai.

The Sword and the Prophet

Ali reports:

> 'I found this inscription on the hilt of the Prophet's sword:
>
> Forgive him who wrongs thee;
> Join him who cuts thee off;
> Do good to whoever does evil to thee;
> And speak the truth even if it be against thee.'

Abdari's Collection.

The Family

In one of his last orations, given at Khumm, between Mecca and Medina, in the tenth year of the Flight, Mohammed the Prophet spoke of his approaching death and emphasised what he was to leave behind for the people:

> 'Know, O People, that I am only a human being: the messenger of my Lord is about to come, and I must answer.
> 'And I am leaving you two important [momentous] things:
> 'The first is the Book of Allah: in it is the guidance and the light, so take the Book of Allah and hold it ...
> 'And my family. I remind you, by Allah, of my family. I remind you, by Allah, of my family. I remind you, by Allah, of my family.'

From the collection of three thousand Authoritative Traditions called the *Sahih of Imam Muslim* (826 – 883 of the Christian Era).

Generosity is Sacred

The Sheikh, The Thief, and The Arab Steed

Once upon a time there lived a Sheikh called Ibrahim, who was the owner of a most beautiful Arab horse. Its eyes were large and its neck was proudly arched, its coat was of a snowy white. In the whole of Arabia it was said that no other horse could match it.

Now, this story came to the ears of a notorious horse-thief, one Abdulla, and he resolved to try to steal the horse.

Accordingly, one day he disguised himself as a beggar, and came to the place where the Sheikh lived.

He lay in wait for the Sheikh as he was riding along a certain road, and cried out, 'Let me up upon your horse, O Sheikh, for I am lame and too weary to walk another step!'

The horse was as beautiful as he had been told, and it made the eyes of the horse-thief gleam with anticipation.

'Once I am upon the saddle,' he thought, 'the horse will be mine, and the Sheikh will have to bear the loss as best he may.'

Sheikh Ibrahim dismounted, his heart touched by the words of the tattered beggar, and said, 'Come, brother, you shall ride the next few miles to the town, and I will assist you in every way I can to restore your fortunes, if Allah wills.'

He helped the other into the saddle, and put the reins into his hands.

No sooner had he done so than the thief threw off his torn cloak and said: 'Now I claim this animal for myself, for I am none other than Abdulla the Horse-Thief, so farewell, this is indeed my lucky day!'

And Abdulla applied his heels to the horse's sides; and, wheeling about, galloped off in a cloud of dust.

The Sheikh ran after him, calling out in great distress, but the horse-thief raced faster and was soon lost from sight.

Wearily, the Sheikh sat down upon a rock and bitterly regretted his action in allowing the beggar to mount his horse.

But, within a few moments, a cloud of dust on the horizon caused him to shade his eyes and stare into the distance.

To his great surprise, it was the horse-thief, Abdulla, and the horse once more.

The thief rode the animal to within a few feet of the Sheikh and, jumping from the saddle, placed the reins in its owner's hands.

'What has happened? Are there soldiers approaching, that you should return like this, in such haste?' asked the Sheikh.

'Noble Sheikh,' said the thief, 'forgive me for what I have done, and let me go in peace. For I realized that, had I ridden away with your stallion like this, no-one would again give a lame beggar a lift upon his horse, and generosity would cease. So, let me go, and ride back to your home without thinking of me as an abuser of the rules of our Faith.'

Then Sheikh Ibrahim forgave Abdulla the horse-thief and let him go upon his way.

Faithfulness

> Well known among Arab writers is the account of the trustworthiness of the Emir Al-Samau'al – Samuel, Chief of a Jewish tribe in the south of Arabia, in the fifth century. The tale is told as one of the highest examples of fidelity to trust.

A friend of the Emir went on a journey and entrusted him with a suit of the finest armour. He was, however, killed in battle, and a Syrian king claimed the armour from Samau'al.

The Emir refused to yield the property except to his friend's lawful heir, and the Syrian besieged him in one of his castles.

After a time, Samau'al's son was captured by the Syrian king, who held him hostage against the surrender of the armour.

Receiving a negative answer, the tyrant had the young man killed before his father's eyes.

Emir Samau'al continued the fight until the siege was raised, and the arms were handed over to the heirs.

The King, The Dog and The Golden Bowl

Once upon a time there lived a merchant, called Hasan, who was wealthy and generous, happy and fortunate.

But, one day, disaster stared him in the face. His ships, bearing great loads of treasure from afar, were captured by pirates, and his warehouse – containing many valuables – was burned down. Unable to face his friends, he sold his house and his remaining belongings, and set off in search of his fortune.

But good luck had deserted Hasan, for a thief stole his remaining money while he was asleep in a caravanserai, and this time he found himself without a single coin to his name, and in a strange town.

He went to the mosque-keeper, and asked for alms to see him on his way, and felt very ashamed of himself. How was he ever to hold his head up again, he wondered, and asked the mosque-keeper what he should do. 'My brother,' said the old man, 'go three days' march from here, and you will arrive at such and such a place. The king there is generous and kind, and you may be able to put your case before him, and ask help of a more substantial nature than that which I am able to present you with from our limited resources.' And he gave Hasan a handful of coins from the poor-box.

Hasan thanked him, and set off, after buying a few dates to eat upon the journey. The way was rough and hard, and Hasan was tired, thirsty and dusty by the time he arrived at the walled town. The shop-keepers which Hasan saw were richly clad and contented of mind. He walked wearily towards the palace, where the old mosque-keeper had told him a generous king fed hundreds of people each night. But when he finally got there he was so ashamed of his rags, and so fearful of presenting himself in such a state before the monarch, that he hid behind a pillar, from which vantage-point he could look upon the scene.

There was a great concourse of people, young and old, being given food and money by the generous monarch, who sat upon a great golden throne in the middle of the lofty hall.

Suddenly from his hiding-place, Hasan saw three great hounds being brought to a space a few feet away from him; and an attendant placed three bowls of finest meat before each of the dogs. The man then went away, and Hasan found his eyes fixed upon the delicious meat which had been given to the dogs. As he was thinking that he could with joy have fed from even the leaving of the animals, so great was his hunger, the dog nearest to him raised its eyes to his, and – looking at him in an almost human fashion – pushed its jewelled golden bowl towards Hasan. The famished man, unable to wait a second longer, helped himself to one of the pieces of meat, and pushed the bowl back to the dog. But, with its paw, the animal again pushed it over to Hasan, until he had eaten to his heart's content. Then the intelligent creature ate, and after it had licked the bowl clean, it pushed it back towards Hasan. The man saw that it was offering him the bowl, and when he took it in his hands and then hid the precious object under his tattered cloak, the animal seemed to nod its head in agreement.

Hasan realised that if he sold the bowl, and bought himself new clothes, he would at least have a chance to approach a merchant for some sort of work.

He patted the hound gratefully on the head, and slipped away from the crowd. Next day, he sold the bowl, which, being studded with precious jewels, brought him in such a good price, that he was able to set up in business for himself.

By clever buying and selling, soon he had enough merchandise to take back to his native town, where his friends greeted him with much joy.

His good luck having returned, Hasan became a successful trader, and before long was once more as rich as he had ever been.

Some years later, he felt the urge to return to that town where he had been shown such kindness by the dog, and he made up his mind to replace the golden food bowl which he had taken away.

Within a few days, a replica of the bowl was ready, and Hasan, on his best horse, with flowing robes and boots of the finest leather, set off.

At last he arrived, and once more saw the old wall which was built around the town. But, upon riding inside the gates, he saw with amazement that the glory of the palace was no more; it lay wide open to the sky, roofless and ruined, its beautiful pillars broken as if destroyed by Mongol hordes.

The wrecked houses were silent and empty, the shops where rich and contented merchants had sat were despoiled of all their merchandise, and there seemed to be no living thing in the whole place.

Sorrowfully, Hasan was mounting his horse to ride away, when a great hound darted out of the palace ruins and was followed by two others. Hasan recognised them as the fine dogs which had been brought by the attendant to feed from the golden bowls when he was a beggar in that very place.

Then an old man appeared, in a rough woollen robe, and with a stick in his hand, upon which he leant heavily.

'Greetings, my son,' said the old man. 'What brings you to this place?'

'Some time ago I came here in rags,' said Hasan, 'and was fortunate enough to be given the meat from its bowl by this dog here. When I left I took the bowl, sold it, and replenished my fortunes, and now I have come to repay the debt, and return this bowl.'

'All those times are gone,' said the old man, 'the vanity and pomp which was once my Court has vanished.'

Hasan now saw that this was indeed that generous king whom he had seen feeding the poor and needy in the great palace long ago.

'Your Majesty,' said he, 'please take this golden bowl which I have brought.'

'No,' said the old king, 'I have no need for anything, except that which I have here. My hounds catch game for my one daily meal, and my old gardener has remained with me and continues to grow some roses and vegetables for me; and together, he, I and the hounds, manage to enjoy our lives. After my enemies destroyed my town and my people were taken away I have lived very simply here.'

'But, but, the bowl, the golden bowl,' whispered Hasan. 'May I not leave it for your Majesty?'

'If a dog of mine thought fit to give away his bowl,' said the king, 'it is not for me to take it back. I am sure that he has no need of it now. Go, return from whence you came, we are sufficiently provided for at the present time.'

So, bowing to the king, Hasan mounted his horse and rode away. He looked back, and saw the old man, leaning upon his stick, wave a last farewell, and then disappear back into the ruins, with his three hounds about him.

And Hasan, in after days, often told the story, that men should not forget the tale of the King, the Dog and the Golden Bowl.

The Arabian Nights.

Hatim Tai

Once upon a time, long long ago, there lived in the land of Arabia a most kind and generous king, who was called Hatim Tai. In his stables were the finest stallions and mares, in his tents the most beautiful carpets, in his army the bravest fighting men. Songs were sung from one end of his dominions to the other, accompanied by tambours and flutes, of the many generous deeds in war and peace which he had done.

In the whole of that part of Arabia which came under his control, all men were brothers, and all women sisters of their monarch, Hatim Tai. Children came running to him when he passed through the lines of their tents, and boys, as soon as they were old enough, begged to join the élite corps of his camel riders, formed to bring news from far regions to the court of Hatim Tai.

There was food for every mouth in the whole land, and much treasure in the coffers, and many rich oases for travellers and merchants.

Every man had the right to stop him when he rode upon his milk-white mare, Jamalia, and ask him a favour, which was always granted, whatever it might be. 'O Hatim Tai,' cried the supplicant, pulling at his royal cloak, 'I beg a boon.' And the king stopped, listened, smiled gently, and granted the request.

From far and wide came visitors to eat at his feasts, sit upon his priceless carpets, gaze at the numbers of his fighting men, their long spears, their glittering daggers, their tremendous size.

But, one was jealous of him, another king of lands bordering upon his own, whose name was Jaleel, and he sent his herald to Hatim Tai, with this message:

'I am mightier and bolder than you will ever be, O Hatim Tai, and lord of many more tents and men. Therefore, I want to possess myself of your land, your people, and all that you own, so tell me when we shall do battle, and all our young men shall be tested, at that time. My warriors will certainly destroy yours, for we have many horses and spears, and you shall be as nothing after the fight which will ensue!'

Around him, his wazirs and amirs, counsellors and princes, raised their hands to Heaven and declared that they and all Arabians under his flag would fight to the death to preserve him and his family, whatever the cost in blood.

The armed men took up the cry, and came thronging to his tent to demand the hour of the battle.

But Hatim Tai thought for a few moments, then he shook his head.

'Brothers,' said he, 'this is not your fight. I will not have battle joined for such a trivial matter as my life. I shall disappear into the mountains, and the conqueror can enter these dominions without killing one living thing. You will not suffer, nor will children lose their fathers, for it is my life that King Jaleel wants. He will not do anything except ride here and take up his position in my tent, and this I will gladly give up to him. For I can live as a dervish, without any of the trappings of the Court, as many another has done before me.'

So, wrapping up some dates and nuts in a small sack, he said farewell to all his family, and walked away.

Jaleel the conqueror came in great state, with much blowing of trumpets and beating of drums, and took over the entire country of Hatim Tai.

Some time passed, during which the new king searched far and wide for Hatim Tai. But no sign of him was to be found. There was not one man, woman or child in all that vast area who would have betrayed the lonely king in his hiding place. Many went by night and took him food, and helped him in every way possible to survive.

At court, with his advisers, King Jaleel sat, surrounded by much luxury and beauty, boasting of his conquest.

'Men of Arabia!' he shouted, 'I took this country without one person raising a hand against me, without shedding one drop of blood. That coward, Hatim Tai, dare not show his face to me, and is now hidden from view, or running still, I have no doubt!' And he laughed loudly, applauded by all his followers.

He saw the downcast face of Hatim Tai's advisers, who were also at the festivities, and cried:

'What have you to say, O Wise Ones, about the cowardice of this late monarch of yours, behaving like a woman?'

One, braver than the rest, spoke out:

'O King, our monarch Hatim Tai is the most generous man in the world. He told us not to fight, but to let you enter these dominions unchallenged, so that we would live. He went away to give us that chance; if my life is to be forfeit, I must say this!'

The new king was nonplussed. Here was Hatim Tai, doing yet

another generous thing, so that the people thought more of him that of their new ruler! Whispered tales about Hatim Tai's deeds were still circulating, nothing good had yet been said about Jaleel, his spies told him. How could he capture the hearts of his subjects? He got very angry, and ordered that whomsoever could capture Hatim Tai and bring him to the Court should be given many bags of gold. The loyal subjects were even more determined to save their king from the tyrant, and no hint of where Hatim Tai was hiding was given to the seekers. But one day, when a very old couple were collecting firewood near the fugitive's cave, they began talking to each other, and Hatim, watchful as ever when he heard voices, could not help listening.

'If only life were not so hard,' said the ancient man. 'The new king makes so many demands upon us, taxing us so cruelly, and taking all the boys into his army. There seems to be less and less wood here: what shall we do when it is all gone?'

'Find Hatim Tai and get the bags of gold, then, old man!' said the shrewish old wife. 'I hear that they have put the ransom money up higher even this very day! Why, we could live to the end of our days in great comfort if we were to take him in ...'

At that moment, Hatim Tai stepped forward and said, 'Then you shall live in comfort for the rest of your days. Take me there and say no more about it.'

'O generous Hatim Tai!' cried the old man, 'never in a million years, if I were to be tempted by the houris of Paradise, would I betray you! My wife is an old fool, forgive her, good Hatim!'

While they were arguing, several of the soldiers who belonged to the usurper's army, came up, and seized them all. They were brought before the king, and Hatim said, 'Your Majesty, give this old woodcutter the money for my discovery, for it was he who found me.'

Then the old man, with great dismay, told of how Hatim Tai had offered himself so that they would be comfortable for the rest of their lives. King Jaleel was so amazed by this great act of generosity, that he decided to make a generous gesture, too. He bade Hatim Tai return to his royal tent, embraced him as a brother, and returned to his own country, taking his soldiers with him, promising to live in peace for all his days.

And Hatim Tai, too, lived in peace until he was called to Paradise at last.

Wisdom of Women

The Reward

A party of travellers came upon an encampment of bedouins. One of them who was very ugly, squint-eyed and with a long white beard, was engaged in beating his wife, a beautiful young woman.

Naturally, says Ibrahim Al Mausili, who recounts this tale, the travellers intervened to stop the beating.

'Leave him alone,' cried the lady, 'for he must have done some good action, and I must have committed some sin: otherwise he would not have been made *my* punishment, and I would not have been *his* reward!'

Muhammad ibn Ibrahim Al Mausili (of Mosul) in Nahfat Al Yaman.

The Demon

Al-Jahiz, who was regarded as very ugly, used to say that there was only once when he was made ashamed.

'One day,' he recounted, 'I was near a woman in the street, when she said: "I need you, if you wish to follow me".

'I followed her until she arrived at a goldsmith's shop, and went in after her.

'She said to the goldsmith, "It has to be like this," and she walked out of the shop.

'I stood there in amazement, until I managed to ask the shopman what had been happening.

'He smiled and said: "That woman has some badly-behaved children. She wants me to make a model of a demon to frighten them with. I told her that I did not know what it should look like, so she said she would bring me an example to copy".'

Nahfat Al Yaman.

The Tale of the Oppressed Girl

> People find it difficult or impossible to link the threads of
> happenings in their lives – and often doubt if such linking
> is possible at all. They tend to look on events in isolation,
> though few events are, in fact, isolated rather than con-
> nected to other things. Similarly, people try to understand
> their own mentality by seeking explanations for their
> behaviour and thoughts and those of others. Again, to do
> this they have to choose a dogma, religious or psychologi-
> cal usually, to bring order into their problem. But there is
> another way of reflecting both worldly events and
> thought-processes. This tale is one of those ways.

There was once a merchant who travelled a great deal, and had a
daughter, Laila, and an adopted son, Adnan. For these children he
arranged for a certain Mulla to live in his house and be their tutor.

When the two children had reached the ages of fifteen and sixteen, the merchant went on a journey to a remote land, to spend
several months there in the course of his business affairs. The Mulla,
however, had fallen in love with the girl, and made advances to
her.

Laila would have nothing to do with the objectionable Mulla;
and in the end was forced to drive him off with a stick, bruising him
severely.

But the enraged Mulla had his revenge. He at once wrote to the
girl's father, claiming that she had become completely degenerate,
and that he was unable to prevent her from committing the most
abominable acts.

The merchant, as is often the case, believed the word of the man
whom he trusted. Without deep enough thought on the matter, he
said to himself, 'This woman has dishonoured herself and all of us. I
must take the law into my hands to preserve her and others from
more evil.'

His solution was that Laila was to be killed. He wrote to Adnan,
telling him to take her into a wilderness, slay her and bury the body
where it would not be found.

Now Adnan was obedient but not foolish, so he asked himself
whether there had not perhaps been some mistake. When he and
Laila had reached a lonely spot in the desert, he sat down and asked

277

her why her father might want her killed on the complaint of the Mulla. 'I repulsed his advances. He has evidently concocted a story about me and written it to my father, who, believing it, has ordered you to murder me,' she said.

Adnan reflected, and then said: 'Have the wise down the ages not said, "If you seek a rapid way to a conclusion, beware that the just conclusion is afflicted by the overwhelming desire for rapidness."? The Mulla tried to press you with haste. Frustrated in this, he tried to get your father to produce a conclusion by similarly rapid decision. If we do not reduce this impetus, innocent blood will be shed. Haste and failure to take all factors into consideration ignore both your honesty and my need to uphold justice as well as to obey orders. Go into the wilderness and live as best you can, keep away from us – and I shall pretend that I have killed you.'

He returned home and smeared one of Laila's garments with the blood of an animal, and showed this to the merchant when he returned to his house.

Now Laila made her life in the wilderness. She slept in trees and lived off whatever berries and plants she could find in the inhospitable wastes, fearful of showing herself to other people, in case word should go back to her father that she was still alive, and he might send someone else to kill her.

After a year of this life, a certain Prince Salim was out hunting when he became separated from his retinue, as he pursued a gazelle. Coming to a pool in the jungle he decided to slake his thirst and took a long drink from the cool, refreshing water. When he had drunk, he rolled over to rest, and saw, in the branches of a tree above him, the form of a beautiful young girl.

'Are you a human being or a spirit?' he called up to her. 'Whatever you are, come down and let us talk.'

'I am a human being,' said the girl, 'and if you give me something to wear, for I am naked, I shall come down to you.'

He handed her his shawl, and she climbed to the ground. Loneliness had made her speak to him, but she was still afraid to tell him who she was, and he agreed not to ask her. He took her, however, back to his palace and, having fallen in love with her, he married her.

They had two children, and then, after several years, Laila was seized with a strong desire to see her parents again, and became doleful and agitated by turn.

When she told her husband how she felt, he suggested that she should go and visit her father and mother, and show them her children. He sent his best friend, together with a suitable escort, and they set off.

After a few days, when they had camped in a wood, the Prince's companion, forgetting his duty, developed a passion for Laila and threatened her. 'If you do not yield to me, I shall kill your two sons.' She still refused, and he was as good as his word. Somehow Laila managed to run away and lose herself in the darkness, having snatched up a bag of gold which was among the party's baggage.

She made her way through the night, and as dawn broke she saw a shepherd with his flock on a hillside.

'Are you an apparition or a human?' he called out, in some distress, for they were miles from anywhere, and Laila was dressed like a princess.

'I am a human being,' she answered, 'and I am tired and hungry, and I beg of you to kill a sheep and roast some meat for me before I faint away.'

'These are not my sheep, and I cannot use them for meat,' said the shepherd. So Laila gave him a handful of gold, and he at once killed a sheep and made a meal.

'Now,' said Laila, 'give me your clothes for this extra handful of gold, and I shall give you mine to wear.' Acting on an impulse, she sent the shepherd for water, and while he was away, she let his sheep wander and went on her way. After a great deal of wandering, wearing the clothes of a man, she arrived at her father's house and went to the door of the kitchen, where she was engaged as a cook. She worked so well that she was eventually put in charge of the whole household, though nobody, of course, suspected who she was.

Meanwhile, the Prince's trusted friend had formed a plan to explain the murder of the two lads. Weeping and wailing, he claimed that bandits had attacked the camp, had killed the children, and had carried off Laila.

When he arrived back at the palace, the Prince vowed that he would track down the murderer of his sons and find his wife. He dressed himself and his friend in the garb of wandering dervishes, and they set off on their quest.

In the meantime the shepherd found that all his flock had

disappeared and, afraid to return to his master, he dressed himself as a wandering dervish and set out to see what life might have in store for him.

Before long, he came across the Prince and his friend, also disguised as dervishes, and they decided to travel together.

One night, when they were sitting by the fire in a caravanserai, the Prince said: 'The night is long, let us pass it by telling tales.'

His companion spoke first. He said:

'Once a young Prince found a girl in the wilderness. She was beautiful, and he fell in love with her and they were married. She went on a journey with her children and a friend, but they were attacked by bandits. They killed the boys and took the Princess away. The Prince and his companion then dressed themselves as dervishes and started to wander the earth, seeking her.'

Now the shepherd told his tale:

'A certain shepherd once saw a beautiful young woman on a hillside at dawn. She paid him much gold for a meal, took his clothes and let his sheep wander. Now he had no livelihood, and, dressing as a wandering dervish, he set out on his travels to see what fate might have in store for him.'

'I am the Prince,' said the Prince, 'and this is my friend and companion.'

'And I am the shepherd,' said the shepherd.

'Let us continue as travelling companions, and make our way around the world, telling strange tales,' said the Prince. They continued on their way, relating stories in the market-places of the towns which they visited in their search, and collecting small sums of money from the townsfolk who gathered to listen to them.

Now, to return to the Princess Laila, disguised as a servant in her father's house. One day, when she was in the town buying the food for the day, she saw three dervishes in the market-place, with a number of people listening to their tales. As she went closer, she realised that they were none other than her husband, the Prince, his friend and the shepherd. Acting on an impulse from where she did not know, she went home and spoke to her father:

'May I invite some guests to eat with us tonight? I know that I am only a servant, but these are holy wayfarers, and I feel that their presence will bring us *baraka*, a blessing.'

Her father answered:

'You are one of us, do not think of yourself as a servant. Invite whomever you choose.'

So the girl, still disguised as a major-domo, returned to the town square. 'Respected Dervishes,' she said, 'our household seeks the honour of your presence and the blessing which comes from attending to the teachings of the People of the Path.'

The three agreed to go; and Laila also invited the local dignitaries, including the Prince of the city, the local judge and the commander of the police force.

After a lavish and delicious repast, Laila addressed the company thus:

'Dear friends! The ancient sages have informed us that in tales there is wisdom, and that so long as the stories of the marvels of the earth are repeated, so long will there be a possibility that man's true state and his understanding may be revealed. I propose, therefore, that for the following few nights each one of us should tell a tale. Since the tales of the Ultimate Reality are those which are preserved and presented by the noble people of the Dervish Way, let us attend carefully, if you permit, to the accounts of their travels by these three wise men.'

Everyone agreed, except that, for purposes of etiquette it was decided that the first story should be recited by the master of the house.

Now the merchant said:

'Distinguished and respected company! Let it be known to you that I had a daughter and also an adopted son: the one was named Laila and the other Adnan. I engaged a Mulla as tutor to these children as they grew up, and this Mulla is still with us. He is, in fact, the Mulla who is at this moment sitting in our company.

'I went on a long journey in the course of my commercial activities; and the Mulla wrote to inform me that a calamity had occurred. The girl had become vitiated: and I therefore instructed, in the heat of my grief and confusion, this young man, Adnan, to kill her. He brought back a bloodstained garment as proof that he had obeyed my orders. But our grief and confusion, remorse and sin, surround us still.'

Everyone went home, sobered by this sad tale.

The following night the Mulla confirmed the recital in his own

281

words, and the company withdrew in a state of even deeper gloom than before.

The third night was the turn of the Prince in dervish robes. He said:

'Excellent friends and wearers of the Dervish Cloak! One day a certain man, who was a prince, was hunting when a gazelle eluded him beside a pool of pure water. He took a drink, saw a beautiful girl in a nearby tree, fell in love with her and married her. After they had produced two children she began to pine for her parents, so the Prince sent her with his trusted friend and two innocent sons to visit her father's house. On the way robbers killed the children and abducted the Princess. Disguised as a wandering Man of the Way, the distracted Prince, having vowed to find the criminals, set out on this quest. That Prince is me!'

Now it was the turn of the 'major domo', and Laila recited the complete story of the girl's adventures, although the Mulla, somehow feeling threatened, tried to stop her, saying: 'This is a woman's story, not yours. Why should we have irrelevancies in what should be coherence?' – in the manner of certain hypocrites. The others overruled him, and she completed her tale.

The Princess Laila concluded:

'... And then the chief servant of the household invited the dervishes and others of significance to a meal, this meal, so that the truth might be manifested ... and so let justice be done.'

And it was.

Three Wishes – The Emir's Wife

Three men met together; one of them expressed a wish to obtain a thousand pieces of gold, so that he might trade with them; the other wished for an appointment under the Emir of the Muslims; the third wished to possess the Emir's wife, who was the handsomest of women, and had great political influence. Yusuf bin Tashifin, the Emir of the Muslins, being informed of what they said, sent for the men, bestowed one thousand dinars on him who wished for that sum, gave an appointment to the other, and said to him who wished to possess the lady: 'Foolish man! What induced you to wish for that which you can never obtain?' He then sent him to her, and she placed him in a tent, where he remained three days, receiving each day, one and the same kind of food. She had him then brought to her, and said: 'What did you eat these days past?' He replied: 'Always the same thing.' 'Well,' said she, 'all women are the same thing!' She then ordered some money and a dress to be given him, after which she dismissed him.

From Ibn Khallikan's celebrated *Biographical Dictionary*.

The Sufi Wise Ones

The Crooked Palace

It is related that the king of the Eastern Roman Empire (Shaam and Roum) sent a messenger to the Court of King Anushirwan of Faaris – Persia – at his great Court at Ctesephon.

This messenger noticed that the palace was not straight on one side, and he asked his interpreter about this.

It was explained to him that when the palace was being built, an old woman whose house was in the way did not want to sell it. The king refused to force her to give way, so the palace was built so that the lady's house remained on one side of it.

The messenger from Roum said: 'This crookedness is better than any other straightness. I swear that what this king has done has not been recorded of any monarch in the past, nor will it be done by one in the future.'

The Caesar was delighted with this remark, and he rewarded the man.

Nahfat al Yaman.

Faith

'The best part of faith,' said the Prophet, 'is to say, "There is no God but God". The least of it is to remove harmful things from the roadway.'

Abu Huraira, in the *Collections of Bukhari and Muslim.*

What Is Given Can Be Taken

There was once a wise man who was approached by a youth, who said to him:

'Why do the wise not give good advice to all, so that we could all act in accordance with it, and prosper? If there are so many illuminated ones who can heal the sick, why do they not do it for everyone, so that we might banish disease from the earth?'

The wise man said:

'Come with me on a journey, and I will show you how matters really stand, for they are otherwise than you think.'

So the two set off on their travels.

They arrived at a village where a man was trying to milk a miserable goat, but could hardly get any milk from her.

The wise man said to him:

'What would you like most of all?'

The man answered:

'I would like a herd of good goats, so that I could hold up my head, and feed my family, and be content.'

The wise man said:

'Would you not rather be worthy of all this first?'

'No,' said the poor man, 'because poverty produces misery and plenty is a blessing which produces benevolence.'

The wise man waved his hand, and suddenly the poor peasant found that he was the owner of many flocks of beautiful goats.

The two travellers went on their way.

The next person they met was a woman, who was sitting disconsolately beside a well. The wise man asked her what was wrong, and she said:

'I am ugly and nobody will marry me, which means that I am doomed to pass the rest of my life in misery, since hereabouts it is considered undesirable to be unmarried.'

The wise man said:

'Would you rather be beautiful or really useful in this world, and able to serve other people?'

'I would rather be beautiful,' she said, 'because if I were, it would not be hard to do good. As it is, others do evil to me.'

The wise man waved his hand, and by his knowledge of the superior realms, the woman was transformed into a ravishing beauty.

The two went on their way.

The next man they met was a scholar, dressed in sumptuous robes.

After some conversation, the wise man asked him:

285

'Is there anything which you need? It appears not, since you have been blessed with so much. You have cattle, houses, the respect of your students...'

The scholar said:

'None of these is of any account. What I really need is that I should be regarded as the greatest scholar in the world.'

'But,' said the wise man, 'would you not rather be known as the most useful man in the world?'

'I do not think so,' said the scholar, 'for nobody can decide whether anyone really is useful: they can only believe it.'

The wise man waved his hand, and, in a trice, the scholar was transformed into the most famous and distinguished sage in the world.

After some months of travelling, the wise man changed his dress and appearance, and those of the disciple, so that they looked entirely different. Now he said:

'Let us retrace our steps and see how our advice and actions have taken effect.'

In due time they came upon the man with the goats, and found that he had become a tyrant, whom everyone feared. 'People,' said the wise man, 'imagine that they need affluence to be good, whereas it may make them worse, for it can give them opportunities which they did not have before.'

Then they saw the woman, who was now married but spent all her time titivating herself. 'If she had been told to make herself better before becoming beautiful, she would not have taken any notice,' said the wise man.

Finally they arrived at the house of the teacher, who was so surrounded by admirers that they had difficulty in gaining an audience.

'Tell me,' said the wise man, 'did you attain this importance by yourself, or was it perhaps through the wonder-working of one of those wise men?'

'Wise men?' said the scholar; 'there is no such thing. Wonder-workers, indeed! Be off with you!'

Now the wise man waved his hand again, and all the people returned to where they had been at the beginning.

'The advice which people need before they can improve and make use of healing and of good counsel, and of good fortune,' he told his pupil, 'is already available to them, and has been repeated for centuries.

'When they start in large numbers to take heed of this, then the wise will be able to give them further direction. Until then, it is only those few who want to learn, not those who want to gain, who will remain the responsibility of the wise. And it is these people who obtain the gifts which the wise can give.'